IRISH SOCIAL SERVICES

JOHN CURRY

FOURTH EDITION

INSTITUTE OF PUBLIC ADMINISTRATION

First published 1980
Second edition 1993
Reprinted 1994
Reprinted 1997
Third edition 1998
Reprinted 2003
Fourth edition 2003

Institute of Public Administration
57–61 Lansdowne Road
Dublin 4
Ireland

ISBN 1 904541 00 3
(ISBN 0 902173 97 9 first edition)
(ISBN 1 872002 07 2 second edition)
(ISBN 1 902448 01 4 third edition)

British Library Cataloguing-in-Publication Data

A catalogue record for this book is available
from the British Library

Cover design by Alice Campbell, Dublin
Typeset in 11/12 Baskerville by Datapage International Ltd, Dublin
Printed by ColourBooks, Ireland

Contents

Tables

Preface to Fourth Edition

Since the first edition of *Irish Social Services* was published over two decades ago in 1980, much has changed. There has been continuing evolutionary development in each of the main areas – housing, income maintenance, health services and education. In all cases, the services now provided are considerably better than two decades ago.

Since the publication of the third edition in 1998, the pace of change in Ireland has quickened even further. Unprecedented levels of economic growth and a more favourable demographic structure appeared to augur well for the future funding of the social services at the beginning of the new millennium. This was in marked contrast to the situation in the late 1980s. A downturn in the economy in 2002, however, has put a halt to almost unbridled investment in the social services. Yet advances had been made during those years that are likely to have an enduring impact.

The purpose of this book is to provide the reader with a broad, informed overview of the evolution, nature and scope of the key social services in Ireland. Because of the scope of the areas covered, it has not been possible to treat each of them in depth. Many issues can be pursued further with the aid of the bibliography. Statistics used throughout the book are provided mainly to indicate trends and these can be readily updated by reference to the source material.

The past few years have been characterised by a wide range of policy reports and legislation. While it is not possible to document in depth the wide variety of developments and discussion on issues, it is hoped that this edition captures the essential elements of the evolving situation.

This edition differs from the previous one in that a chapter on equality issues has been included. There has also been a restructuring of other chapters.

While many have helped in various ways with this publication, none is responsible for any views or unintentional errors.

John Curry
17 April 2003

1

Introduction

The social services are the main instruments of social policy. They are provided by the State and other agencies to improve individual and community welfare. The main social services are income maintenance, housing, education, health and welfare or personal social services. Before considering the general relevance of these services in Irish society it is useful to examine the background against which social services developed and the broad objectives behind the services.

What is social policy?

Donnison, in a report in the mid-1970s for the National Economic and Social Council (NESC), defined social policy as:

> Those actions of government which deliberately or accidentally affect the distribution of resources, status, opportunities and life chances among social groups and categories of people within the country and thus help to shape the general character and equity of its social relations.[1]

By this definition it could be argued that virtually all government policies or programmes have some implications for the well-being of the population. Consequently, all government programmes could be assessed in terms of their contribution to the achievement of national social objectives. Certain public programmes, specifically those of income maintenance, housing, education and health, have been traditionally regarded as the main constituent elements of social policy since they are the most visible instruments of achieving the distributive aims of government. In addition to these public programmes there are others, such as fiscal (e.g. taxation) and occupational (e.g. benefits relating to a particular employment) measures that could also be included since they too provide benefits for individuals and the community at large. The primary focus of this book, however, is on the four main social service areas outlined, i.e. income maintenance, housing, education and health. Other areas such as the welfare of certain groups, poverty and equality issues are also considered.

The NESC has indicated that government intervention by means of social policy is a response to four factors.[2]

i.   A socially acceptable distribution of income and other resources could not be guaranteed by a market economy, i.e. one in which the state does not intervene. A market economy would not, for example, guarantee an income to those unable to earn a living in the labour market. In any case the distribution of incomes guaranteed in the market may be the result of many factors, some of which are accidental and have little to do with equity.

ii. A socially desirable level of provision of some particular goods and services and their consumption by different groups will not necessarily be achieved through the market. For example, the attainment of certain levels of education and the utilisation of health care services confer benefits not only on the individual but also on the community in general. If left to market forces alone the utilisation of certain services would be less than optimal since many would not be in a position to afford them.

iii. The states of dependency in which people may find themselves, such as unemployment or illness, are social risks that are a hazard for the entire community and are not necessarily due to individual shortcomings. Governments can ensure, through appropriate social policy measures, that the community as a whole shares the burden of dependency.

iv. The concept of citizenship has evolved from a purely legal status of belonging to a particular country to one that confers rights to participation in the well-being of the community, including social services provided as an expression of social solidarity.

Over several decades, intervention by governments in developed countries has, in general, increased in relation to social policy.

Aims of social policy

If the above are the main factors accounting for government intervention in the social services area, the precise objectives of such intervention are not always clarified. This is certainly true of Ireland. In the absence of explicit objectives, Kennedy examined various official sources to determine what the aims of social policy were in post-war Ireland.[3] She concluded that three main aims were discernible:

- the relief of poverty and the provision of a minimum standard of living for all
- equalisation of opportunity
- increased productivity and economic growth.

These, according to Kennedy, could be described as the humanitarian, egalitarian and economic aims of social policy respectively.

In 1981 the NESC outlined what it considered to be the aims of social policy.[4] These were as follows:

- the reduction in inequalities of income and wealth by transferring resources to those in need and by equitably distributing the burden of such support
- the elimination of inequalities of opportunity that arise from inherited social and economic differences
- the provision of employment for those seeking work
- the provision of access for all, irrespective of income, to certain specified services
- the development of services that make provision for particular disadvantaged groups in the community
- the development of responsible citizenship based on an explicit recognition of the network of mutual obligations in the community.

Interestingly, these aims were referred to, though not necessarily endorsed, by the Fine Gael/Labour Coalition Government of 1982–1987 in its national plan *Building on Reality*.[5]

The aims as outlined by the NESC are being met to a greater or lesser degree. The extent to which they are being achieved will be referred to, as appropriate, in the following chapters.

Importance and relevance of social services
There are several reasons why the social services are an integral part of Irish society. These include the extent of utilisation of the services and the level of public expenditure on them.

The social services are availed of by practically everyone in Irish society. Two-fifths of the population are in receipt of weekly income maintenance payments and at some stage the members of practically every household avail themselves of a scheme or schemes administered by the Department of Social and Family Affairs. One-quarter of the population is engaged in full-time education. Most of the housing stock has been either provided directly or subsidised by the state. While one-third of the population has entitlement to the full range of health services, approximately one in every five persons is treated in acute hospitals annually.

Over two-thirds of government current expenditure is spent on the social services, with health accounting for the highest share of the four social services areas. It should be noted that expenditure on housing is an area subject to fluctuation depending on the demand for housing and other related factors.

For the general public, therefore, the social services can be vitally important, with some people dependent on them for their very livelihood. For government, the social services are a commitment to society, accounting for a considerable proportion of public expenditure.

Factors influencing type and level of social service provision
In most countries social service provision will have evolved over a period of time. Coughlan has summarised the situation as follows:

> Most people are aware of the *ad hoc* and fragmentary way in which the social services came into being; they were largely a piecemeal growth, introduced at different times to cover different categories of need and in response to different pressures, the result of a wide variety of motives – humanitarianism, social idealism, political expediency, the desire to damp down social discontent, the response to the spread of democracy and universal suffrage, the need to provide an environment conducive to industrial development. Seldom were they the expression of a coherent philosophical outlook.[6]

While broadly similar social services exist in most developed countries there are considerable differences in emphasis, the type of services provided and the priorities given to certain services. Thus, in relation to health services, for example, the extent to which free services are available to all or part of the population can vary greatly.

In Ireland, the development of the social services has also been piecemeal, as the following chapters will illustrate. Developments normally occur for a variety of reasons in response to various needs and demands, with the government having regard to cost considerations.

Once governments decide to provide social services, various factors come into play to influence the shape, the precise nature and the future development of the services. A number of key factors have been identified which determine the type and level of services provided in any country.[7] These include socio-demographic, economic and ideological factors. In examining the development of Irish social policy a number of factors are briefly examined. It should be stressed, however, that the interplay of all these factors is important rather than the primacy of any one in particular.

Socio-demographic factors
It is axiomatic that changes in the total population and changes in the composition of the population will determine or influence certain priorities. Thus, very simply, whether the population is increasing or declining will have implications for social services in general but education and housing in particular. In the 1950s when net outward migration was running at an annual average of 40,000, it was deemed that housing demand had been virtually met and consequently housing output declined (see Chapter 3). Within a decade, however, the situation had been reversed, the population increased for the first time since the 1840s, emigration declined steadily, the demand for housing increased and housing output rose.

Apart from trends in the total population, provision of services is also influenced by changes in the birth rate and life expectancy. Increases or decreases in the birth rate have obvious implications for child care services, educational facilities and income supports for children. One of the notable features of the Irish demographic situation in recent decades has been the steady decline in the birth rate from a peak of 22.8 per 1,000 population in 1971 to 13.4 in 1994. The actual number of births fell from 74,000 in 1980 to 48,000 in 1994 (a decline of 35 per cent). Since 1994, however, there has been a gradual increase in the number of births to 58,000 in 2001. The fall in the birth rate since 1980 has already had an impact on first and second level education where numbers enrolled have declined after reaching peaks in 1985 and 1990 respectively. Life expectancy increased throughout the twentieth century and this has implications for the provision of pensions as well as health and welfare services for older people.

Over the last few decades there has been a dramatic change in the age structure of the population (Table 1.1). One of the features has been the decline in the young population (under 14 years) due to the sharp decline in the birth rate. By contrast, the number of people in the prime working age group (25–44 years) has increased by over 60 per cent. The number in the 45–64 year age group has increased by 15 per cent, and the number of older persons (65+) has increased by 25 per cent. The age dependency ratio (the ratio between the working age groups, i.e. ages 15–64 and the groups aged under 15 and over 65) has fallen from 100:74 in 1971 to 100:54 in 1996. This ratio indicates the relative burden of providing services that benefit the young and old. Those in the working age group have to bear the burden, through direct or indirect taxation, of providing services for the dependent groups. The real burden of dependency (i.e. the ratio between those

Table 1.1: Age structure of population 1971–1996

Age groups	0–14	15–19	20–24	25–44	45–64	65+	Total
1971							
Number (000s)	931	268	215	626	608	330	2,978
Percentage	31.3	9.0	7.2	21.0	20.4	11.1	100.0
1981							
Number (000s)	1,044	326	276	838	591	369	3,444
Percentage	30.3	9.5	8.0	24.3	17.2	10.7	100.0
1991							
Number (000s)	963	333	265	949	618	395	3,523
Percentage	27.3	9.5	7.5	26.9	17.6	11.2	100.0
1996							
Number (000s)	859	340	293	1,016	704	414	3,626
Percentage	23.7	9.4	8.1	28.0	19.4	11.4	100.0

Source: Census of Population

actually at work and others) is much greater. In 1991 it was 100:214, and this had been exacerbated by the steady rise in unemployment throughout the 1970s and 1980s. By 2001, however, it was down to 100:123.

The distribution of population between urban and rural areas and the density of population also has important implications for the social services. It is less costly per unit, for example, to provide certain services such as water supply in high-density urban areas than in sparsely populated rural areas. Specialised services such as hospitals are usually located in the larger urban areas, making access difficult for those living in remote rural areas. Approximately three-fifths of the population in Ireland live in urban areas (towns with 1,500 persons or more). Many rural areas contain disproportionate numbers of older people, a legacy mainly of persistent and selective outmigration over a period of time. This has implications for the provision of services for older people.

In a study commissioned by the Combat Poverty Agency and published in 1997, the Economic and Social Research Institute considered the welfare implications of demographic change into the early part of the present century. The study, *Welfare Implications of Demographic Trends*, pointed out that concerns about the rising burden of welfare in the context of a falling population were unfounded. In support of this it claimed that the real burden of dependency would fall to 100 workers per 133 dependants by the year 2010 (from 100:220 in the mid 1980s); that the number of people at work would continue to rise and the unemployment rate would be halved by 2010; and that the savings in unemployment payments would make up for any increase in the cost of pensions. The study, having traced the impact of population decline up to the 1960s and the demographic features of recent decades, concluded:

> For the first time in the modern era, it is possible for Ireland to look forward with some confidence to a period of well-balanced population performance combined with economic progress ... The policy challenge in Ireland as far as population trends and their effects on welfare and support is not so much to prepare for imminent threat as to make the best use of the unprecedented opportunities which are now developing.[8]

Within a few years of the publication of the report, the demographic situation had changed even more markedly than the authors had predicted. The worker/dependency ratio was

100:123 by 2001 (ten years in advance of and less than that forecast), unemployment had been more than halved by 2001 and state revenue continued to grow due to a combination of increased workforce and unprecedented growth in the economy.

Economic factors
The financial resources available influence the level of state involvement in social service provision. In a period of economic growth it is likely that developments and expansion of social services will occur. By contrast, when there is little or no economic growth the aim may well be to simply retain, if not reduce, the existing level of services. Kennedy has outlined different social policy phases, both expansionary and regressive, in Ireland between the end of World War II and the 1970s.[9] Thus the 1950s was a period of relative economic stagnation with few developments in the social service area. By contrast, the period from the mid-1960s to the early 1970s was one of economic growth accompanied by a series of developments across the social services.

One of the features of the Irish economy over the past few decades has been the rise in unemployment. The average annual number on the live register of unemployment rose steadily from 70,300 (1974) to 109,000 (1977) to 254,000 (1991) and to 294,300 (1993). The rise in unemployment not only resulted in a drop in revenue to the state through taxes, but also an increase in state expenditure on income support schemes for the unemployed and their families. The substantial increase over the past few decades in the population in receipt of social welfare payments is largely accounted for by the rise in unemployment (see Chapter 2). The NESC identified the creation of employment and the consequent reduction of unemployment and involuntary emigration as primary objectives in the strategic issues for the 1990s.[10] By the mid-1990s, there was a sharp upturn in the Irish economy with unprecedented levels of economic growth and job creation.

Because of economic growth since the mid-1990s, employment has risen (from 1.16 million persons at work in 1990 to 1.72 million in 2001) while unemployment has fallen sharply (the annual average number on the live register of unemployment fell from a peak of 294,300 in 1993 to 142,300 in 2001). By 2001 the unemployment rate had fallen below 4.0 per cent, a level generally regarded as the equivalent of full employment.

Party political factors

While party political ideology may have influenced the shape of social service provision in other countries, its impact in Ireland has not been significant. In general, there are no fundamental differences between the Irish political parties on matters of social policy. This is not to deny that there has been different emphasis given to developments or priorities to others depending on the party or parties in power. What is obvious, however, is that there is a broad continuity in relation to social policy irrespective of the parties or combination of parties in government. There has not been any major social policy development which opposition parties may have criticised while the necessary legislation was being passed but which on gaining power themselves they have been prepared to undo. All too frequently, however, there has been opposition but this has largely been of a politically opportunist nature, involving point scoring, rather than the principled type. A classic case in point is afforded by the family planning legislation introduced in 1978 by the Fianna Fáil government to allow for the availability of contraceptives, hitherto banned. In 1985 the Fine Gael/Labour coalition government amended the 1978 Act in order to make contraceptives more readily available. Fianna Fáil, the then main opposition party, opposed this. Yet, ironically, in 1991/1992 Fianna Fáil, by then in government in coalition with the Progressive Democrats, were in a position to liberalise the law further (albeit against a background of an increase in AIDS) in order to make contraceptives even more widely available.

It would be difficult to describe any of the Irish political parties as having strong ideologies in relation to social policy. Most tend to be pragmatic and to reflect the attitudes of the population towards social service provision in general and towards specific developments required. Furthermore, there is broad support among the population at large for services provided either directly by the state or by other agencies with state support.

While the differences in ideology between parties on social policy issues may be negligible, individual politicians have made significant contributions to the development of social services. An example is Donogh O'Malley, TD, who, as Minister for Education, was responsible for introducing free post-primary education in 1967, several years before its introduction was planned for and without sufficient reference to the cost implications from the viewpoint of the Department of Finance. Without his unorthodox initiative, it has been asserted, it is unlikely that free post-primary education in its present form would ever have been introduced.[11] In this way, Donogh O'Malley made a far greater impact during his short term as Minister for Education than some of his predecessors or successors.

The role of the Catholic Church
Until relatively recently, one of the more notable features of Irish society has been the pre-eminence of Catholic social teaching. In the past this emphasised the principle of subsidiarity, i.e. that the state should not undertake functions that could be fulfilled by individuals on their own or by the local community, and that the state's role should be to supplement, not to supplant. The debate over the proposed Mother and Child Scheme in the late 1940s illustrated the importance of this issue (see Chapter 5). Since Vatican Council II (1962–1965), the Catholic Church has been concerning itself increasingly with inadequacies in social policy and social provision. It has been urging the introduction of measures designed not simply to ameliorate the effects of disadvantage and poverty in society but also the removal of the cause of these problems. This renewed emphasis on social issues by the Catholic Church has been exemplified by the sentiments expressed in the hierarchy's pastoral, *The Work of Justice* (1977), and several reports by the Council for Social Welfare (a sub-committee of the Catholic hierarchy). The Conference of Religious of Ireland (CORI, formerly the Conference of Major Religious Superiors) has also been to the forefront, not only in highlighting issues of social concern but also in proposing alternative policies.

Vocational and lobby groups
The influence of vocational and lobby groups should not be ignored in the development of social service provision in Ireland. In some countries, the trade union movement has had a formative influence on social service developments. In Ireland this role has probably been more limited, but it has been significant none-theless. While the primary concern of trade unions has been the remuneration and general working conditions of their members, as one of the main social partners they have been to the forefront in pressing for social reforms. The National Understandings

between government, employers and trade unions in the early 1980s followed a period of national wage agreements and contained a number of commitments related to social policy. More recently, the trade unions have had a significant input in various national partnership agreements – the *Plan for National Recovery* (1987), the *Programme for Economic and Social Progress* (1991), the *Programme for Competitiveness and Work* (1993), *Partnership 2000* (1996), the *Programme for Prosperity and Fairness* (2000) and *Sustaining Progress* (2003). These documents (agreed between government and the social partners) contain extensive and detailed commitments to social policy developments. The inclusion of these commitments is attributable largely to the influence of the trade union movement. The discussions prior to the agreement on *Partnership 2000* marked a new departure with the involvement of representatives of community and voluntary groups, such as the Irish National Organisation of the Unemployed, the Conference of Religious of Ireland (CORI) and the Society of Saint Vincent de Paul, in the consultative process. This process was continued with the *Programme for Prosperity and Fairness* (2000) and *Sustaining Progress* (2003). The notion of consultation and partnership involving the four different 'pillars' (employers, trade unions, farmers, voluntary/community sector) has now become such an integral part of policy making that it is difficult to imagine developments outside this framework in the future.

Many voluntary bodies involved in providing services also have a lobby role and frequently press for changes in areas under their remit. Some of these have representative umbrella organisations that perform this particular function on behalf of their members. Lobbying usually takes place in advance of proposed legislation and, more commonly, in the form of pre-Budget submissions.

Historical and external influences
British governments laid the foundations of many existing social services in Ireland before independence had been achieved in the 1920s. Examples of early state intervention in various social services include primary education (1831), children's services (1908), non-contributory pensions (1908), and unemployment and sickness benefits (1911).

The influence of the Poor Law, which came into effect in Ireland in 1838, on the development of social services, must also be stressed. It was out of the Poor Law, for example, that the public hospital system developed. The initial central feature of the Poor Law was the workhouse, which was designed for the very destitute. The philosophy of the Poor Law was based on the concept of less eligibility, i.e. the conditions of persons within the workhouse should be less eligible than those of the lowest paid worker outside. While many of the workhouses, the visible signs and reminders of the mid-nineteenth century Poor Law, were demolished and remodelled for other purposes such as county homes after independence in the early 1920s, some of the other services which the Poor Law spawned remained until the 1970s. These include the dispensary system, replaced by the choice-of-doctor scheme in 1972 and outdoor relief/ home assistance replaced by the supplementary welfare allowance scheme in 1977.

The British influence continued long after independence: the contiguity of Britain and the free flow of labour between the countries (mostly to Britain) inevitably meant that comparisons would be made between the social services in each country. Consequently, there had been a general tendency to look to Britain as the first reference point when a new scheme or development was being considered. Not infrequently, modified versions of schemes already in existence in Britain have been introduced in Ireland.

While it can be difficult to make general comparisons between the social services in different countries, it appears that over the past few decades differences in the range and quality of services between Northern Ireland and the Republic have narrowed. By 1990, a comparative study of the social security systems in Northern Ireland and the Republic indicated that: '. . . the same contingencies are catered for under both systems and, taken overall, the differences are not substantial'.[12] It is at least arguable that this has been the result of a continuous and conscious process to remove some of the obvious or perceived obstacles to the eventual unity of the two parts of Ireland.

Ireland's entry to the European Community in 1973 also had an impact on social service provision. If nothing else it served to heighten comparisons between Ireland and other member states and to provide wider reference points than heretofore. The influence of membership of the European Union (EU) has been of a direct and indirect nature. The direct influence has been exemplified by EU directives, such as the directive in 1978 on the equal treatment of men and women in matters of social security.

The indirect influence is more difficult to determine but it is nonetheless important. While it was never the intention of the EU to secure uniformity in social service provision, obvious gaps in social security coverage, for example, became apparent from the time Ireland became a member. The publication of a Green Paper (a discussion document) by the Department of Social Welfare on *Social Insurance for the Self-Employed* (1978) was undoubtedly influenced by the fact that Ireland was the only EU country that did not extend social insurance cover to the self-employed.

Recent interest in social policy
Over the past few decades there has been increased interest in social policy in Ireland. This is reflected in the output of publications dealing with social services and social issues in general. Several of these have helped to create and increase public awareness of social issues. Reference must first be made, however, to an early pioneering work – a paper on *Social Security* read by Dr Dignan, Bishop of Clonfert and Chairman of the National Health Insurance Society, to the management committee of the Society in 1944. In his paper Dr Dignan outlined what at the time appeared to be radical proposals for reform of the Irish social security system.

It is only since the mid-1960s that publications containing analysis of the various social services began to emerge in Ireland. These works include Coughlan's *Aims of Social Policy* (1966), the publications of Kaim-Caudle in the 1960s and early 1970s, especially *Social Policy in the Irish Republic* (1967), Ó Cinnéide's *A Law for the Poor* (1970) and *The Extent of Poverty in Ireland* (1972).

The publications of several agencies have also contributed to the debate on social services. At one level, governments have commissioned reports on the various aspects of the social services, e.g. *Investment in Education (1965), Report of the Commission on Inquiry into Mental Illness (1966), Report on the Industrial and Reformatory School System (1970), Report of the Commission on Social Welfare (1986), Report of the Commission on Health Funding (1989),* and *Report of the Commission on the Status of People with Disabilities (1996).*

At another level, various advisory and research agencies have been established and through their publications have contributed to the growing debate on social issues. In 1973 the National Economic and Social Council (NESC) was established, its main task being 'to provide a forum for discussion on the principles relating to the efficient development of the national economy and the achievement of social justice and to advise the government on their application.'

The reports of the NESC, as well as being invaluable sources of information, have raised important social policy issues and have contributed to a continuing debate on social problems and policies. The same could be said of many publications emanating from the Economic and Social Research Institute (ESRI), e.g. the report by Tussing on *Irish Educational Expenditures – Past, Present and Future* (1978).

In 1992, the National Economic and Social Forum (NESF) was established by government with a broader base of representation than the NESC. Apart from the traditional social partners (employers, trade unions and farmers) the membership also includes representatives from political parties and community/voluntary groups. The NESF, charged with developing economic and social policy initiatives, especially initiatives to combat unemployment, has also published a number of reports that have helped to contribute to the formation of a national consensus on social and economic matters.

The work of the Combat Poverty Agency, a statutory body established in 1986, which succeeded the non-statutory National Committee on Pilot Schemes to Combat Poverty (1974–1980), has highlighted the extent and nature of poverty in Irish society. The Agency has published a number of reports dealing with different aspects of poverty.

The Conference of Religious of Ireland (CORI, formerly the Conference of Major Religious Superiors) has become an increasingly influential body in the social policy area since the mid-1980s. It too has been responsible for a number of important publications, e.g. *Social Policy in Ireland: Principles, Practices and Problems* (1998).

The above illustrates the growing interest in and concern with social policy in Ireland and the need to assess the impact of the social services. It is in marked contrast to the situation several decades ago when the same services were rarely subjected to any serious debate or analysis.

Notes

1. NESC Report No. 8, *An Approach to Social Policy* (Stationery Office, Dublin, 1975), p. 30.
2. NESC Report No. 61, *Irish Social Policies: Priorities for Future Development*, (Stationery Office, Dublin, 1981), pp. 12–30.
3. F. Kennedy, *Public Social Expenditure in Ireland* (Economic and Social Research Institute, Dublin, 1975), pp. 54–58.
4. NESC Report No. 61, op. cit., pp. 15–20.
5. *Building on Reality* (Stationery Office, Dublin, 1984), pp. 87–88.
6. A. Coughlan, *Aims of Social Policy* (Tuairim Pamphlet, No. 14, Dublin, 1966), p. 4.
7. See J. Higgins, *States of Welfare: Comparative Analysis in Social Policy* (Basil Blackwell and Martin Robertson, Oxford, 1981), Chapter 4.
8. T. Fahey and J. FitzGerald, *Welfare Implications of Demographic Trends* (Combat Poverty Agency, Dublin, 1997), pp. 116–117.
9. F. Kennedy, op. cit., pp. 11–20.
10. NESC Report No. 89, *A Strategy for the Nineties: Economic Stability and Structural Change* (Stationery Office, Dublin, 1990), p. 6.
11. S. O'Connor, *A Troubled Sky: Reflections of the Irish Educational Scene 1957–1968* (Education Research Centre, St Patrick's College, Dublin 1986) pp. 152–153.
12. *Social Security Benefits: Northern Ireland and Republic of Ireland* (Department of Social Welfare, Dublin, 1991), p. 2.

2

Income Maintenance

Introduction

In this chapter the term 'income maintenance' is used to describe the system of cash payments made to people who experience certain contingencies, such as unemployment and sickness. This system is more popularly referred to in Ireland as 'social welfare' and that terminology is derived from the fact that it is the Department of Social and Family Affairs (formerly the Department of Social Welfare) that is responsible for the administration of the vast majority of the cash payments (and some benefits in kind). The term 'social welfare', however, may have a much broader meaning in other countries. It should also be noted that in many other countries the term 'social security' is used to describe the system of cash payments and, additionally, in some, eligibility for health services.

The basic purpose of an income maintenance system is to provide income support for people who, for whatever reason, experience a loss of income or whose existing income is regarded as being insufficient. In this context it is useful to make a broad distinction between those in the labour market and those outside it. Examples of those in the labour market who experience an income loss would be the unemployed and the short-term ill, while the retired and chronically ill are examples of those outside the labour market.

Over several decades, the types of income contingencies catered for have become accepted in most industrialised countries. They include unemployment, retirement, widowhood and invalidity. It is not unusual, however, for countries to have special measures for other categories. This is true of Ireland where a special scheme was introduced for deserted wives in the 1970s.

Types of income maintenance scheme

There are three main types of income maintenance schemes, i.e. social insurance, social assistance (means tested) and universal.

The distinguishing feature of social insurance schemes is that eligibility is determined on the basis of social insurance contributions paid. They are financed by compulsory contributions on employers, employees and the self-employed. Once the contribution conditions are satisfied, there is an intrinsic entitlement to benefit irrespective of any other income the person may have.

In the case of social assistance or means-tested schemes, eligibility is determined by an assessment of means. Only if the means are below the threshold set for the particular scheme is the claimant entitled to a payment. Partial rather than maximum payment will be paid where the means are greater than the minimum floor set. In general, claimants of social assistance will have either no social insurance contribution record or a broken social insurance record, which effectively disqualifies them from social insurance payments. Means-tested schemes are financed from general taxation.

Under a universal scheme there are neither social insurance contribution conditions nor a means test and a payment is made without respect to income. The most important universal scheme in Ireland is that of child benefit, payable in respect of all children up to a specified age.

The Irish income maintenance system embraces the three types of schemes referred to above. For some time the trend has been to extend the social insurance base and, consequently, the social insurance schemes now account for the larger share of expenditure. Nonetheless the social assistance schemes are likely to be an important element of the system for many decades to come.

Social insurance and social assistance schemes are often referred to as contributory and non-contributory schemes respectively. This is because of the way in which they are funded. In many instances there are complementary social insurance and social assistance schemes. For example, there are widow's and old age contributory pensions for those who satisfy the contribution conditions, while on the social assistance side there are widow's and old age non-contributory pensions for those who do not satisfy the contribution conditions and who qualify on the basis of a means test. The payments under social insurance are invariably higher than those for social assistance although the difference is not consistent across schemes.

Evolution of income maintenance system

The income maintenance system evolved over several decades. Schemes were introduced at different times in response either to an increased emphasis on the needs of particular groups or to newly emerging needs.

An outline of the chronological development of the main income maintenance schemes is given in Table 2.1. This is not meant to be comprehensive but is simply indicative of the piecemeal nature of the development of the system.

Since the background to the development of the income maintenance schemes is given elsewhere,[1] only a broad outline is presented here.

Under the Irish Poor Law system that originated in 1838, workhouses were established throughout the country. The Poor Law was never intended by its founders to be a system of income support but due to various circumstances, involvement in this area was grudgingly and reluctantly conceded. The central philosophy of the Poor Law was that destitution could only be relieved in the workhouses and no help whatsoever was to be made available outside of the workhouse. The circumstances of the great famine in the 1840s, which led to overcrowding of the workhouses and widespread destitution, forced the Poor Law Commissioners to concede the granting of help (in the form of Outdoor Relief) outside of the workhouses. While this was only a temporary measure it eventually became an established part of the Poor Law system. By the beginning of the twentieth century, the only resort of those on low incomes was to Outdoor Relief of the Poor Law. In the 1920s the system of Outdoor Relief was renamed Home Assistance.[2] Gradually, reliance on the Poor Law was diminished as separate schemes were introduced for different categories of claimants.

The first categorical scheme of income maintenance was the old age non-contributory pension that came into effect in 1909 following the passing of the Old Age Pension Act the previous year. This was a landmark development, achieved after twenty years of campaigning by social reformers and several unsuccessful attempts to introduce the necessary legislation.[3] Since then, various schemes for other categories have been introduced, as

Table 2.1: Chronological development of main social welfare schemes

Year	Insurance schemes	Assistance schemes	Other schemes
1838			Poor Law
1909		Old age pension	
1911	Unemployment benefit Sickness benefit		
1920		Blind pension	
1933		Unemployment benefit	
1935	Widow's and orphan's pensions	Widow's and orphan's pensions	
1942			Cheap fuel scheme
1944			Children's allowance Cheap footwear
1947	Department of Social Welfare established		
1961	Old age pension		
1966		Smallholder's assistance	
1967	Occupational injuries		Free travel Electricity allowance
1968			Free TV licence
1970	Retirement pension Invalidity pension	Deserted wife's allowance	
1973	Deserted wife's benefit	Unmarried mother's allowance	
1974	Payment-related benefit	Single woman's allowance Prisoner's wife's allowance	
1977		Supplementary welfare allowance	
1980			National fuel scheme
1984		Family income supplement	
1989		Lone parent's allowance	
1990		Carer's allowance	
1994	Widower's pension		
1997		Widower's pension	

Table 2.1 illustrates. It is interesting to note that the complementary old age contributory pension was not introduced until over half a century later in 1961.

There is no pattern to the way in which the various schemes were introduced. Particular circumstances frequently surrounded the introduction of each scheme. It should be obvious from Table

2.1 that the development of the system was not planned in a coherent manner. At best it can be said that schemes were introduced at different times to meet different needs.

The widow's and orphan's pensions (contributory and non-contributory) were introduced in 1935 following a report of the Poor Law Commission in 1927. The social insurance based unemployment benefits scheme (1911) provided benefit only for short-term unemployment, whereas the widespread and prolonged unemployment of the early 1930s inevitably led to the introduction of a means-tested assistance scheme to enable the unemployed, who had exhausted their unemployment benefit, to continue to receive a payment (albeit at a reduced rate subject to a means test). The introduction of schemes for women in the early 1970s must be considered against the background of the burgeoning women's movement in Ireland and elsewhere at the time and the recommendations of the report of the *Commission on the Status of Women* (1972).

With the introduction of the various categorical schemes, the Home Assistance scheme (derived from the Poor Law) became more and more marginal. Its highly discretionary nature was due to the fact that local authorities administered it without formal guidelines from central level.[4] It was a scheme of last resort and one to cater for emergencies. Home Assistance, the last link with the nineteenth-century Poor Law, was finally replaced in 1977 by supplementary welfare allowance, administered by health boards subject to the control of the Minister for Social Welfare.

In Table 2.1 a number of schemes that are neither social assistance nor social insurance, may be noted. Two of these, i.e. children's allowance (renamed child benefit in 1986) and free travel, are universal schemes. The former, as already indicated, is a scheme whereby monthly payments are made in respect of each child up to age sixteen – or age eighteen if in full-time education (see later section on child income support). Under the free travel scheme all persons of old age pension qualifying age (66 years) and certain other categories are entitled to use public transport facilities (with some exceptions during peak hours in urban areas) free of charge. The electricity allowance is mainly confined to recipients of old age pension living alone and qualification for this allowance automatically gives entitlement to a free TV licence. The cheap fuel scheme was introduced during World War II when fuel was scarce and its application was confined to recipients of certain social welfare payments in urban areas mainly along the eastern seaboard. The scheme remained in existence long after the war and eventually the demand for a similar scheme for the rest of the country was met in 1980 with the introduction of a national fuel scheme. Two separate fuel schemes existed until, in 1988, a unified scheme was introduced for the entire country.

Modifications have been made to schemes since their introduction. This has mainly related to the easement of eligibility conditions. For example, the old age non-contributory pension, introduced in 1909, was described, with some justification, as 'a pension too low at an age too high after a means test which was too severe'.[5] The present situation is quite different; the qualifying age has been reduced from 70 years to 66 years (between 1973 and 1977) and the means test has been eased considerably. Apart from increases in the rates of payment, the eligibility criteria for all schemes have been modified since their inception.

Main features of social insurance schemes

As already indicated, eligibility for the social insurance schemes is based on social insurance contributions. Up to 1974 the social insurance contribution was in the form of a 'stamp' at a flat rate irrespective of income. In that year a partial pay-related social insurance system (PRSI) was introduced and in 1979 a more comprehensive system was introduced. Contributions are based on a percentage of earnings up to a certain ceiling. In 2003 the standard rate of contribution for employees was 4.0 per cent and the ceiling was €40,420. In a year of uninterrupted employment an insured person will have fifty-two contributions paid. The maximum rate of contribution for employers in 2003 was 10.75 per cent of employee income with no ceiling (the ceiling was abolished in 2001).

The qualifying conditions vary from scheme to scheme. In general, however, a contribution record over a relatively long period is required for the long-term payments, such as the old age pension. This is usually in the form of an average number of contributions paid or credited (see later) over a number of years. For example, in order to qualify for the maximum rate of old age pension, an average number of 48 weeks' PRSI paid or credited from 1953 or from the time insurable employment commenced to the end of the tax year before reaching pensionable age is required.

Qualification for short-term benefits, such as unemployment and disability (sickness), is based on a contribution record of a shorter duration than for the long-term benefits. For example, unemployment benefit is payable if the claimant has at least 39 weeks' PRSI paid and at least 39 weeks' PRSI paid or credited in the governing tax year; 48 weeks' PRSI paid or credited are required in the governing tax year in order to obtain benefit at the maximum rate.

Apart from contributions that have been paid, provision is also made for credited contributions that apply in certain circumstances. A person on unemployment benefit, for example, may continue to receive credited contributions that, in effect, are the equivalent of paid contributions. Credits help to maintain a social insurance record over a period of unemployment and are an important means of qualifying for long-term benefits.

There are a number of different social insurance classes that determine the rate of contribution. Persons in Class A account for the majority of contributors who pay the standard rate of 4.0 per cent. Persons in this class are entitled to the full range of social insurance benefits. There are special social insurance categories for others who are not entitled to the same range of benefits. For example, permanent and pensionable civil servants who were employed in the civil service prior to October 1995 pay a contribution of 0.9 per cent and in return are entitled to a limited number of benefits. The rationale behind the classification of the population into different social insurance classes is related to work status. In the case of civil servants employed prior to 1995, the rationale for not paying the full contribution would appear to be that, having secure employment and consequently being most unlikely to become unemployed and having adequate occupational pensions, it was unnecessary for them to contribute towards such benefits. The end result is a rather complex system of social insurance classes. In 2001, the insured population was 2.4 million and three-quarters were in Class A.

A full description of the contribution conditions attached to the various social insurance schemes and details of the social insurance classes are given in *Guide to Social Welfare Services*, published by the Department of Social and Family Affairs.

Main features of social assistance schemes

Eligibility for all social assistance schemes is determined on the basis of a means test. The amount of means will determine whether a person is entitled to maximum benefit, or reduced benefit, or is ineligible for any benefit. Officers of the Department of Social and Family Affairs assess means.

In the assessment of means a number of items are taken into account. These include cash income less certain allowances and the value of investments.

A portion of earnings is disregarded in the calculation of means for certain assistance schemes, such as blind pension and lone parents payments. The income derived from a dwelling through letting and, in the case of farmers, the value of all saleable produce from the farm is taken into account.

Up to 2001 different methods were used for calculating interest from investments (such as bank deposits, stocks and shares) for various social assistance schemes. Since then, however, the same formula applies to all. Under this formula a certain amount of savings (€12,697 in 2003) is disregarded and a notional value is applied to the balance on a sliding scale. The amount of savings will determine whether a peron is entitled to the maximum assistance, or partial assistance, or is ineligible for assistance.

The details of the means requirements for particular schemes are given in *Guide to Social Welfare Services* published by the Department of Social and Family Affairs.

While a number of modifications to the means test took place in the early 1970s it was not until 1997 that further substantial amendments were made especially to the formulae for the assessment of savings. Following further simplification in 2002 the same formula now applies to all claimant categories. Despite these improvements, the system of means test can only be described as complex and it is extremely doubtful if it is fully understood by many claimants.

Other social welfare schemes

Apart from the social insurance and social assistance schemes, reference has already been made to a number of miscellaneous schemes administered by the Department of Social and Family Affairs. The most notable of these is the system of child benefit, formerly known as children's allowance (see later section on child income support). Others include the various 'free' schemes such as electricity allowance and telephone rental for certain categories of recipients.

Beneficiaries of social welfare

An important feature of the Irish income maintenance system is that once a claimant has established entitlement, payments are also generally made in respect of any adult and child dependants. This has been a traditional feature of the system and was only modified following the implementation of an EC Directive in 1986 on the equal treatment of men and women. Up to then spouses (married women mostly) were regarded as being financially dependent. With the greater participation by married women in the labour force, however, the situation had changed over a period of time but this change was not reflected in the income maintenance system. For example, if a man became unemployed and qualified for unemployment benefit, he received a personal rate of payment together with an adult dependant rate even if his wife was employed and earning a relatively high income. In compliance with the Directive, this situation was changed amid considerable controversy at the end of 1986.

An adult dependant is now defined as someone who is either not earning or whose weekly earning falls below a specified threshold. The situation with regard to payment for child dependants has also altered. If a full personal rate and full adult dependant allowance is payable, then the full child dependant allowance is payable. If, however, the spouse is not regarded as an adult dependant (as defined above), then only half the child dependant allowance is payable for each child.

The above brief description of the situation in relation to dependants in the income maintenance system is a necessary prelude to understanding trends in the number of beneficiaries. Recipients together with their adult and child dependants constitute the beneficiaries.

Over the past thirty years or so the number of beneficiaries has almost trebled (Table 2.2). Recipients of child benefit are not included in these figures. In 1966 the 566,000 beneficiaries accounted for just under 20 per cent of the population and by 2001 this had increased to 1,460,000 or 38.0 per cent of the population. Over this period the peak number of beneficiaries was 1,486,000 in 1997.

Table 2.2: Total number of beneficiaries* of weekly social welfare payments, selected years 1966–2001

Year	Beneficiaries	Percentage of total population
1966	566,400	19.6
1982	1,110,900	32.3
1996	1,485,500	41.0
2001	1,460,000	38.0

* Recipients, adult dependants and child dependants. The figures do not include recipients of child benefit.

Source: Statistical Information on Social Welfare Services

This does not imply, of course, that about two fifths of the population is solely dependent on social welfare payments. For example, some of those in receipt of social insurance payments, such as old age contributory pensions, may well have another source of income. It is only those on the maximum rates of social assistance payments who rely almost exclusively on social welfare payments for their livelihood. Just over half (52.8 per cent) of beneficiaries in 2001 were in receipt of social assistance payments.

The growth in the number of beneficiaries is accounted for by a number of factors. Of these, the increase in unemployment is by far the most significant, accounting for half of the growth between 1966 and 1996. Other factors include the introduction of new schemes over this period such as lone parent's allowance and modification of eligibility conditions such as the lowering of the qualifying age for old age pensions.

The growth in unemployment is reflected in the composition of the social welfare population. In 1966 the unemployed and their dependants accounted for one-quarter of the total; by 1996 this had increased to two-fifths but by 2001 had fallen to one-sixth. Beneficiaries of old age and retirement pensions accounted for one-quarter of the total in 2001 as compared with one-third in 1966.

Financing and expenditure

As already indicated, a distinction can be made between the financing of the social insurance schemes and the financing of the social assistance schemes.

Social insurance schemes are financed from pay-related social insurance contributions from employers and employees, with the state making good any deficit on outgoings from general taxation.

Financing of social assistance schemes is from general taxation. Employer and employee PRSI contributions as well as those from the self-employed go into the social insurance fund (see Table 2.3). The tripartite system of funding (employers/workers/state) is not based on any set formula. In practice, the shares have fluctuated over time. The *White Paper on Social Security* (1949) argued that the fund should be financed equally by employers, employees and the state.[6] This recommendation was not acted upon. In 1975, the Minister for Finance, Richie Ryan, TD, stated:

> The Government have decided in principle to transfer the exchequer contribution towards the cost of social insurance to the other contributors to the social insurance fund over a period of six years or so.[7]

This was not acted upon either. The employer share is now more than double what it was three decades ago.

Since 1998, due to the substantial increase in employment and the consequent increase in the flow of contributions from employers, employees and self-employed, the social insurance fund has been in surplus for the first time. In 2001 there was an estimated surplus of €630 million. The increase in contributions to the fund also allowed for a reduction in the standard rate of PRSI from 5.5 per cent of reckonable income in 1998 to 4.0 per cent in 2001.

Table 2.3: Sources of income for social insurance fund, selected years 1967–2001* (%)

	1967 *(€44m)*	*1980* *(€636m)*	*1996* *(€2,399m)*	*2001* *(€4,306m)*
Employer	30.5	53.2	64.5	75.1
Employee	29.1	22.1	25.2	19.5
Self-employed	-	-	5.0	4.4
State	38.1	24.5	5.3	-
Other receipts	2.3	0.2	0.0	1.1
	100.0	100.0	100.0	100.0

* Up to 1990 the occupational injuries insurance was not included in the above figures. It was funded solely by employers from a separate fund. In 1990 this fund was amalgamated with the social insurance fund and this accounts for the increase in the employers' share and the drop in the state's share.
Source: Statistical Information on Social Welfare Services

Table 2.4: Sources of income for all expenditure on social welfare, selected years 1967–2001* (%)

	1967 *(€86m)*	*1980* *(€1,108m)*	*1996* *(€5,771m)*	*2001* *(€7,842m)*
Employer	18.4	31.8	27.8	
Employee	14.5	12.4	10.9	46.8**
Self Employed	-	-	2.1	
State	65.3	55.4	59.0	52.7
Other receipts	1.8	0.4	0.1	0.5
	100.0	100.0	100.0	100.0

* The occupational injuries insurance was not included in these figures until 1990.
** Social insurance fund
Source: Statistical Information on Social Welfare Services

When the financing of the social assistance schemes is allied to that of the social insurance schemes, the state's contribution to the total system is relatively high (Table 2.4).

Administration
Prior to the National Insurance Act, 1911, a number of friendly societies provided schemes for sickness benefit. Following the Act, sickness and unemployment schemes continued to be operated mainly by the existing societies under the general supervision of the Irish Insurance Commissioners. A statutory condition of admittance to the scheme was that a society be non-profit making. Commercial insurance companies, which formed separate non-profit making branches, also became involved in the scheme. By 1933 the number of insured persons in the state was about 474,000 and these were catered for by 65 approved societies with membership ranging from 55 in a small mutual benefit society up to over 100,000 in a central society covering the whole country.[8] These societies had considerable freedom in selecting workers to be admitted to membership and some societies were relatively more prosperous than others. The latter, by accumulating reserves, were able to increase the statutory cash benefits while at the other end of the scale some small societies had difficulty even in meeting the statutory benefits. Apart from these differences between societies, the administrative costs of the scheme were also relatively high.

The National Health Insurance Act, 1933 made provision for the amalgamation of all societies into a single agency – the National Health Insurance Society. In 1947 the Department of Social Welfare was established and all social insurance and assistance functions previously performed by the Departments of Local Government and Public Health (e.g. old age pensions, widow's and orphan's pensions) and by Industry and Commerce (e.g. unemployment assistance, children's allowance) were transferred to the new department. The National Health Insurance Society was dissolved in 1950 and its functions taken over by the Minister for Social Welfare. The Social Welfare Act, 1952 established a unified social insurance scheme, replacing the separate schemes for unemployment, national health and widow's and orphan's pensions. The net effect of these changes was not only to simplify administrative procedures and reduce costs but also to ensure that one government minister was responsible for the direction of all social insurance and assistance schemes.

While the Department of Social and Family Affairs has overall responsibility, the co-operation of other government agencies is essential to the administration of the income maintenance system. An Post, through its extensive network of post offices, provides outlets for payments such as child benefit and old age pensions. The Department of Justice, Equality and Law Reform, through the Garda Síochána, also assists by certifying evidence of unemployment for claimants who live more than six miles from a social welfare office. The Revenue Commissioners collect the pay-related social insurance (PRSI) contributions from employers, employees and the self-employed.

Appeals system
An important element of the administration of the income maintenance system is the right to appeal. This is designed to safeguard the rights of claimants who feel they have been unfairly refused payment or awarded less than the maximum payment. Appeals are dealt with by appeals officers and may be decided summarily (especially those dealing with contribution records) or orally.

The number of appeals constitutes a relatively small proportion of the total number of annual claims (Table 2.5). The 12,353 appeals in 1995 accounted for 0.8 per cent of total claims (1,516,801). Statistics on the number of claims have not been

Table 2.5: Number of social welfare claims* and appeals, selected years, 1985–2001

	Claims	*Appeals*
1985	1,174,050	17,288
1990	1,080,873	15,871
1995	1,516,801	12,353
2001	n/a	15,961

* Excluding claims for 'free schemes', such as free travel, electricity allowance and free phone rental.
Sources: Statistical Information on Social Welfare Services; Reports of Social Welfare Appeals Office

published in recent years. It had not been the practice of the Department of Social Welfare to publish statistics on the outcome of appeals but since the establishment in 1990 of a separate Appeals Office (see later section) in line with the recommendations of the Commission on Social Welfare, this has been done. The 2001 report indicated that of the 16,525 appeals decided, just over two-fifths were resolved in favour of the appellant.[9] Since the establishment of the Appeals Office there has been a sharp downward trend in the number of appeals – from 19,314 in 1991 to 12,353 in 1995. Much of this is attributed to the improved claim procedures as recommended by that Office. The recent increase in the number of appeals may be partly attributed to the increase in new schemes and the transfer of appeals on supplementary welfare from health boards to the Appeals Office.

Commission on Social Welfare
Despite the central role of the income maintenance schemes in the lives of so many people, the considerable public expenditure involved and the piecemeal development of the system, it is surprising that no fundamental review had taken place before the establishment of the Commission on Social Welfare in 1983. This is in marked contrast to other areas such as health and education. Admittedly, three official reports on the system were published: a White Paper, *Social Security* (1949), and two Green Papers, *A National Income-Related Pension Scheme* (1976) and *Social Insurance for Self Employed* (1978). In addition, a special committee was established to examine the system of workmen's compensation arising from occupational injuries and its report was published in 1962. Otherwise, the system was not subject to the periodic

review that has been characteristic of other areas. Nor was there any popular demand for reform. The main areas of concern to particular groups were the rates of payment and these would normally be the subjects of pre-Budget submissions. In 1982 the National Social Services Board in its pre-Budget submission called for the establishment of a commission to carry out a fundamental review of the system.[10] A commitment to establish such a commission was part of the programme of the Fine Gael/ Labour Coalition Government which came into office in December 1982. The Commission on Social Welfare was established in 1983.

The Commission's report, published in 1986, opted for an evolutionary rather than a radical change to the system. It envisaged reforms within the framework of the existing system rather than replacing that system. At no stage had any guiding principles been laid down for the income maintenance system. The Commission therefore considered that the principles that should guide the development of the system were adequacy, redistribution, comprehensiveness, consistency, and simplicity. The reformed system, as proposed by the Commission, reflected a mix of these principles but with a special emphasis on the principle of adequacy.

The four key elements of the reformed system proposed by the Commission concerned the payment structure, social insurance, social assistance and financing.

The payment structure
The most fundamental issue facing the Commission was the adequacy of payments. There had never been any official attempt to establish what a minimally adequate income for a person dependent on income maintenance should be. The payment structure had simply evolved without any explicit reference to particular indicators such as wage levels. Since the early 1970s, however, there has been a conscious attempt to ensure that increases in payments are in line with inflation.

By using a number of indicators the Commission estimated that a minimally adequate income for a single person in 1985 was in the range of £50 to £60 per week (the top point being equivalent to approximately half the net average industrial earnings). The Commission recognised that its calculation of a minimally adequate income could be open to criticism but stated:

... in the absence of any explicit official criteria and because of the limitations of available data we had no option but to attempt to establish a minimally adequate income. Not to have done so would, in our view, have been a serious omission. Furthermore, if our approach is considered to be deficient then an acceptable alternative should be provided.[11]

Some of the existing payments were well below the estimated minimally adequate income while others were at or near the top part of the range. The Commission was faced with a variety of payment levels for different categories and contingencies for which there was no apparent rationale. The lowest payment (unemployment assistance) in the system for a single person was 60 per cent of the highest payment (old age contributory pension). Inevitably, incongruous situations arose where, for example, a person long-term unemployed with a dependent spouse and two children received considerably less than a couple on old age pension.

The variation in rates of payment for different categories mainly arose from piecemeal changes over time rather than any systematic evaluation of the income needs of particular categories. The result was a payment structure that was not only complex but also discriminated against individuals and families with similar financial needs. A hierarchical system existed, with the highest payments going to older people, followed by widows and with the unemployed at the bottom. Insofar as there was any rationale for the different rates of payment it may have had more to do with popular notions of need in Irish society and of attitudes towards groups that were regarded as 'deserving' and 'undeserving' poor. The Commission recommended that, in general, the same basic payment should apply to all recipients, with the main difference being a differential of the order of 10 per cent between insurance and assistance payments.

A number of other issues arose in the context of the payment structure. The Commission made recommendations on each of these, designed to bring a greater degree of consistency into the system. Thus, for example, there were no less than 36 different rates of child dependant payments depending on the birth order of the child and the recipient category of the parent. The lowest child dependant payment was 42 per cent of the highest and children of widows attracted the highest amounts. In the Commission's view, the range was unjustified and it recommended a rationalisation of child dependant payments. Similarly, the Commission argued that the existing limited pay-related element (associated with some payments only) should be phased out and the priority should be the attainment of a minimally adequate income for all recipients.

Social insurance
The Commission favoured the retention of the social insurance system. The *raison d'etre* of social insurance had never been sufficiently articulated in Ireland. For this reason the Commission emphasised that social insurance was an expression of social solidarity and citizenship in which the risks, costs and benefits are spread as widely as possible in the community. Furthermore, in the Commission's view, social insurance contributions create a sense of entitlement to benefit and generate support among the community for these benefits. The Commission recommended that all income earners should therefore contribute to and benefit where appropriate from social insurance. The main group outside the social insurance system when the report was published was the self-employed, including farmers, who accounted for about 20 per cent of the labour force.

Apart from the self-employed, there were other smaller groups not liable for social insurance contributions, such as members of religious orders and certain ministers of religion. Furthermore, public servants were liable only for a modified rate of contribution on grounds that their conditions of employment did not warrant coverage for all benefits. The Commission recommended that all public servants be liable for the full rate of contribution.

Social assistance
The widening of coverage for social insurance as proposed by the Commission would lead to a decline in the need for means-tested social assistance payments. Social assistance would then be a residual element in the income maintenance system.

The Commission recommended that there should be a comprehensive social assistance scheme for those who, for whatever reason, do not qualify for social insurance. The main condition would be the establishment of an income need irrespective of the cause of that need. This would lead to the elimination of the unnecessary categorical social assistance schemes that existed (e.g. lone parent's allowance, widow's pension, prisoner's wives allowance). The income need would be established by reference to a means test. The Commission recommended that the means test be rationalised and simplified and that the main constituents be better publicised.

Financing
It has already been noted that the social insurance system in Ireland is funded on a tripartite basis by employers, workers and the state and that social assistance is funded entirely out of general taxation. There is no set formula which determines the apportionment of costs between the three partners to the social insurance fund nor did the Commission support the notion of pre-stated shares.

While the Commission recognised that social insurance is not directly comparable with private commercial insurance, it nevertheless has a significant insurance dimension that is not outweighed by the absence of an actuarial link between benefits and contributions. The Commission also considered the question of the employment effects of employers' social insurance contributions, a subject of debate on a number of occasions in the recent past. In the Commission's view, the evidence concerning the effects on employment was inconclusive. Nor did it justify a departure from the payroll base of contributions that the Commission concluded was the broadest, most clearly identifiable and predictable base available.

On grounds of redistribution the Commission concluded that the income ceiling on contributions should be gradually abolished. This move would need to be co-ordinated with the evolution of earnings and income tax.

Other issues
The Commission also considered a series of issues related to the key elements of the proposed reform. These included issues affecting particular groups such as the unemployed, older people and lone parents. In relation to the unemployed, for example, the Commission did not consider the administrative procedures governing conditions of entitlement to unemployment payments to be appropriate given the high level of unemployment at the time. This applied especially to those which require the unemployed to attend at an employment exchange at least once weekly in order to 'sign on', indicate their availability for

employment, and collect their payment. The Commission recommended a more flexible approach and the need to provide all recipients with the greatest possible choice in relation to method of payment.

A considerable degree of duplication of functions exists between the Department of Social and Family Affairs (formerly the Department of Social Welfare) and the Department of Health and Children (formerly the Department of Health). While the Department of Social and Family Affairs is mainly concerned with providing a range of cash benefits, it is also responsible for 'treatment benefits' (dental, ophthalmic and aural) based on social insurance contributions. These are more properly health functions. Similarly, the Department of Health and Children, through the health boards, administers a number of cash payments. This in turn gives rise to a lack of consistency and uniformity in the application of guidelines since, in effect, the health boards are autonomous agencies. Particular problems arise in the case of the supplementary welfare allowance scheme (formerly home assistance), administered by health boards, where discretion is an important element. The Commission recommended that all income maintenance functions be transferred to the Department of Social Welfare, and the 'treatment benefits' transferred to the Department of Health. Ironically, when the views of the two Departments on this matter were sought by the Commission, it emerged that the principle of the transfer of functions had been agreed for some time but no concrete steps had been taken to effect the transfer.

Because of the nature of the service, the Commission's view was that the income maintenance system should be organised to respond in an efficient manner to the client population. A survey based on the experiences and perceptions of claimants was commissioned and this highlighted a number of deficiencies, especially the delay in processing claims. The Commission considered that computerisation was a key factor in the development of a more efficient and more localised service and envisaged a situation where the entire application process could be conducted locally. Delays were encountered because of the transfer of claimant files to and from central offices in Dublin. The efficient delivery of the service should be balanced by a need for control measures, and a number of recommendations designed to limit the scope for fraud were made.

The appeals function is an important aspect of the income maintenance system. In the Commission's view there was a perception that the appeals system was not independent since it operated within the Department of Social Welfare. Furthermore, statistics on appeals were published as part of the Department's biennial reports but consisted of numbers of appeals under different categories, without information on the outcome of appeals. The Commission recommended the establishment of an Appeals Office as a separate executive office with a requirement that it publish an annual report containing not only comprehensive statistics but also, where necessary, policy recommendations.

Progress on implementation
While the Commission had estimated that additional revenue could be generated from broadening the social insurance base, there would be a net cost to the exchequer from implementing its recommendations. Partly, though not exclusively for cost reasons, the Commission recommended that the development of the reformed system be undertaken on a gradual basis and it listed areas requiring priority attention. These included improvement in the basic rate of payment for those on the lowest social welfare rates and a broadening of the social insurance base.

The government statement issued on publication of the Commission's report in August 1986 noted that:

> in present circumstances and for the immediate future it would be beyond the capacity of the country to fully implement the Commission's proposals. This is an unpalatable reality but it must be borne in mind in the context of considering all the Commission's proposals.

This statement gave the impression that the Commission's report was going to be ignored by government. Subsequently, Gemma Hussey, TD, Minister for Social Welfare, stated in the Dáil that:

> ... there is no question of the report being dismissed or ignored. There is absolutely no doubt that radical changes will be necessary over the next few years in the social welfare system ...While we must be selective in bringing forward proposals for additional expenditure, there is considerable scope for reform of the system in line with the general approach which the Commission has adopted.[12]

While the government's initial reaction to the report appeared to be hostile, there was a general welcome for the thrust of its recommendations from a variety of organisations. The apparent rejection of the report by the government led to the formation of a coalition of over 20 voluntary groups – Campaign for Welfare Reform – to lobby for the implementation of its recommendations. The notion of the minimally adequate income was highlighted in the debate that ensued and the figure proposed by the Commission was not challenged.

Following the change of government in 1987 some progress began to be made on the recommendations. The Budgets of 1989 to 1992 provided for higher increases for those on the lowest payment levels and this had the effect of significantly narrowing the gap between the highest and lowest payment (see Table 2.6). In the Budgets of 1997 to 2002, however, higher increases were given to recipients of old age pensions, with the result that the narrowing of the gap has been halted. The lowest weekly personal payment (unemployment assistance) is now three-quarters of that of the highest personal weekly payment (old age contributory pension aged over 80 years).

Table 2.6: Trends in highest and lowest weekly payments (€) 1985–2002

	1985	*1988*	*1990*	*2002*	*Increase 1985–2002*
A: Highest payment (contributory old age pension, over 80 years)	69.70	77.00	83.30	153.70	120.5%
B: Lowest payment (unemployment assistance short duration)	41.60	49.50	57.15	118.80	185.6%
B as percentage of A	60%	64%	69%	77%	

* Up to 1989 there was a distinction in the personal and married rates for unemployment assistance between urban and rural areas. In 1985 the rural personal rate was €40.30. The distinction was abolished in 1989 and the rural rate increased to the same level as the urban.

The number of different rates of payment for dependent children was rationalised considerably – from 36 rates in 1988 to 3 rates in 1991. In 1988, the self-employed, members of religious orders and all ministers of religion became liable for social insurance contributions. This was perhaps the most significant development in the income maintenance system in decades as it had seemed, for some time, that the political will to bring these groups into the system was lacking. Other developments were the introduction of a lone parent social assistance scheme in 1989 and a carer's allowance in 1990. The lone parent scheme represented a move towards a more rational system of income support for lone parents, including male lone parents with dependent children.

The Social Welfare Act, 1990 provided for the establishment of a separate Appeals Office, headed by a Director and Chief Appeals Officer, as an executive office of the Department of Social Welfare. The establishment of the Appeals Office was designed to emphasise the independence of the appeals system and to ensure that it was perceived to be impartial and independent. In accordance with the Commission's recommendations, the Appeals Office is obliged to publish an annual report on its activities with comment, where necessary, on the workings of the social welfare system and the implications of its decisions for policy making.

In the decade following publication, various groups used the *Report of the Commission on Social Welfare* in their pre-budget submissions and as a yardstick to evaluate reforms in the system. Of greatest significance perhaps was the commitment made in the *Programme for Economic and Social Progress* (1991), agreed between government and the social partners, to implement the priority recommendations of the report over a three-year period. This was the first commitment at official level to implement the Commission's recommendations on a minimally adequate income and came five years after the report's publication. It was followed by further commitments in the *Programme for Competitiveness and Work* (1993) and *Partnership 2000* (1996). These commitments were largely due to the influence of the trade union movement. By the Budget of 1998, Charlie McCreevy, TD, Minister for Finance, could state that the rates of payment for all but two categories (unemployment assistance and supplementary welfare allowance) were above the minimum rates recommended by the Commission.

Following decades of piecemeal development, the *Report of the Commission on Social Welfare* provided a blueprint for the rational development of the income maintenance system.

Income adequacy

One of the central features of the Commission's report was the emphasis on a minimally adequate income. This was the first time that the adequacy of social welfare payments had been subjected to critical scrutiny. In 1996 the Economic and Social Research Institute published a review of the Commission's minimum adequate income. The fact that the Department of Social Welfare commissioned the review was in itself significant. It represented an acknowledgement that the Commission's emphasis on adequacy was justified. The review pointed out that no method of measuring adequacy could 'allow one to derive in an unproblematic, objective and scientific way, estimates of adequacy which would be universally acceptable and convincing'.[13]

The review pointed out that social welfare payments in Ireland were generally above those in the United Kingdom relative to average earnings but below the average for EU countries as a whole.

The National Anti-Poverty Strategy (NAPS) was published by government in 1997 (see Chapter 8). One of the five key areas selected for attention over the ten-year life span of the strategy was income adequacy. The objective was to ensure that all policies in relation to income support (e.g. unemployment, tax, social welfare, pensions) provide sufficient income for a person to move out of poverty and live in a manner compatible with human dignity.

The *Programme for Prosperity and Fairness* (PPF) (2000) contained the following commitments over the three-year term of that programme:

- to increase all social welfare payments in real terms
- substantial progress to be made towards a target of €127 per week for the lowest rate of social welfare.

The PPF also stated:

> Recognising the complex issues involved in developing a benchmark for adequacy of adult and child social welfare payments, including the implications of adopting a specific approach to the ongoing up-rating or indexation of payments, a Working Group will be established with an independent chairperson to examine the issues ... and to report by April 2001.

The Working Group, the Social Welfare Benchmarking and Indexation Group, completed its report in September 2001. The majority of the group proposed a formal linkage between adult social welfare rates and average earnings in order to ensure that the income of social welfare recipients keep pace with those of the wider population. While recognising that the exact rate was a matter for government, the Group proposed that a target of 27 per cent of gross average industrial earnings (on a current year basis) be established. This target should be met by 2007. A minority of the Group felt it was inappropriate to establish a formal benchmark and that existing arrangements should continue to apply.

The revised National Anti-Poverty Strategy (under the PPF) 2002 contained a commitment by government to increase the lowest rates of social welfare to €150 per week in 2002 terms, by 2007, but it did not refer to any formal link with gross average industrial earnings.

The Commission on Social Welfare was first to raise in a fundamental manner the adequacy of social welfare payments. By establishing a target for a minimally adequate income for social welfare recipients in the mid-1980s it had raised the debate to a hitherto unprecedented level. Subsequent developments indicate that by doing so it ensured that the issue of adequacy remained a feature of the wider social policy agenda.

Basic income
For some time it has been suggested that the income tax and social welfare systems should be so integrated as to eliminate the need for the latter. This would involve the payment of a basic income to be granted, unconditionally, to everyone on an individual basis, irrespective of income from other sources. This new system, it is argued, would eliminate the poverty and unemployment traps inherent in the present systems. Because it would be neutral as to the work status of the individual, it would facilitate the free movement of persons between employment and unemployment without creating any disincentives.

Variants of this basic income have been propounded in various reports. The NESC, for example, published a consultant's report on this subject in 1979 but did not recommend its adoption. The Commission on Social Welfare also examined the feasibility of its introduction but opted for reform of the existing social welfare system rather than the more radical reform inherent in the basic income.

Arising from a commitment in the *Programme for Partnership Government* between the Fianna Fáil and Labour parties in 1992, 'to study in consultation with the social partners the integration of the tax and social welfare codes', an Expert Working Group was established. Its report, *Integrating Tax and Social Welfare*, was published in 1996. The Expert Group assessed a number of options ranging from full integration of the tax and social welfare systems in the form of a basic income to options which provided for better co-ordination of the systems. The Expert Group did not recommend a basic income mainly because the rate of income tax required to fund it – 68 per cent – was considered too high. This in turn was considered likely to have a negative impact on employment. Having examined a range of associated issues, the Expert Group did, however, recommend a simplification and co-ordination of the tax and social welfare systems.

In 1997 the Conference of Religious of Ireland (CORI) published a study, *Pathways to a Basic Income*, in which it argued that its proposals for a basic income could be funded by a tax rate of between 44 per cent and 49 per cent. The *Irish Times* commented that:

> On the face of it, the kind of payments favoured by CORI would appear to require substantial tax increases – especially for the top 30 per cent of earners on a scale which no political party has the courage to propose at this time.

Partnership 2000, agreed between government and the social partners, contained a commitment that 'a further independent appraisal of the concept of, and the full implications of introducing a basic income payment for all citizens will be undertaken'.

In keeping with this commitment a Green Paper, *Basic Income*, was published in 2002.

The Green Paper outlined the essential elements of a basic income:

- It would be an unconditional amount paid by government to each individual in the state
- The payment would be tax free
- All other income, for example, from a job, would be taxed

- It would involve replacing the existing social welfare and income tax systems with a universal payment to all adults and a lesser amount to children
- A flat rate of income tax would apply
- A social solidarity fund would be established to compensate persons on low-income who would lose out from the abolition of social welfare payments.

The Green Paper indicated that 'there is a considerable element of uncertainty in predicting the likely dynamic effects of the introduction of a basic income system'.[14]

In announcing the publication of the Green Paper, the Taoiseach, Bertie Ahern, TD, indicated that it 'honours the commitment to inform and widen future public consideration of the concept'. The overriding impression, however, is that publication of the Green Paper had more to do with honouring a commitment than with any intention of introducing basic income in the future.

Child income support
Child income support is an essential yet complex aspect of the Irish income maintenance system. Part of the complexity stems from the fact that there are now three forms of child income support:

- the universal child benefit (formerly children's allowance)
- child dependant allowances paid to recipients of weekly social welfare payments
- family income supplement.

Children's allowance was introduced in 1944 and the monthly allowance was paid in respect of the third and subsequent children. In introducing the Bill in the Dáil, Séan Lemass, TD, Minister for Industry and Commerce, gave the following as the rationale for the scheme:

> The basis of the argument in favour of the establishment of a children's allowance scheme is that among the causes of want, apart from unemployment, ill-health (etc) there is the fact that in an economic system such as ours, where wages are related to standards of productivity or determined by supply and demand, the amount the wage earner can obtain is frequently inadequate to provide for the reasonable requirements of a large family ... it is, I think, necessary

to emphasise that the basis of the whole case for the establishment of a children's allowance service is the need of large families.[15]

Subsequently, various changes were made to the scheme and it became payable to the second child in 1952 and to the first child in 1963.

Parallel to the scheme of children's allowance was a tax allowance for each child. In 1984 the government pledged to introduce a unified system of child benefit.[16] This unified system, however, was not introduced but the tax allowance, whose value had been reduced over a period of time, was eventually abolished in 1986 and children's allowance was renamed child benefit.

One of the important differences between child benefit and other social welfare payments is that increases in the rates of payment of child benefit are treated quite separately. In other words, increases in general social welfare payments are not necessarily applied in the case of child benefit.

A further feature of child benefit is that due to the decline in the birth rate over a few decades the number of beneficiaries has declined substantially, from 1,187,465 in 1985 to 1,014,340 in 2001 (a decline of 14.6 per cent).

The basic objective of the family income supplement (FIS) introduced in 1984 was to increase the difference between take-home pay for those on low income and the unemployment payments that those on low pay would be entitled to if they were unemployed. In this way there is a supplement or top up to take-home pay. At the time of the introduction of FIS the perception was that those with large families were only marginally better off when working on low pay by comparison with being in receipt of unemployment support payments and thus would have little incentive to take up low paid employment. In the Budget of 1983, John Bruton, TD, Minister for Finance, indicated that an estimated 20,000 families would benefit from FIS. By the end of 1985, after one full year in operation, only 4,664 families had availed themselves of FIS. Subsequently, the scheme was widely advertised by the Department of Social Welfare, the eligibility conditions were eased and higher rates of payment introduced. By 2001 the number of recipient families was 11,570.

Ideally, the preferred system of child income support would be one which did not have regard to whether the recipient was in receipt of social welfare payments or not. But to move to that situation may be difficult and costly. The main cost arises from increasing child benefit to such an extent that it is possible to abolish child dependant allowances while at the same time ensuring that the families in receipt of them do not experience a drop in income as a result.

The Fine Gael, Labour and Democratic Left parties assumed office in December 1994 just as the Child Benefit Review Committee was completing its report for the outgoing government. In their joint programme, *A Government of Renewal*, the three parties pledged:

> We will work towards a basic income system for children by systematic improvements in child benefit and the creation of a child benefit supplement to all social welfare recipients and to low and middle income families. It will replace child dependant allowances currently payable to social welfare recipients and family income supplement which is currently payable to many low-income families.

While the precise nature of the child benefit supplements was not clear, government policy in the budgets of 1995 to 1997 was to enhance the value of child benefit. At the same time as the child benefit was increased substantially, the child dependant allowances were effectively frozen, with no increases since 1994.

Child benefit has frequently been the subject of criticism on the grounds that it should be applied more selectively rather than applied to all income groups. Furthermore, the rationale for child benefit has strayed somewhat from its original purpose and over time various policies have been ascribed to it. The Child Benefit Review Committee (1995) was of the view that child benefit fulfilled a number of roles, the most important of which were:

- assistance to all households with children in recognition of the higher costs incurred
- the alleviation, without contributing to labour market disincentives, of household poverty associated with children.[17]

At times it has been suggested that child benefit is essentially a payment to mothers for whom it may be the only source of independent income. This fact has been highlighted on occasions when any form of targeting has been suggested. There has been strong opposition to treating child benefit either as taxable income, or introducing some form of means test such as a qualifying income ceiling. In the Budget of 1989, for example, Albert Reynolds, TD, Minister for Finance, referred to the unselective nature of child benefit and indicated that the government wished to target resources by confining the payment to families with incomes below a certain level. Nothing came of these proposals.

More recently, child benefit has been viewed as a means of helping to contribute towards the cost of child care. The child care issue gained particular prominence in the late 1990s as more women with children participated in the work force. While various suggestions were made as to how this situation might be addressed, the government's decision was to provide capital for the expansion of the number of childcare places rather than directly subsidise the cost of such care to parents through tax allowances. Allied with this, however, was an unprecedented increase in child benefit payments by the Fianna Fáil/Progressive Democrat government of 1997 to 2002. During that period the payment for the first and second child increased from €38.09 to €117.60 and the payment for the third and subsequent children increased from €49.52 to €147.30. But the confused purpose of child benefit was evident in the 2001 Budget speech by Charlie McCreevy, TD, Minister for Finance. He referred to the diversity of views held in relation to the childcare issue and that the government's objective was to offer real choice to parents. The substantial increases in child benefit would therefore 'help all parents with the cost of rearing their children and represent a major move towards ending child poverty'. In other words the policy now was that child benefit would serve a dual purpose – to deal with the costs of child care and the relief of child poverty.

There is a lack of clarity in relation to policy for child income support. If anything the situation has got worse and the objectives seem to be even more confused. The recent trends may be summarised as follows:

- Improvement in child benefit
- Improvement in family income supplement
- The effective freezing of child dependant allowances since 1994.

It is not clear if the purpose is to eventually eliminate the child dependant allowance.

Notes

1. See D. Farley, *Social Insurance and Social Assistance in Ireland* (Institute of Public Administration, Dublin, 1964); *Report of the Commission on Social Welfare* (Stationery Office, Dublin, 1986), Chapter 2.
2. For an excellent account of the evolution of the income support aspect of the Poor Law system see S. Ó Cinnéide, 'The Development of Home Assistance Service', *Administration*, Vol.17, No. 3, 1969.
3. See C. Carney, 'A Case Study in Social Policy – The Non-Contributory Old Age Pension', *Administration*, Vol. 33, No. 4. (1985), pp. 483–527.
4. See S. Ó Cinnéide, *A Law for the Poor* (Institute of Public Administration, Dublin, 1970).
5. Quoted in P. Kaim-Caudle, *Comparative Social Policy and Social Security: A Ten Country Study* (Martin Robertson, London, 1973), p. 167.
6. *Social Security* (Stationery Office, Dublin, 1949), p. 37.
7. *Budget 1975* (Stationery Office, Dublin, 1975), p. 23.
8. Farley, op. cit., p. 71.
9. *Annual Report 2001*, Social Welfare Appeals Office, p. 10.
10. *Relate*, Vol. 9, No. 4 (National Social Service Board, Dublin, 1982), p. 4.
11. Report of the Commission on Social Welfare, op. cit., pp. 193–194.
12. *Dáil Debate*, 20 June, 1986.
13. T. Callan, B. Nolan and C.T. Whelan, *A Review of the Commission on Social Welfare's Minimum Adequate Income* (Economic and Social Research Institute, Dublin, 1996).
14. *Basic Income, A Green Paper* (Department of the Taoiseach, 2002), p. 44.
15. *Dáil Debate*, Vol. 92, 23 November, 1943.
16. *Building on Reality* (Stationery Office, Dublin, 1984), p. 105.
17. *Child Benefit Review: Report to the Minister for Social Welfare* (Department of Social Welfare, 1995) p. 4.

3

Housing

Introduction
One of the central features of the Irish housing system is the
predominance of owner occupation or privately owned dwellings.
This is due in part to the promotion of owner occupation by
successive governments through various measures. There has
been state intervention in housing since the middle of the
nineteenth century and such intervention is now very extensive.

At a general level it can be said that government intervention in
the housing area is necessary to ensure that certain standards are
maintained, that environmental interests are protected, and that
persons without sufficient income are provided with housing.

The provision of adequate housing for all has been a central
aim of government policy that has been enunciated in various
policy documents:

> The government are committed to pursuing housing policies with the
> broad objective of ensuring that every household has a dwelling
> suitable to its needs, located in an acceptable environment, at a price
> or rent it can afford.[1]

The general strategy for realising this aim is that those who can
afford to do so should provide housing for themselves with the aid
of the various supports available and that those who cannot afford
housing from their own resources should have access to social
housing provided by local authorities or to income support to
secure accommodation in the private rented sector.

Administration
The Department of the Environment and Local Government,
established in 1924, is the central authority responsible for
national housing policy. It exercises a general supervision over

the social, financial and technical aspects of local authority and private housing and is responsible for the distribution of most of the capital and subsidies for housing provided by the state. The Department also promotes legislation on housing, co-ordinates the activities of local authorities and is responsible for legislation on building standards.

There are 90 local authorities engaged in the provision of public housing – five city councils, five borough councils, 31 county councils and 49 town councils.[2] A number of other government departments are concerned with housing, though this is only a minor element of their work. These include, for example, the Department of Community, Rural and Gaeltacht Affairs, which pays grants for the building and improvement of dwellings in the Gaeltacht (Irish-speaking) areas.

Major trends in housing output
In this section the major trends in housing development are outlined.[3]

Housing prior to 1921
Urban housing. The first series of legislative enactments dealing with housing was passed in the 1850s and 1860s. While these and other Acts passed in the 1870s provided a legislative basis for a housing drive, little was accomplished under these Acts except in Dublin city. The Housing of the Working Classes Act, 1890 was a more comprehensive measure which repealed practically all the preceding Acts and represented an attempt to deal with the problems of urban housing and slum clearance. The next important piece of legislation dealing with urban housing was the Housing of the Working Classes (Ireland) Act, 1908. This Act set up the first subsidy system for urban housing. The Irish Housing Fund was established, a sum of £180,000 invested, and the income directed towards the cost of dwellings erected after the 1908 Act. By 1919, however, only 8,700 houses had been provided under the Housing of the Working Classes Act.

The housing situation in Dublin had deteriorated through the latter part of the nineteenth century as former Georgian houses were subdivided into multiple single-room dwellings to house low-income families. These became tenements and certain districts in the city became 'slumlands'. By 1900, almost 22,000 families (representing one-third of the city's population) lived in single-room dwellings condemned by Dublin Corporation as unfit for occupation.[4]

In 1921 the problem of urban housing still remained unsolved. A survey of housing needs in municipal areas carried out in 1919 estimated that 46,416 houses were required, one-third of them to replace inhabited houses unfit and incapable of being made fit for human habitation.

Rural housing. The first attempts to improve rural housing in Ireland were aimed at getting landlords to take the initiative in building cottages for their own tenants. The Dwellings for Labouring Classes (Ireland) Act, 1860 enabled landlords to obtain loans for the provision of cottages.

The Census of 1881 indicated that there were 215,000 cottiers and the majority of dwellings in which they lived were single-room cabins with mud walls and thatched roofs. Under the Labourers (Ireland) Act, 1883, housing operations were to be carried out locally by the rural sanitary authorities, the Boards of Guardians, under the general supervision of the Local Government Board for Ireland. The provision of cottages was no longer left to the initiative of individual landlords or farmers. By 1921 approximately 48,000 cottages had been built.

Fahey has indicated that for decades, the primary focus was on the improvement in rural public housing for farm labourers and that this was a direct link with the process of agrarian reform which ultimately led to tenant farmers becoming owners of land. It was only later (especially with the Housing Act, 1908) that corresponding, though less generous, measures were introduced for the hitherto neglected urban dwellers.[5]

Private housing. The demand for private dwellings was stimulated by the Small Dwellings Acquisition Act, 1899 which enabled local authorities to advance loans for the purchase of existing houses. Another source providing finance for house purchase was the building societies and the main Act governing these societies was passed in 1874. Banks and insurance companies also provided finance in this period. The total number of owner-occupiers at the time, however, was small and most of the houses were purchased by investors and let to tenants. A significant development was the introduction, under the Housing Act, 1919, of a scheme of grants for persons who constructed houses in accordance with prescribed conditions. The political conditions of the time prevented the extensive use of the scheme. Nevertheless, the scheme marks one of the first steps in direct state aid to the house purchaser, a policy which was sustained throughout the rest of the century and which accounts, in part, for the relatively high proportion of owner-occupied dwellings in Ireland at present.

Housing in the 1920s
The first real attempt to provide houses on a large scale was made by the Free State government that initiated what is referred to as the 'Million Pound Scheme'. Under this scheme local authorities were required to provide £125,000 from rates (local taxation) and raise a further sum of £375,000 by way of short-term loans from banks, giving a total of £0.5 million. This was matched by £1 million in state aid and enabled 2,000 houses to be built at an average total cost of £750 per house. The majority of local authority housing provided in the early years of independence was confined to Dublin and Cork.[6]

Under the Housing Act, 1924, grants were again made available to people constructing their own dwellings. This Act also empowered local authorities to supplement the state grants by further grants or loans and also free or cheap sites for development work. It provided for the partial remission of rates (local taxation) over 19 years on grant-aided houses. Reconstruction grants were also made available under the 1924 Act.

The housing problem of urban areas, however, remained to be tackled in earnest. A survey carried out by urban authorities in 1929 indicated that almost 44,000 houses were needed and highlighted the need for slum clearance.

Housing in the 1930s
The main drive against slums was begun in the 1930s. The Housing Acts, 1931 and 1932 were particularly important, giving effect to the recommendations of previous commissions of enquiry on slum clearance and compulsory acquisition of land and providing greater financial assistance to local authorities for rehousing displaced families.

The output of housing rose steadily during the 1930s reaching a peak of 17,000 in the year ended 31 March 1939. Between 1931 and 1942 a total of 82,000 dwellings were built. During the same period over 11,000 condemned houses were demolished by local authorities as well as an unknown number by private people. This period was one of the most productive ever in the building of

Corporation houses in Dublin. The estates of the southwest, centring on Crumlin, which constitute the largest concentration of municipal housing in Dublin, were built at this time. Progress was not confined to Dublin, however, and in the main urban areas overcrowded tenement buildings were replaced by new flats or by new housing on what was then the outskirts of the built-up area. In smaller towns the same process was continued mainly in the form of new estates on the fringes.

The housing initiatives of the early 1930s and in particular the slum clearance which continued into the 1940s were taken by the Fianna Fáil party which first came into power in 1932. Fahey has noted that:

> The success of this programme has since gone down in history as one of the great social achievements of the day – and incidentally also as one of the main bases for Fianna Fáil's claim to be a progressive populist party.[7]

Housing in the post-war period
During the wartime period, output of new housing sank to a low level and only 1,300 dwellings were built in 1946.

In 1948 a White Paper was issued containing an estimate of the number of houses needed. Despite pre-war accomplishments it was estimated that 61,000 dwellings were required, 44,500 in urban areas and the remainder in rural areas. The major problem was in Dublin where the requirement was for an estimated 23,500 dwellings (approximately 40 per cent of the national need).

The Housing (Amendment) Acts, 1948 to 1952, provided among other things for more generous grants for private dwellings, particularly for people building dwellings for their own occupation, for higher loans to house purchasers and for the strengthening of local authority powers to deal with special housing problems. These measures had a stimulating effect on the housing programme and in the early 1950s an annual average of 14,500 dwellings were erected.

By the late 1950s, however, a downward trend was again evident. This was partly due to the belief (later found to be erroneous) that sufficient progress had been made with the satisfaction of housing needs throughout the country. It was also due to cutbacks in local authority capital expenditure on housing. In 1959 the report, *Economic Development*, stated:

Private housing needs have been largely met, while local authority housing programmes have already been completed in a number of areas and are expected to be completed in all areas outside Dublin within three or four years.[8]

Between 1956 and 1958, capital expenditure on housing by public authorities was halved, from £14.3 million to £7.5 million.[9] In the late 1950s the population of the Republic was falling by about 10,000 per annum, net outward migration was running at over 40,000 annually and some local authority housing estates were reporting vacancies. There was a dramatic rise in the number of vacancies in Dublin Corporation estates from 1954 onwards which reached a peak of over 1,200 per year between 1958 and 1961 and rapidly declined again later in the 1960s. Output of local authority housing in Dublin declined from a high point of 2,600 in 1951 to 279 in 1961.

Housing in the 1960s
In the 1960s, economic growth was accelerated and led to an upsurge in social spending. Furthermore, significant demographic changes occurred giving rise to an increased demand for housing, particularly in urban areas.

In 1964 a White Paper, *Housing: Progress and Prospects*, estimated that 50,000 dwellings were required to cater for existing needs and 8,000 for future needs. In the following year Dublin Corporation initiated the Ballymun scheme, one of the largest single housing projects in Europe at the time. The construction of over 3,000 dwellings was a formidable achievement and helped to alleviate housing needs in the Dublin area.

In 1969 the government issued another White Paper, *Housing in the Seventies*, which estimated that the number of dwellings required to cater for accumulated needs was 59,000, while the annual prospective need was 9,000 for the period 1966–1971 and 11,500 for the mid-1970s.

Housing in the 1970s and 1980s
During the 1960s output of housing increased steadily and in the early 1970s increased further, reaching what was then a peak of almost 27,000 in 1975. Thereafter there was a slight decline until 1981 when almost 29,000 dwellings were built. Throughout the 1980s there was a steady decline in housing output. Much of this was accounted for by a policy to reduce investment in local

authority dwellings and by the increase in emigration that led to reduced demand. In the latter part of the 1980s emigration began to rise steadily with a net outward migration of over 40,000 in 1988 and 1989. In 1988 the number of units built was 15,654, the lowest for two decades.

Housing since 1990

From the beginning of the 1990s output began to steadily increase. This rate accelerated especially from the mid-1990s onwards, and record numbers were achieved in each successive year, reaching 57,695 in 2002 (provisional figures suggest even higher output in 2003). It should be noted that the number built in 2002 was almost double that for 1998, a mere five years earlier. In the latter part of the 1990s, demand far exceeded supply, leading to unprecedented increases in house prices (see later section). This coincided with unprecedented growth in the economy, leading among other things to a substantial increase in employment. Output has continued to rise in the early years of the twenty-first century and projections are that a high level of completions (approximately 50,000 per annum) needs to be achieved up to 2010.

The number of dwellings completed for selected years over the past three decades is set out in Table 3.1.

Table 3.1: Output of dwellings, selected years 1971–2002

1971	15,380
1975	26,892
1981	28,917
1985	23,948
1991	19,652
1995	30,575
2001	52,602
2002	57,695

Source: Annual Housing Statistics Bulletin, Department of the Environment and Local

Housing stock

The total housing stock increased by over one-third between the end of World War II and 1991. During that period the owner-occupied sector continued to increase its share of the total stock while that of the local authority rented sector and especially the private rented sector declined (Table 3.2). The decline of the local

Table 3.2: Tenure structure of Irish housing 1946–1991

Sector	1946 %	1961 %	1971 %	1981 %	1991 %
Owner-occupied	52.7	59.8	68.8	76.1	80.2
Local authority rented	16.5	26.1	17.2	13.3	9.7
Private rented	26.1	17.2	13.3	8.1	7.0
Other	4.7	4.6	2.4	3.1	-
Total housing stock	662,654	676,402	726,363	896,000	1,006,506

Source: Census of Population

authority rented sector is partly accounted for by the relatively high volume of sales of dwellings to tenants that has brought them into the owner-occupied sector (see later section).

Between 1991 and 2002, approximately 422,000 units were added to the housing stock, bringing the total to over 1.4 million. A result of the recent increased output is that the housing stock is relatively new with over 40 per cent built since 1981.

Factors in planning housing needs

The principal factors affecting housing needs are a matter of concern for each local authority and for the state in general. Each housing authority is expected to ascertain the extent of the need for dwellings in its area and to assess the adequacy of the supply and prospective demand for housing.

In general, two kinds of housing needs may be recognised: accummulated or existing needs, and prospective needs. Accumulated needs refers to the existing replacement requirements arising from the necessity (a) to replace unfit dwellings, (b) to relieve overcrowding, and (c) to provide housing for certain categories of people on medical or other grounds, e.g. homelessness. Prospective need refers to future need that can arise mainly from replacements and increase in households. One of the more important factors affecting housing needs is demographic change and, in particular, changes in household-forming age groups. In 1976 and in 1983 the NESC published reports on projected new dwelling needs.[10]

The *National Development Plan* (1999) estimated that 500,000 houses would be required over the period 2000 to 2010 to meet demand arising from the increased proportion of the population in the household formation age, falling household sizes, immigration and obsolescence.[11] The Plan estimated that 70 per cent of the demand would arise in the southern and eastern regions. It also noted that Ireland's housing stock, at 327 per thousand population, was the lowest in the EU where the average was 450 per thousand.

Tenure sectors
In this section the salient features of the different tenure sectors (owner-occupied, local authority and private rented) are outlined.

Owner-occupied sector
By comparison with other European countries Ireland has a relatively high proportion of owner-occupied dwellings. This is due to a number of factors. Chief among these are historical and cultural factors and the schemes of state aid to the owner-occupier.

It has been suggested that the legacy of the land reform measures in the late nineteenth century and early decades of the twentieth century has influenced the pattern of owner occupation.[12] During that period farmers, who had been tenants of their land, became owner-occupiers.

While it is difficult to measure the extent of the influence of cultural factors on the level of owner occupation in Ireland, there is little doubt that the state has also contributed to Ireland's relatively high proportion of owner-occupiers by a system of financial aid, part of which originated in the latter part of the nineteenth century. This system includes grants and loans, provided by local authorities and income tax relief on the interest element of mortgages.

Grants. Since the introduction of grants for the provision of new dwellings in 1919, the grants levels have been increased on several occasions and the system has been altered to respond to the needs of particular sections of the community. In July 1977, for example, all previous grant schemes (state and local authority) were rescinded and a new £1,000 grant for first time buyers of new houses was introduced. In 1985 this grant was increased to £2,000 and to £3,000 in 1993. There was no further increase in the grant and it was abolished amid public and political disquiet in November 2002 as provided for in the government's book of estimates for 2003.

There have been other forms of grants made available in recent decades, for example the mortgage subsidy scheme and a surrender grant of £5,000 available to local authority tenants who moved into the private sector to purchase a dwelling. The provision of grants for new dwellings has undoubtedly helped people to meet the costs of buying or providing a house but it has also provided a stimulus to the production of houses. In fact it can be argued that, for long periods, the grants system was designed as much to help the building industry as to help persons to acquire houses of their own.

Grants have also been provided from time to time by the state for the reconstruction and improvement of existing houses. These grants have usually operated for certain defined periods. The most recent scheme was introduced in 1985 but was terminated in 1987.

Income tax relief. The interest element of a mortgage is allowable against income tax, subject to certain limits. This concession to house purchase is a consequence of the income tax code and was not intended as a specific housing subsidy. Prior to 1982, tax relief was available on all forms of interest but it was then confined to housing purposes. Over the period 1992 to 1997 the value of tax relief was gradually reduced to the standard rate of tax (20 per cent in 2003), thus remedying the situation whereby those on the highest rate benefited most.

Other aids. Apart from the grants and the system of tax relief there are a number of other means designed to help owner occupation. Thus, for example, there is no stamp duty payable by a first-time purchaser of a new house. In the case of second-hand houses, however, there is a liability for stamp duty where the price exceeds a certain ceiling.

Financing of private housing. Apart from state and local authority investment in housing, a number of other agencies are involved in the provision of house purchase loans. Of these, the building societies have played the most important role. Up to the 1970s, assurance companies also had a substantial role to play but their contribution in this area is now almost negligible. In the supplementary budget of 1975, the Minister for Finance directed the associated banks to provide house purchase loans totalling £40 million over the following two years. This directive was intended to provide a stimulus to the construction industry during a difficult period, as well as providing an additional source of loans to the house purchaser. The banks, while exceeding the figure stipulated by the Minister, continued to provide loans beyond this period and they have now surpassed the building societies as a main source of finance for house purchasers. Up to the 1970s local authorities were also an important source of finance especially for persons on low or relatively low incomes but their role has also declined sharply in this area since then.

In 2001, banks accounted for 76.5 per cent of the value of loans paid, building societies for 23.4 per cent and local authorities for 0.1 per cent.

Local authority rented sector
Local authorities are mainly concerned with providing dwellings for renting to people living in unfit and overcrowded conditions and to those whose income does not allow them to provide adequate accommodation for themselves. They also provide special housing for older people and people with disabilities.

Output of local authority housing. As a proportion of total housing output, that of local authorities has fluctuated over several decades. In 1949/50 local authority output constituted two-thirds of the total output of 8,113 dwellings. In subsequent years the output constituted one-fifth to a quarter of the total. All that was to change from the late 1980s onwards as the output began a downward spiral. In 1989, when investment in local authority dwellings was scaled down considerably, output accounted for as little as 4.4 per cent of 18,068 dwellings built. Throughout the 1990s annual output was consistently less than 10 per cent. While housing needs increased in the latter part of the 1990s due to rising house prices, and as the total number of dwellings built began to rise to unprecedented levels, the output of local authority dwellings plummeted even further. In 2001, only 3,622 local authority dwellings were built out of a total of 52,602 new dwellings (representing 6.9 per cent).

The stock of local authority dwellings available for renting has fluctuated over the past few decades (see Table 3.3). The fact that the stock has not increased continuously over that period is mainly due to the sales of local authority dwellings to tenants (see later section), thus removing those dwellings from the stock available for renting. The decline is especially noticeable from the late 1980s due to a particularly attractive purchase scheme introduced in 1988 that resulted in over 28,000 dwellings being taken out of

Table 3.3: Number of local authority dwellings available for renting, selected years 1975–2001

1975	105,000
1981	104,000
1985	114,364
1988	116,270
1992	93,283
1995	97,219
1999	99,163
2001	102,789

Source: Annual Housing Statistics Bulletin, Department of the Environment and Local Government

the rented category. It is also due to the relatively low output of local authority dwellings, by historical standards, from the mid-1990s onwards.

Financing. Prior to 1988 local authorities obtained loans from the Local Loans Fund and were liable for the loan charges (interest and capital repayments). Their increasing inability to meet these charges, however, and the consequent increase in subsidy to them from the Department of the Environment to meet these charges, led to a change in January 1988. Since then, capital for the house-building programme of local authorities is made by way of grants rather than fully subsidised loans.

Rents. The majority of local authority dwellings are now let on what is termed a differential rent system, i.e. a rent related to household income. The letting of dwellings at fixed rents was a feature of local authority housing in the past and the tenant's capacity to pay was not a consideration irrespective of changes in household income. In 1934 income-related rents were first introduced in Cork city, the rent being based on one-sixth of family income less certain deductions and subject to review with changes in that income. Since 1967 all new lettings of local authority dwellings throughout the country have been let on the differential rent system. For each local authority dwelling minimum and maximum rents are set and within this range the tenant pays a proportion of income in rent. If household income increases, so does the rent (up to the maximum set) and if household income is reduced, so also is the rent (down to the minimum set).

Prior to 1973 differential rent schemes varied from one local authority area to another, principally in regard to allowances deductible from household income. In 1973, however, following a prolonged strike by the National Association of Tenants Organisations, a new national differential rents scheme was introduced. In effect, subsequent reviews were initiated and the Department of the Environment established the terms of schemes. In 1983 the Minister for the Environment decreed that local authorities should themselves decide on the basis of the rent schemes. Consequently there may well be differences between local authorities in the details of the schemes. In general, rent is based on a percentage of the principal earner's assessable income (less certain allowances). Income of other household members is also taken into account up to a certain limit.

Since the introduction nationally of differential rents in 1967, the proportion of local authority dwellings let on these rents has increased steadily as those on fixed rents have been phased out. In 1966/67 just over half (54 per cent of local authority dwellings) were let on fixed rents. By 1990, however, 96 per cent were let on differential rents. No comparable figures have been published in recent years but it can be assumed that virtually all tenants now pay differential rents.

The average weekly rent of local authority dwellings is relatively low – €26.33 in 2001 (Table 3.4). Furthermore rental income does not meet the cost of maintenance and management of the local authority stock. In 2001 the rental income was €141.21 million and accounted for 70 per cent of the cost of maintenance and management which came to €202.59 million.

Table 3.4: Rents of local authority dwellings, selected years 1975–2001

	Annual rental income €m	Average weekly rent €
1975	11.01	2.02
1980	26.90	5.04
1985	53.41	8.77
1990	57.72	11.76
1995	80.90	16.00
1998	101.49	19.66
1999	109.63	21.26
2001	141.21	26.33

Source: Annual Housing Statistics Bulletin, Department of the Environment and Local Government

Part of the reason for the low average rent is that over a period of time the higher income tenants have availed themselves of schemes to purchase their dwellings. Increasingly, therefore, the population in the local authority sector is comprised mainly of either low-income earners or recipients of social welfare payments. Consequently, because of the differential rent scheme, where rent is related to income, few are paying the maximum rents. The report of the *Dublin Lord Mayor's Commission on Housing* (1993) estimated that 80 per cent of the 31,000 rent-paying tenants in the housing stock of Dublin Corporation area were dependent on social welfare payments as their main source of income. It is likely that a broadly similar situation pertains in other local authority areas throughout the country.

Purchase schemes. Despite the considerable output of local authority dwellings over several decades, there has not been a commensurate increase in the stock of dwellings, i.e. the total number available for letting (see Table 3.3). This is due to the fact that since the 1930s local authorities have operated purchase schemes to allow tenants to purchase their dwellings, with a discount on the market or replacement value of the house. For example, between 1970 and 1979 a total 60,630 local authority dwellings were built while 60,026 were sold through purchase schemes, so there was no net gain to the stock. During the early 1980s the trend was reversed as building exceeded sales. In 1988, a specially attractive purchase scheme was introduced which allowed 40 per cent discount on the market value of a local authority dwelling (50 per cent in the case of those built prior to 1961) together with a £2,000 grant available to purchasers of new houses. The scheme was popularly known within civil service and local authority circles as 'the sale of the century'. It resulted in the sale of 28,241 local authority dwellings between 1989 and 1992. Over the same period the number built was 5,883. The net effect of this special purchase scheme coupled with a low output of local authority dwellings was to reduce the national stock available for letting from 116,270 in 1998 to 93,283 in 1992 (Table 3.3). Since then there has been an increase in the number available for letting to 102,789 in 2001.

The number of local authority dwellings built up to 2000 was 335,100 while the number of these sold off to tenants was 235,100.[13] This amounts to 70 per cent of the total local authority housing stock.

The sale of local authority dwellings over a period of time has helped to account for the high proportion of owner-occupied dwellings but it is a system that has met with some criticism. On the one hand it is argued that the capacity of local authorities to meet housing needs would be improved in the long run if much less of the stock was sold to tenants and if such sales were at less generous discounts. On the other hand it is argued that the sale of local authority dwellings encourages better maintenance and improvement of individual dwellings and therefore of the housing stock; it provides a pool of reasonably priced houses suitable to the needs of first-time purchasers and reduces the maintenance and management burden on the local authorities.[14] Since rents meet only a proportion of the total housing costs for local authorities it has even been suggested that it would make financial sense for the state to give away the entire local authority stock to the tenants free of charge and actually save money in the process.[15]

For several decades, purchase schemes were introduced periodically on a once-off basis with a closing date for applications. Since 1994 there has been an open-ended scheme in operation so that tenants may apply at any stage. Under the terms of the current scheme a tenant who has been in occupation for over one year may opt to purchase. From the market value of the house there is a discount of 3 per cent per annum for each year of tenancy up to a maximum of 30 per cent (ten years tenancy).

Priority in letting of dwellings. Prior to the passing of the 1988 Housing Act, local authorities had to establish a scheme of priority in the letting of dwellings so that families or persons most in need of housing received prompt attention. Overall priority was given to families living in dangerous premises; families that became homeless through emergency situations such as fire or flood, families that required housing on medical grounds, and families evicted or displaced from areas required for redevelopment.

Some local authorities have had to operate a points system in order to establish priority. In practice this would apply mainly in the large urban areas. The highest number of points was generally allocated to those families living in unfit or overcrowded dwellings.

Under the Housing Act, 1988, local authorities are obliged to assess the extent of need for local authority accommodation and to revise their scheme of letting priorities. The aim of the scheme of priorities is to ensure equal opportunity for different categories of need in relation to housing accommodation. The Housing Act, 1988 stipulated that the needs of homeless persons should be provided for. In order to ensure equality of treatment a local authority can set aside a proportion of the dwellings available for renting to particular categories of people, including homeless persons.

Waiting lists. During the period 1981–1988 the total number of households on local authority waiting lists fell from 27,000 to 17,700.[16] This accounts in part for the decline in capital expenditure on local authority housing and the decline in output of local authority dwellings.

In 1989 there was an upturn in the numbers on the waiting lists and the first assessment of housing needs under the Housing Act, 1988 indicated that 19,376 households (including homeless and travellers) were qualified for local authority housing. With one exception, each subsequent assessment has indicated an inexorable rise in the waiting list numbers (Table 3.5). By 2002 the numbers had reached 48,413 and the increase between 1996 and 2002 was 76 per cent. Ironically, this had occurred against a background of unprecedented growth in the economy.

Each of the assessments categorises the households. In the assessments of 1989 and 1991 almost half the households were living in overcrowded or unfit conditions. By 2002, however, the proportions in these combined categories had declined to about 25 per cent (although the actual numbers were far higher than in 1989 or 1991). The highest proportionate increase by category over the 1989–2002 period was among households 'unable to meet the costs of existing accommodation', which increased from 15 per cent of the total in 1989 to 44 per cent of the total in 2002.

The factors accounting for the substantial increase in the numbers on the waiting lists for local authority housing include

Table 3.5: Assessment of housing needs, 1989–2002

	Households
1989	19,376
1990	23,342
1993	28,624
1996	27,427
1997	39,176
2002	48,413

Source: A Plan for Social Housing, 1991 and *Annual Housing Statistics Bulletin*, Department of the Environment and Local Government

the decline in output of local authority dwellings during the 1990s, the unprecedented rise in house prices from the mid-1990s and the consequent increase in rents in the private rented sector. All of these factors combined to swell the numbers of those unable to provide housing from their own resources.

Private rented sector

There has been a constant decline in the dwellings available for private renting up to the 1990s when an upturn in this sector occurred. Up to 1982, a distinction could be made within the private rented sector between two categories, i.e. dwellings whose rents were controlled (restricted) and those whose rents were uncontrolled (unrestricted). While market forces largely determined the rents of tenants in uncontrolled dwellings, rents were controlled for certain dwellings under the Rent Restrictions Acts, 1960 and 1967. The categories of dwellings excluded from rent control were complex but, for example, all furnished lettings and dwellings built since 1941 were excluded.

In 1982 the High Court ruled that sections of the Rent Restrictions Acts were unconstitutional. This decision was appealed to the Supreme Court that upheld the decision of the High Court.

As a result of this, the government was obliged to introduce the Housing Act, 1982 in order to protect the interests of tenants in dwellings that had been subject to rent control. The Act provided for security of tenure for existing tenants and also provided a mechanism by which the rents could be reviewed. If landlord and tenant agreed on any increase in rent then there would not be any intervention by the state; otherwise the rent could be established by a district court. For various reasons, this court system was found to be unsatisfactory and was replaced by Rent Tribunals in 1983.

In order to avoid any hardship that could arise for tenants faced with a substantial increase in rent following decontrol, the Department of Social Welfare introduced a rent allowance scheme. This allowance was confined to tenants, mostly older people, in the former rent controlled dwellings, subject to a means test, the maximum allowance being the difference between the old and the new rent. Over the years the number of recipients of this allowance has gradually declined from 1,348 in 1986 to 433 in 2001.

The general decline in private rented dwellings throughout much of the twentieth century inevitably meant that the needs and potential of this sector were neglected in housing policy. It was not until the 1980s that this was highlighted:

> The Irish private rented sector remains virtually unregulated; its tenants are afforded less protection than any other such group in Europe – and less state subsidies.[17]

For some time, Threshold, a voluntary organisation providing a service for those in the private rented sector, highlighted the lack of government policy in this area. In 1982 it published *Private Rented, the Forgotten Sector*, and it consistently argued, for example, that tenants should have greater security of tenure and that minimum standards of accommodation should be introduced.[18]

In response to these demands, a number of changes were announced in *A Plan for Social Housing* (1991) and provided for in the Housing Miscellaneous Provisions Act, 1992. Subsequently, regulations were introduced under this Act for rent books (1993), standards for rented dwellings (1993), and registration of rented houses (1996). These changes constitute a Charter for Rented Housing. It is generally recognised that the registration system has not progressed satisfactorily and by 2002 only 25,000 out of an estimated 150,000 accommodation units were registered with local authorities.

Commission on the Private Rented Residential Sector
In 1999 a Commission on the Private Rented Residential Sector was established and its report was published in July 2000. The report highlighted what the Commission regarded as the two main issues concerning the private rented sector. The first concerned the shortage of suitable accommodation whether for owner-occupation or renting. The second was the complex issue of providing an appropriate balance of rights between landlords and tenants.

The main proposals (not unanimously accepted by members of the Commission) of the report were:

- to establish a Private Residential Tenancies Board to deal with landlord-tenant disputes
- to provide for security of tenure of up to four years for tenants who have completed six months' tenancy.

The government broadly endorsed the recommendations of the Commission and in January 2001, six months after the publication of the report, Robert Molloy, TD, Minister for Housing and Urban Renewal, announced the government's proposals arising from the recommendations. The proposals were:

- The establishment on an *ad hoc* basis by Autumn 2001 of a Private Residential Tenancies Board to deal primarily with disputes between landlords and tenants and legislation to establish the Board on a statutory basis within two years
- The same legislation would provide for improved security of tenure for tenants and graduated notice to quit periods as recommended by the Commission: rent levels to be no greater than the market rate and reviews no more frequently than once a year.

These changes when implemented will go some way towards resolving outstanding problems in the private rented residential sector.

The Private Residential Tenancies Board was established on an *ad hoc* basis in October 2001.

Voluntary and special housing
In recent years attention has begun to be focused on the issue of accommodation for persons with special needs, such as older people and people with disabilities. This particular type of housing need has been largely met by organisations and housing associations providing housing on a non-profit basis. It has been pointed out that Ireland has not shared in the development of the social housing movement which has characterised many European countries over the past few decades and that state support for social housing organisations has been a peripheral aspect of housing policy.[19]

In 1984 the Department of the Environment introduced a scheme – the capital assistance scheme for non-profit and voluntary housing – to assist approved voluntary housing associations with the capital funding cost of housing projects for certain categories of persons with special housing needs. Under the scheme, 80 per cent of the capital cost in building or renovating a property for the accommodation in self-contained units of older people and people with disabilities was provided. Subsequently, the scheme was extended to include projects for homeless persons and the level of funding was also increased. With this assistance, a number of housing units have been provided by different organisations within the past decade. Examples include HAIL (Housing Association for Integrated Living), and Focus Housing Association, which have provided units for homeless and socially vulnerable persons such as those who have been hospitalised for some time and have no adequate accommodation to return to. While capital assistance is available to social housing organisations, they are responsible for the ongoing running costs such as maintenance, management and social support. A further scheme for voluntary housing was announced as part of the *Plan for Social Housing*. The rental subsidy scheme, which provides housing for renting particularly to meet the needs of low-income families, was introduced in 1991. The Housing Centre functions as an advisory body for new housing associations or voluntary organisations wishing to develop a housing service. By 2002 there were approximately 800 voluntary housing associations.

In 2001 the output from the voluntary housing sector amounted to 1,253 units or just over 2.0 per cent of total output that year.

Homelessness
It is generally recognised that the extent of homelessness has increased in recent decades. The Simon Community and other groups who have campaigned for government action and legislation have highlighted the plight of the homeless. For some time, confusion existed as to which state agency (health board or local authority) had statutory responsibility for providing accommodation for the homeless. In 1983, Senator Brendan Ryan introduced a Homeless Persons Bill in the Seanad in order to bring greater clarity to the situation. However, the government opposed his Bill and introduced its own in 1985 but this lapsed with the dissolution of the Dáil in January 1987.

The Housing Bill 1988 was passed with two main objectives:

• to revive and update the statutory basis for the provision, improvement, management and letting of local authority housing, so as to ensure that the needs of categories of persons such as the homeless, the aged, the disabled and travellers get due priority

- to increase the powers of housing authorities in regard to the accommodation of homeless persons.

The definition of homelessness in section 2 of the Housing Act, 1988 is as follows:

> A person shall be regarded by a housing authority as being homeless for the purpose of this Act if: (a) there is no accommodation available which, in the opinion of the authority, he together with any other person who resides with him or who might reasonably be expected to reside with him, can reasonably occupy or remain in occupation of, or (b) he is living in a hospital, county home, night shelter or other such institution, and is so living because he has no accommodation of the kind referred to in paragraph (a).

The Housing Act, 1988 did not place a statutory duty on local authorities to provide accommodation for homeless persons but it did empower them either on their own or in conjunction with other agencies to provide a range of suitable accommodation. The Department of the Environment, which encouraged local authorities to operate the new powers available to them in a flexible and sensitive manner, issued guidelines and these guidelines stressed the desirability of planning, liaison and consultation with health boards and voluntary organisations in implementing the Act. Within a relatively short time it became clear that some local authorities were either unwilling or unable because of lack of finance to comply with these guidelines.

The lack of response to implementing the guidelines was criticised in *A Plan for Social Housing* and it indicated that steps would be taken by the Minister for the Environment to prevail on local authorities to utilise fully their powers under the Housing Act, 1988 to secure accommodation for homeless persons.[20]

What has emerged as result of the Housing Act, 1988 is that local authorities have responsibility for the provision of emergency, temporary and permanent accommodation for homeless persons over 18 years, while health boards have responsibility for the health and in-house care needs of such persons.

In 2000 in response to the growing numbers of homeless persons the government published *Homelessness, An Integrated Strategy*. The report indicated that in 1999 there were 5,234 homeless persons in the country and that the majority (70 per cent) were in Dublin.[21] The key proposals of the Strategy were as follows:

- Local authorities and health boards, in full partnership with the voluntary bodies, to draw up action plans on a county-by-county basis to provide a more coherent and integrated delivery of services by all agencies dealing with homelessness
- Homeless fora, comprising representatives of the local authority, health and the voluntary sector, to be established in every county
- Local authorities to be responsible for the provision of accommodation, including emergency hostel accommodation for homeless persons, and health boards to be responsible for their in-house care and health needs.

The action plan for homelessness in Dublin was published in 2001. The plan indicated that:

> Homelessness in Dublin is a persistent problem and one which has grown in recent years with higher levels of families, young people and rough sleepers ... Services for people are provided by different voluntary and statutory agencies, with no overall co-ordination. As a result there has been no systematic or integrated response and people will go from one agency to another in order to access different services. Furthermore, there has been no emphasis on getting people out of homelessness and many people are homeless on a long-term basis.[22]

The action plan set out a range of measures over the period 2001–2003 and a new approach to the delivery of services. Part of this was the establishment of the Homeless Agency, responsible for the planning, co-ordination and management of services. The approach is based on the principle of a continuum of care that will ensure that all the needs of homeless persons are met in an integrated manner and in a way that ensures that they move from homelessness into long-term housing. Rather optimistically, the action plan noted that the Homeless Agency would not be a permanent structure and that in the effective achievement of its aims, it would make itself redundant.[23]

The focus of the *Homeless Preventative Strategy* (2002) is on the prevention of adult homelessness and is aimed at target groups at risk of homelessness, particularly those leaving custodial or health-related care. For example, it proposed that records would be kept of the number of patients being discharged from psychiatric hospitals and the type of accommodation into which they are being discharged.[24]

A Plan for Social Housing

It is only within the past few decades that housing policy has been subjected to critical analysis. In 1977, for example, the NESC published a report on housing subsidies. This was the first attempt to quantify the value of subsidies, both explicit (e.g. grants) and implicit (e.g. income tax relief on the interest element of a mortgage) to the various sectors within the housing system. The report estimated that in 1975 the highest subsidy on a household basis went to those who purchased their local authority dwellings while the average household subsidy varied little between owner occupier and local authority tenants.[25]

Baker and O'Brien (1979) presented an excellent overview of the housing system with reference to efficiency and equity.[26] They argued that while the system was tolerably efficient at providing accommodation, it was also seriously unfair in that it favoured those who already owned or rented houses at the expense of those seeking housing. They referred to the wide variation in the quality of dwellings and housing costs within each tenure. Some of their recommendations for improvements have been implemented since then, for example the greater availability of local authority housing for single persons and the abolition of rent control.

Blackwell (1981) argued that most elements of housing policy did not work to the achievement of either horizontal or vertical equity.[27] By horizontal equity is meant that households with broadly similar income and household characteristics (e.g. family size) should obtain equal net benefits from the system. Vertical equity is concerned with the implications of policy for those who are not equal and with the extent to which there is a transfer of resources in a progressive manner, i.e. that those on the lowest income should benefit most. In relation to horizontal equity Blackwell pointed out, for example, that there was a considerable difference in benefit between those purchasing new houses (where grant and stamp duty exemption applied) and those purchasing second-hand houses.

While there have been various criticisms of elements of housing policy and while a number of adjustments to policy have been made in response to these, a few key areas have been constantly highlighted.

Firstly, in addition to the stated objectives, housing policy was designed to help the building industry. This is exemplified by the fact that grants for first-time purchasers were confined to new houses only. Furthermore, various schemes have been introduced from time to time to provide a boost to the building industry, e.g. the home improvement grants scheme (introduced in 1985, abolished in 1987) and the builders' grants for new dwellings (introduced in 1986, abolished in 1987).

Secondly, there was increasing concern that the secondary objective of housing policy, i.e. the promotion of owner occupation, had been pursued to the detriment of those on the fringes of the housing system and not, therefore, in a position to benefit from the public subsidies available. Now that four-fifths of dwellings were owner occupied it was argued that greater attention should be focused on marginal groups and the needs of those in the private rented sector.

The NESC, in various reports, consistently questioned the validity of existing policy and argued for a more balanced housing strategy. In 1990 the NESC stated:

> The central thrust of housing policy has always been the encourage-
> ment of owner occupation. In the Council's view, owner occupation
> *per se* should not be an end in itself, but one of a series of instruments
> to achieve the goal of adequate housing, in an acceptable environ-
> ment, at an affordable price or rent.[28]

The NESC argued that it was necessary to achieve a better balance between tenures and that, while owner occupation remains the main tenure, the other tenures (local authority, private rented and voluntary/social housing) should play an appropriate role. This, according to the NESC, should be the fundamental aim of housing policy.

Some of the criticisms made by the NESC and others were responded to, in part, by the Minister for the Environment in *A Plan for Social Housing*, published in 1991. While reiterating the broad objective of housing policy as enunciated by successive governments, the Plan went on to indicate that future strategy would include:

• promoting owner occupation as a form of tenure preferred by most people

- developing and implementing responses appropriate to changing social housing need
- mitigating the extent and effects of social segregation in housing.

The Plan provided for a number of policy changes. In relation to local authority housing, for example, it indicated that the approach of local authorities would be broader and more diverse than its traditional role. The new measures envisaged for local authorities included the following:

- to avoid building large housing estates which have 'reinforced social segregation with adverse consequences'
- to purchase private houses or existing houses in need of refurbishment where it is more economic than building new houses
- to carry out improvements to existing local authority dwellings as opposed to providing new houses
- to introduce a system of shared ownership with tenants in which the local authority would take a 50 per cent share
- to introduce a new mortgage allowance (over five years) for tenants moving to private houses.

A Plan for Social Housing also contained proposals for initiatives in relation to homeless and travelling people, voluntary and co-operative housing, home ownership and, as already indicated, the private rented sector.

A Plan for Social Housing was the most comprehensive government statement on housing since the White Paper of 1969 and was a response to the changing housing needs in society. It addressed the key issues that had been of concern for some time and proposed policy changes especially in the local authority sector. The legislative base for these changes was provided for in the Housing Miscellaneous Provisions Act, 1992.

A review of *A Plan for Social Housing* was commenced in 1993 by the Department of the Environment and the resulting report, *Social Housing – The Way Ahead*, was published in 1995. The report recorded progress in relation to different schemes and indicated ways in which these might be improved further.

One of the main changes arising from the two reports was to provide for a more diverse role for local authorities in meeting housing need compared with the traditional response of new large housing estates. Thus, from 1992 to 2001, the shared ownership scheme has been taken up by 11,277 and, over the same period, 6,920 second-hand houses have been purchased for local authority tenants.

The two reports did nothing to alter the predominant position of owner occupation. In fact they reinforced that position by introducing new schemes (shared ownership, mortgage allowance) and continuing existing schemes (tenant purchase and local authority house purchase loans).

Quality of housing

A general indication of quality of housing stock and housing conditions may be obtained by reference to the degree of overcrowding and presence of basic amenities.[29]

If overcrowding is defined as two or more persons per room then the improvement has been substantial. In 1926 almost two in every five persons (37.1 per cent) lived in overcrowded conditions, but by 1991 this had declined to one in fifty (2.0 per cent). Related to this has been the decline in the average household size from 4.48 in 1926 to 3.54 in 1991. Over the same period the average number of persons per room in private households declined from 1.19 to 0.64.

Similarly, there has been a dramatic improvement in the proportion of dwellings with basic amenities, such as piped water supply, from 38.7 per cent in 1946 to 98.7 per cent in 1981. A considerable disparity existed until recently between urban and rural areas, with the latter lagging far behind. Part of the reason for this, however, was the fact that it was more difficult and costly to provide schemes in rural areas with a scattered settlement pattern as compared with high-density urban areas. With the expansion of group water schemes, especially during the 1970s, the disparity between rural and urban areas was reduced. The same type of disparity between areas also existed in relation to the provision of electricity. By 1981, however, virtually all dwellings had electricity as compared with 83 per cent in 1961.

Despite the improvement in housing conditions an NESC Report in 1988 concluded:

> ... certain groups have benefited little, or not at all, from the general improvement in housing conditions over the past decade or so. This is indicated by the stagnation, or even deterioration, in housing conditions which has occurred among those with the poorest quality

of dwellings or with none at all. There has been an increasing
disparity between the quality of housing services enjoyed by most
households, and those obtained by those at the bottom end of the
housing market.[30]

Among the evidence given in support of the above was a reference
to the situation in some local authority estates in certain urban
areas, which are characterised by a combination of poor
community facilities, lack of accessibility to jobs and shopping,
poorly maintained fabric, and design problems which have led to
difficulties with security and vandalism.

Rising house prices

In the late 1990s house prices (for both new and second-hand
houses) began to rise at an unprecedented level (Table 3.6). This
applied in particular in the Dublin area but gradually began to
affect all parts of the country. In the period 1995 to 2001 the
average price of all new houses for which loans were approved
more than doubled, while the price of second-hand houses in
Dublin trebled. The reasons for this increase, according to the
National Economic and Social Forum in its report *Social and
Affordable Housing* (2000),[31] included:

- demographic and household formation changes
- economic growth with particular impact on employment
  growth
- increased disposable income and lower direct taxes
- low mortgage interest rates

Table 3.6: Average house prices*, 1995–2001

	1995 €	1997 €	2001 €	Increase %
New				
National	77,994	102,222	182,863	134.5
Dublin	86,671	122,036	243,095	180.5
Second-hand				
National	74,312	102,712	206,117	177.4
Dublin	88,938	131,258	267,939	201.3

*   For which loans were approved
Source: Annual Housing Statistics, Department of the Environment and Local
Government

- a shortage of serviced development land
- increases in the price of development land
- labour shortages including those in the planning sections of local authorities
- investor and general speculative activity
- immigration.

In response to the sharp rise in house prices the government commissioned a report from Bacon and Associates, published in April 1998 and usually referred to as Bacon I. This was followed by two further reports, Bacon II (March 1999) and Bacon III (June 2000). The government introduced certain measures to improve the situation following each report. Some of these were designed to take the heat out of the market, improve affordability, curb investor demand and improve the availability of serviced land. The initial measures taken by government in response to Bacon I did not have an immediate impact and hence a second and subsequently a third report were commissioned.

Among the measures adopted by government were exemptions and reductions in stamp duty for first-time buyers of second-hand houses (up to a certain ceiling), imposition of stamp duty on investors buying new houses and measures to ensure early development of large-scale residential developments. One of the measures in response to Bacon III was to provide 1,000 extra local authority houses up to 2006. This would still leave the local authority output well below what was provided less than 20 years earlier and would not be sufficient to significantly reduce waiting lists.

The above measures had some impact especially in discouraging investor speculation in housing in 2001 but the stamp duty impositions on investors were later removed. It is also arguable that they led to a levelling off in prices from the latter part of 2001 although the impact of broader global factors following the Attack on America on 11 September cannot be ignored. Prices resumed an upward spiral throughout 2002 and looked set to continue as long as supply failed to meet demand.

The affordable housing scheme was introduced in March 1999 to enable low-income households purchase their own homes. Under the scheme, local authorities provide additional new houses on land available to them in or near urban centres.

Houses are offered for sale at cost price. There has been a gradual take up of this scheme with a total of 398 houses provided by the end of 2001 and proposals for several thousand houses.

A controversial but very significant step taken by government was contained in the Planning and Development Act, 2000, whereby a developer would be obliged to provide 20 per cent of dwellings in any development for social housing. This was a controversial section of the Bill and it was referred by the President, Mary McAleese, to the Supreme Court for judgement on its constitutionality. The Supreme Court ruled in favour of the section.

The 20 per cent measure did not meet with any enthusiastic co-operative response from developers or from potential purchasers of private dwellings who did not favour 'mixed' housing schemes. By the end of 2002 the government was obliged to amend the legislation to allow a more flexible response by developers towards meeting their requirements. The options would allow developers to build social and affordable housing on a different site to that of private housing, engage in land swaps with the local authority, or provide financial compensation to the local authority for failing to meet their obligations. The amendment to the Planning and Development Act, 2000 following on from other government responses since the unprecedented rise in house prices commenced, led the *Irish Times* to comment:

> Three years ago, the coalition government decided to deal with the growing house crisis by way of taxation measures and regulatory machinery. It became a wild roller coaster response, lacking any coherence. A 60 per cent tax on hoarded land was introduced and then scrapped. Rental income tax breaks were scrapped and then reintroduced. The percentage of homes built by the state drastically declined. Waiting lists ballooned. Prices soared. But the 20 per cent law on social and affordable housing offered some people some hope. Now that too is about to change. And penalties for hoarding development land are being modified. The government's housing policy is a shambles.[32]

As already indicated, some of the effects of rising house prices were to lead to growing numbers on local authority waiting lists and an increase in rents in the private rented residential sector where demand also began to exceed supply.

Notes

1. *A Plan for Social Housing* (Department of the Environment, 1991), p. 1. Similar objectives were outlined, for example, in the White Paper, *Housing in the Seventies* (Stationery Office, Dublin, 1969) p. 3.
2. There are three county councils in Dublin, three in Cork and two in Tipperary.
3. This section contains a summary of developments up to the mid-1960s as outlined by P.J. Meghan, *Housing in Ireland* (Institute of Public Administration, Dublin, 1966).
4. K.C. Kearns, *Dublin Tenement Life: An Oral History* (Gill and Macmillan, Dublin, 1994) pp. 7–8.
5. T. Fahey, 'Housing and Local Government' in M.E. Daly (ed.), *County and Town: One Hundred Years of Local Government in Ireland* (Institute of Public Administration, 2001) pp. 121–122.
6. D. Ferriter, *Lovers of Liberty: Local Government in 20th century Ireland* (National Archives of Ireland, 2001) p. 76.
7. Fahey, op. cit., p. 123.
8. *Economic Development* (Stationery Office, Dublin, 1959), p. 46.
9. F. Kennedy, *Public Social Expenditure in Ireland* (Economic and Social Research Institute, Dublin, 1975), p. 15.
10. NESC Report No. 14, *Population Projections 1971–86: The Implications for Social Planning – Dwelling Needs* (Stationery Office, Dublin, 1976); NESC Report No. 69, *Housing Requirements and Population Change 1981–91* (Stationery Office, Dublin, 1983).
11. *Ireland, National Development Plan 2000–2006* (Stationery Office, Dublin, 1999) p. 69.
12. P. Pfretzschner, *The Dynamics of Irish Housing* (Institute of Public Administration, Dublin, 1965), p. 112.
13. T. Fahey, 'Social Housing in Ireland: The Need for an Expanded Role?' in *Irish Banking Review*, Autumn 1999, pp. 27–28; *Annual Housing Statistics*, Department of the Environment and Local Government.
14. See NESC Report No. 87, *A Review of Housing Policy* (Stationery Office, Dublin, 1989), where the pros and cons of local authority purchase schemes are outlined, pp. 177–181.
15. P. Tansey, 'Housing Subsidies: A Case for Reform' in J. Blackwell (ed.), 1989, op. cit., pp. 31–32.
16. *A Plan for Social Housing*, op. cit., p. 6.
17. B. Harvey and M. Higgins, 'The Links between Housing and Homelessness' in J. Blackwell (ed.), 1989, op. cit., p. 36.
18. L. O'Brien and B. Dillon, *Private Rented: The Forgotten Sector* (Threshold, Dublin, 1982).
19. B. Thompson, 'Social Housing' in J. Blackwell and S. Kennedy (eds), *Focus on Homelessness* (Columba Press, Dubin, 1988), pp. 118–119.
20. *A Plan for Social Housing*, op. cit., p. 15.
21. *Homelessness, An Integrated Strategy* (Department of the Environment and Local Government, Dublin, 2000) pp. 8–9.
22. *Shaping the Future: An Action Plan on Homelessness in Dublin 2001–2003* (Homeless Agency, 2001), p. 1.
23. Ibid. p. 128.

24. *Homeless Preventative Strategy: A strategy to prevent homelessness among: Patients leaving hospital and mental health care, Adult prisoners and young offenders leaving custody, Young people leaving care* (Stationery Office, Dublin, 2002), p. 19.

25. NESC Report No.23, *Report on Housing Subsidies* (Stationery Office, Dublin, 1977), pp. 8–11.

26. T.J. Baker and L.M. O'Brien, *The Irish Housing System: A Critical Overview* (Economic and Social Research Institute, Dublin, 1979).

27. J. Blackwell, 'Do Housing Subsidies Show a Redistribution to the Poor?' in *Conference on Poverty* (Council for Social Welfare, Dublin, 1981), pp. 225–228.

28. NESC Report No 89, *A Strategy for the Nineties: Economic Stability and Structural Change* (Stationery Office, Dublin, 1990), p. 238.

29. Statistics used in this section are derived from the *Census of Population*.

30. NESC Report No. 87, *A Review of Housing Policy* (Stationery Office, Dublin, 1988).

31. NESF Report No.18, *Social and Affordable Housing and Accommodation: Building the Future* (Stationery Office, Dublin, 2000) p. 22.

32. *Irish Times*, 9 December 2002.

4

Education

Introduction

In many respects, the system of education in Ireland is highly complex. Education is carried out at three levels and considerable variation exists not only between these but also within them. The management of first- and second-level schools is different and at first level there are different kinds of primary schools, while at second level there are also distinct sub-sections. Despite the fact that there is substantial state support at all levels, there are few state schools in the accepted sense. The influence of the churches (especially Catholic) on the development of the system has been profound.

The present system represents a curious mixture of state and church interests, particularly at first level and in some parts of second level. Secondary schools, for example, are in receipt of various state subsidies yet are privately owned and managed. Apart from the churches, there are various other interest groups, such as the teachers' unions and, more recently, parents' organisations. The presence of these groups, coupled with the fact that up to recently there was little legislative basis for education, has meant that it has often been difficult to obtain agreement on policy changes. The following pages will illustrate this.

Since the mid-1960s some important changes have occurred in the education system. These include the introduction of free post-primary education, the establishment of new institutions such as comprehensive and community schools at second level and regional technical colleges (later renamed institutes of technology). These innovations have been accompanied by increased rates of participation.

The main features of each of the three levels as well as of adult education are considered in this chapter. Some key issues in education are also considered.

First-level education

Origins of present system
Many basic features of modern Irish primary or first-level education can be traced back to the establishment in 1831 of the National Board of Education.[1] Prior to that there was no uniform system of primary education and while some areas were well served by schools, others had only rudimentary forms of schooling.[2] A number of organisations promoted first-level education in the early decades of the nineteenth century, for example the Kildare Place Society and Catholic religious orders.

In 1831 the British House of Commons voted a sum of £30,000 towards primary education in Ireland. This money was to be administered by the National Board of Education which consisted of seven Commissioners representing the main religious denominations. The Board was given power to contribute to the cost of building schools, pay inspection costs, contribute to teachers' salaries, establish model schools and provide school books. The system was to provide for 'combined moral, literary and separate religious education'. The Board's intention was to establish a multi-denominational rather than a denominational system of education. In other words it did not favour the funding of schools to pursue a particular religious ethos. Schools run by religious orders were to be given the same assistance as other schools provided they complied with the rules of the Board.

Opposition and lack of co-operation, mainly on religious grounds, hindered the Board's early success. In 1837, for example, the Irish Christian Brothers withdrew their schools from connection with the Board. Four years later, however, Pope Gregory XVI encouraged Catholics to support the national schools. While some of the Catholic hierarchy welcomed the new system, others, notably Dr John MacHale, Archbishop of Tuam, were less enthusiastic and forbade their clergy to co-operate with the Board.[3]

The training of teachers for the national schools proved to be another contentious issue. In 1837, the Board established a training school and three model schools at Marlborough Street,

Dublin. Teachers were to be trained on the principle of the 'mixed system', i.e. the teaching of children of all denominations where religious and secular instruction would not be separate. The Catholic hierarchy forbade their clerical managers to appoint teachers trained in the model schools to schools under their control. In 1883 the Board decided to recognise denominational training colleges and two Catholic colleges (St Patrick's, Drumcondra, for men and Our Lady of Mercy, Blackrock, for women) were established in Dublin. A Church of Ireland training college for men and women was affiliated to the Board in the following year. Three other training colleges at Waterford (1891), Belfast (1900), and Limerick (1907), were established.

Notwithstanding its limitations and somewhat tempestuous history, by 1922 when the Commissioners of the National Board of Education were replaced by a branch of the newly-founded Department of Education under an Irish Minister for Education, the national system could claim credit for considerable achievements since its foundation.[4] Perhaps the most important consequence of the national system was that it was the chief means by which the country was transformed from one in which illiteracy predominated into one in which most people could read and write: in 1841 over half (53 per cent) the population aged five years and over could neither read nor write, and by 1901 this proportion had declined to 14 per cent. In the eradication of mass illiteracy, therefore, credit must be given to the national system. The system also ensured that in all parts of the country national schools were established. The number of schools increased from just over 1,000 in 1834 to almost 8,000 in 1921, and the school-going population increased from 107,000 in 1833 to 685,000 in 1891. This occurred despite a decline of over 50 per cent in the total population between 1841 and 1921.

One of the main objectives of the National Board of Education, the establishment of multi-denominational schools, was not achieved. The state system of multi-denominational education established in 1831 had become, by the time the Irish State was founded, a system of denominational education and has remained essentially so ever since. As indicated in the *Rules of National Schools under the Department of Education* (1965), the state gave explicit recognition to the denominational character of these schools well into the twentieth century.

Compulsory schooling

Under the Irish Education Act, 1892, attendance on at least 75 days in each half year was made compulsory for children between the ages of six and fourteen. A number of acceptable excuses for non-attendance were specified by the Act, e.g. sickness, harvesting operations, fishing, any other unavoidable cause, or that the child was already receiving suitable elementary education. Initially the application of the Act was limited to municipal boroughs and towns but in 1898 it was extended to all parts of the country. The enforcement of the Act was particularly difficult in rural areas. School attendance committees set up by local authorities helped to enforce the law but not all local authorities set up such committees.

While the Act may not have had the desired effect, it nevertheless brought about a change in school attendance. In 1902 the average yearly attendance was 63 per cent and this increased to 76 per cent by 1908.

The School Attendance Act, 1926 made further provisions for the enforcement of compulsory schooling and remained the main statute governing school attendance until the Education (Welfare) Act, 2000.

Management and finance

Initially, the National Board of Education was willing to give special consideration to any joint applications for aid from members of different religious denominations within a parish. What happened in practice was that where there were sufficient numbers of children of different denominations, the Catholic or non-Catholic clergy or members of religious orders applied for separate aid in building a school. The pupils, therefore, were concentrated in separate schools under local clerical or religious order management. This was the beginning of the managerial system, which survived up to 1975.

Ironically, while the direct administration of primary schools and the appointment and dismissal of teachers has remained in the hands of local managers, the state has always paid a large share of the cost of building schools and pays the teachers' salaries in full. The non-state character of the school was preserved by the provision of a site from local funds together with a local contribution towards the cost of building the school. The state also contributes towards the maintenance of schools. The situation in relation to the subsidy for school buildings up to the late 1990s has been summarised as follows:

> While in theory the state contributes two-thirds of the approved cost of a primary school building, this contribution is open to negotiation, and in the vast majority of cases is very much higher. The system is not entirely satisfactory, since the amount of the state grant provided often depends on the case put forward in respect of local circumstances.[5]

Prior to 1999, the position was that up to 15 per cent of building costs was provided by the patron except for special schools for children with learning difficulties (intellectual disabilities) and schools in disadvantaged areas where the contribution was 5 per cent.

In January 1999, Micheál Martin, TD, Minister for Education and Science, announced a fundamental change in capital grants for primary schools designed, in part, to relieve fund-raising pressures on local communities. The state would now provide the full cost of a site and 95 per cent of the capital cost. While the local community would be responsible for 5 per cent of capital costs, this would be subject to a ceiling of £50,000. However, the most significant change arising from this policy develop-ment was that, in future, the state would own the school building (hitherto the patron was the effective owner of the building). This applies only to new schools built following the change in policy. The new funding system is likely to be of significant benefit to multi-denominational schools (see later section).

There are approximately 60 private primary schools and these do not receive any state subsidy and are totally financed by parents' fees.

In practice a distinction can be made between primary schools. The majority are referred to as ordinary national schools and are mainly under either Catholic or Protestant clerical patronage. There are also some schools run by religious orders. In addition, there are special schools for children with disabilities, schools in which the curriculum is taught wholly or mainly through the medium of Irish (Gaelscoileanna) and a growing number of multi-denominational schools. There are also a small number of 'model' national schools directly under the control of the Department of Education and Science.

While suggestions were made in the early 1970s to involve parents and teachers formally in school management, little became of these until the world oil crisis of 1973–1974 presented the opportunity. The soaring cost of heating oil meant that the state would have to substantially increase its maintenance subsidy to primary schools, otherwise the burden would fall on the local community. In October 1974, Richard Burke, TD, Minister for Education, announced a new scheme of aid towards the maintenance costs of primary schools. Instead of paying schools a proportion of the maintenance costs, a capitation grant of £6 per pupil (to be matched by an amount equivalent to one-quarter of the state grant to be collected locally) would be given only to those schools that had set up joint management committees by October 1975, composed of four nominees of the patron and two parents. The Minister subsequently indicated that teachers should also be represented on these committees. Schools which had not set up the committees would have to accept a lower subsidy from the Department of Education towards upkeep. From a financial viewpoint, therefore, it was in the manager's interest to establish committees. The manner in which management boards were introduced in primary schools has been aptly described as a form of 'gentle blackmail'.[6] It also illustrated the difficulty of making policy changes in the Irish education system. In the absence of a legislative basis, change was normally introduced by agreement among the various interests involved rather than by legislation. In this instance, a financial carrot achieved in one year something that in all probability would have taken several years to achieve.

While the principle of teacher and parental representation on management boards was accepted, in practice protracted negotiations between the main interests (Irish National Teachers' Organisation, the Catholic hierarchy, the Department of Education and the Catholic Primary School Managers' Association) took place before agreement to establish committees was reached and before the exact functions and composition of the boards of management were agreed. It was not until November 1976 that the constitution and rules of procedure for the management boards were published. Following further negotiations, these rules and the composition of boards were subsequently altered in 1981. Further changes occurred in the 1990s. In schools of seven teachers or more, the board is comprised of a total of eight members, i.e. two nominees of the patron, two parents elected by other parents, a principal teacher and one other teacher elected by teaching staff; these six members then propose two others from the local community (subject to the approval of the patron) to bring the total to eight.

The patron of the school appoints the chairman of the board of management. For the majority of primary schools, the bishop or archbishop (Catholic or Protestant) is normally the patron. The boards are responsible for the maintenance of the school (and up to 2001 they were also responsible for the collection of the local contribution which was introduced as part of the new funding arrangement in 1975). The *Review Body on Primary Education* received submissions which were critical of the management system, e.g. the Department of Education decided on all major matters of policy, the patron played a central role in the appointment of the Board, the chairperson, the principal and assistant teachers, and agreements between trade unions and the Department limited further the autonomy of the board. Having considered alternative proposals, the Review Body did not recommend any change in the composition of the Boards. Instead it recommended that the future of the Boards be reappraised and strengthened, e.g. that they be given greater autonomy in relation to many matters which require the approval of the Department of Education.[7]

The system of capitation grant from the Department of Education, coupled with a local contribution of one-quarter of that grant, introduced in 1975, continued into the 1990s. For example, in 1997/98, the Department grant for ordinary schools was £45 per pupil and the local contribution was £10 (a total of £55 per pupil). Since then, however, the local contribution has been phased out and in 2001 it was abolished. By 2002/03 the capitation grant was €115 (special schools for children with intellectual disabilities and Gaelscoileanna receive higher capitation grants).

In 1997 a significant development took place with the introduction of minor capital grants to primary schools. This grant (€3,000 basic grant plus €13 per pupil in 2002/03) is to cover such items as replacement of windows, roof repairs and purchase of standard furniture. Prior to this, boards of management had to apply to the Department for funding for such purposes.

Rationalisation

A relatively high density of population in the mid-nineteenth century, combined with the fact that education was based on the parish and the lack of speedy transport, encouraged the building of small primary schools serving a rather limited catchment area. As population declined throughout the latter part of the nineteenth century and the first half of the twentieth century, however, many schools, especially those in rural areas, became vulnerable to closure. Since its establishment the Department of Education had sought to amalgamate those schools with the smallest number of pupils. In many areas there was considerable opposition to school closures, reflecting the value of the school as a focal point in the local community.

The *Investment in Education* report (1965) indicated that on a cost-effective basis the one-teacher and two-teacher primary schools were inefficient, for example, in the range of subjects taught and in the rate of pupils' progress through school.[8] This report influenced subsequent policy towards small schools and an intensive programme of primary school rationalisation was embarked upon. Within a decade (1967 to 1977), 471 one-teacher and 1,186 two-teacher schools were closed or amalgamated. During the same period the total number of primary schools fell from 4,625 to 3,372. In 1967, one-teacher and two-teacher schools accounted for almost two-thirds of all primary schools; by 1997, the proportion had fallen to one-quarter (Table 4.1). It should be noted that while small rural schools were being closed or amalgamated, others were being established in the expanding urban areas.

In 1976 a NESC report questioned the efficacy of closing small rural schools and referred to the trend in Scandinavia where the process of rationalisation had been reversed.[9] In 1977, Peter

Table 4.1: Number of small schools and total number of schools at primary level*, 1967–1997

	1967	1977	1997
(a) Number of one and two-teacher schools	2,920	1,263	803
(b) Total numer of primary schools	4,625	3,372	3,186
(a) as % of (b)	63.1	37.4	25.2

*   Special schools for children with disabilities are not included.
Source: *Statistical Reports*, Department of Education and Science

Barry, TD, Minister for Education, announced that the Department of Education would no longer force the amalgamation of small schools into larger units.[10] Inevitably, the closure and amalgamation of small schools in rural areas has continued, reflecting the continuing decline in population in some of those areas.

Denominationalism and primary schools

It has already been noted that despite the intentions of the National Board of Education to establish a non-denominational school structure, what emerged was a system of denominational schools. The preface to the *Rules for National Schools under the Department of Education* (1965) gave recognition to such schools:

> ... the state provides for free primary education for children in national schools, and gives explicit recognition to the denominational character of these schools.[11]

In the mid-1970s a movement to establish multi-denominational schools was initiated by some parents in parts of Dublin. The Department of Education was unco-operative while the Catholic Church opposed the concept. The movement was gradually afforded recognition and state financial support for the establishment of schools was provided. The first multi-denominational school to open was the Dalkey School Project, Dublin, in 1978. Most of the multi-denominational schools are under the aegis of a representative organisation, Educate Together, and in 2003 there were 28 such schools with a number of others at various stages of planning.

The policy in relation to multi-denominational schools has been outlined in the *Programme for Action, 1984–1987*:

> Where the government is convinced that the establishment of a multi-denominational school represents the clear wishes of parents in an area and where such schools can be provided on a viable basis, support will be given to such developments on the same terms that would be available for the establishment of schools under denominational patronage.[12]

Up to 1999 groups of parents who wished to provide a multi-denominational school had to provide a site and up to 15 per cent of the cost of the building (this would have applied to the building of a new school as opposed to the renting of a premises). The

change in policy in 1999 has eased the burden of the fund-raising
required.

Second-level education

Second-level education is conducted mainly in four types of
schools – secondary, vocational, comprehensive and community.
Since the origins, financing, ownership and management structure of these schools differ, each type is considered separately in
this section.

Secondary schools

While state aid was made available for primary education in 1831
it was not made available for secondary education until 1878 and
even then the level of aid was comparatively small. Under the
Intermediate Education Act, 1878, the secondary school education system in its present form took shape. The Act established the
Intermediate Education Board with seven commissioners to
administer funds for examination purposes. The word 'intermediate' was taken to imply a system of education between
elementary or primary instruction and higher education. Junior,
middle and senior grade examinations were established under the
Act and results fees were paid to the managers of schools in which
candidates passed the examinations. The principal means of
obtaining state aid, therefore, was through success in examinations. On the credit side, the new system imposed a uniform
curriculum on secondary schools where variety had predominated. However, since aid available from the state was limited,
schools relied heavily on students' fees to meet capital and current
costs. Unlike the primary school system whereby schools could be
established in practically every area with state support, the
distribution of secondary schools was mainly confined to urban
areas. Consequently, many areas of the country lacked secondary
schools, the greatest concentration being in the Dublin area and
along the east coast generally, while few existed in the province of
Connacht.

The Intermediate Education Board was dissolved in 1922 and
in 1925 its functions were taken over by the Department of
Education. Under the Intermediate Education (Amendment) Act,
1924, the system of paying grants to schools on the results of
public examinations was discontinued. Instead, capitation grants
were paid to schools for pupils over twelve years of age who

followed prescribed courses and who made a certain number of attendances (130 days during the school year). The initial grant was £7 per junior pupil and £10 per senior pupil.

In 1924 the junior, middle and senior grade examinations were replaced by the intermediate and leaving certificate examinations. In 1925, the first year of the new examination system, 2,900 pupils sat for the intermediate certificate examination and 995 for the leaving certificate (the numbers were 59,700 junior certificate and 52,200 leaving certificate in 2000).

Incremental salaries for recognised secondary teachers were introduced in 1925 in schools that fulfilled certain conditions regarding size and staffing ratio.

Finance. The government of the Free State recognised the private ownership of all secondary schools and decided to give neither building nor maintenance grants but to help them indirectly by means of capitation grants. An opportunity was therefore lost of redressing the serious imbalance in the distribution of secondary schools. It was not until 1965 that state capital grants were made available for secondary schools.

Up to 1986, the current expenditure of secondary schools was subsidised by a combination of a capitation grant and a supplemental grant (in lieu of fees charged by schools participating in the free post-primary education scheme introduced in 1967–1968). In 1986 these two grants were combined into a capitation grant based on enrolment. The value of the capitation grant in 2002/03 was €266.

The subsidy for Protestant secondary education is organised on a different basis. The majority of the Protestant secondary schools are not in the free scheme and the Department of Education pays a block grant to the Secondary Education Committee which distributes it, in accordance with a means test, to Protestant parents in order to subsidise their children's attendance at Protestant day or boarding schools.[13]

Free post-primary education scheme. One of the more significant findings of the *Investment in Education* report (1965) was that there were serious inequalities in the numbers from different socio-economic groups in second-level schools. In particular, the report indicated that less than one-third were children of semi-skilled and unskilled workers, while almost three-quarters were the children of professionals, employers, managers and senior salaried employees.[14]

The introduction of the free post-primary education scheme in 1967–1968 was an attempt to ensure equality of access to all seeking education beyond first level. Prior to this, entrance to secondary schools in general depended as much on ability to pay fees as intellectual capacity. It must also be noted, however, that while all secondary schools charged fees prior to the introduction of the scheme, ability to pay fees was not a condition of entry to some schools managed by religious orders. In effect, they operated a free scheme for pupils from low-income families long before the Department of Education took the initiative.

Under the scheme, secondary schools that opted to discontinue charging school fees for pupils would be paid a supplemental grant per pupil equal to the fee charged in the school year 1966–1967. The majority of secondary schools agreed to participate in the free scheme.

The free post-primary education scheme also provided for grants towards free schoolbooks and accessories for necessitous day pupils. Under the scheme, free transport was also provided for pupils living more than three miles from a school in which free education was available.

A limited scheme of free post-primary education had been under consideration in the Department of Education during the 1960s and it was intended that such a scheme be introduced in 1970 to coincide with the raising of the school leaving age to fifteen years. That the scheme was introduced earlier than planned for was due to the intervention of Donogh O'Malley, TD, Minister for Education. Seán O'Connor, Assistant Secretary in the Department of Education at the time, has recounted:

> We, the planners, prepared to introduce free education in tandem with the raising of the school leaving age in 1970 and all our urging and striving for co-ordination and co-operation had that year as a focal point ... I have long been convinced that had matters proceeded according to our plans, when 1970 came, free education would not have been on the agenda at all, or if it had been, it would have been in such attenuated form as scarce to merit the title. Donogh O'Malley shattered our plans and left Ireland in his debt.[15]

The numbers participating in second-level education rose dramatically in the decade following the introduction of free post-primary education. This was due in part to the increase in the young population at the time, but the participation rate by age also increased (see later section on Participation in education).

Some of the increased participation may be attributed to the introduction of the free scheme, and the free transport service undoubtedly led to increased participation in rural areas.

Vocational schools

There was little emphasis in Ireland on technical education prior to the early decades of the twentieth century. The Vocational Education Act, 1930 remained the basic statute governing vocational and technical education until the late 1990s and has provided the framework for development in this area. The subsequent development of vocational schools helped to redress partially the regional imbalance of secondary schools. The important provisions in the Act covered administration and financial arrangements.

Administration. The vocational education system is administered by local Vocational Education Committees (VECs) subject to the general control of the Minister for Education. Membership of the VEC consisted of local authority elected representatives (who constituted the majority) and other representatives of educational, cultural, industrial and commercial interests in the area. A total of 38 VECs were established; one each for the county boroughs (Dublin, Cork, Limerick and Waterford), one for each administrative county and seven for certain urban areas (Bray, Drogheda, Dún Laoghaire, Galway, Sligo, Tralee and Wexford).

The functions of a VEC were to provide, or assist in the provision of, a system of continuation education and a system of technical education in its area. It could establish schools, employ staff and generally perform all the functions of an education authority, within the general powers conferred by the Vocational Education Act. A VEC's programme was subject to the approval of the Minister for Education, but once the basic educational and financial schemes had been approved, a considerable degree of flexibility and discretion was allowed in regard to the actual organisation of courses. Committees were thus in a position to be responsive to local needs.

The financial arrangements of the Vocational Education Act, 1930 provided for a local rate contribution and corresponding grant from the state. In the first year, 1931/32, the total cost of vocational education was £303,000, of which two-thirds was a contribution from the Department of Education. In time, the local rate contribution declined in importance, particularly following the abolition of rates on private dwellings in 1978. At present, almost 90 per cent of the total cost of vocational education is by way of grants from the Department of Education with a miniscule contribution (0.2 per cent) coming from local rates.

The Vocational Education (Amendment) Act, 2001 provided for new structures and accountability, management and financial procedures in order that each VEC can meet the needs of vocational education in the area. The VECs have corporate status. Although their administrative areas are similar to those of the larger government bodies, they do not come within that system. In 1998 the number of VECs was reduced from 38 to 33 (see later section).

Secondary versus vocational schools
Apart from administrative and financing differences between secondary and vocational schools, a number of other important differences also existed. From the outset, vocational schools were inter-denominational and co-educational, whereas secondary schools were mainly denominational and single sex. While vocational schools appear to have a more democratic adminis-trative structure, the Church nevertheless has had some influence on the development of the system. At the time of the passing of the Vocational Education Act, the Catholic hierarchy was given an assurance by Professor John Marcus O'Sullivan, TD, Minister for Education, that the vocational system would not impinge upon the field covered by the denominationally controlled secondary schools.[16] It was intended that the two types of schools were to develop quite separately with no overlap between them.

Coolahan notes that in the 1960s:

> Vocational schools were frequently in unequal competition with the local secondary school, each type of school proceeding in splendid isolation from the other.[17]

With the introduction of leaving certificate courses in vocational schools in the mid-1960s, the social and educational barriers between the two systems have begun to be slowly removed. The vocational system with its emphasis on technical subjects was popularly regarded as a type of educational cul-de-sac where qualifications led to low-paid occupations; the secondary schools, on the other hand, with their emphasis on academic subjects were regarded as having higher social status, their qualifications being passports to third level academic education and more remunerative occupations.

Despite curricular developments, the divisions remained and were such as to have evoked from Gemma Hussey, TD, Minister for Education (1982–1986), the following remark during a visit to a number of schools in north Kerry in 1984:

> The old snob divisions between vocational and secondary are firmly evident. If I was a dictator they would be all mixed up together.[18]

Comprehensive schools

Apart from inequalities based on social groups, the *Investment in Education* report also indicated that there were inequalities based on geographical location in the participation of children in post-primary education.[19] The reasons for this have already been outlined in the foregoing sections. An attempt to remedy this deficiency was the establishment of comprehensive schools, plans for which were first announced in 1963 by Dr Patrick Hillery, TD, Minister for Education. In his policy statement, the Minister referred to:

> ... areas where the population is so scattered as to make the establishment of a secondary or a vocational school a most unlikely event.[20]

What the Minister envisaged was the establishment, in areas where post-primary education was inadequate or non-existent, of schools that would be completely financed by the state. The first four comprehensive schools were to be established at Cootehill (County Cavan), Carraroe (County Galway), Shannon (County Clare), and Glenties (County Donegal). Each of these schools was sited in rural areas and was open to all children within a radius of ten miles.

The comprehensive school also represented an attempt to rectify the division of interest between secondary and vocational schools by combining academic and practical subjects in one broad curriculum. In this way pupils would be offered an education structured to their needs, abilities and interests.

Protestant comprehensives. Because of the absence of any Protestant equivalent of the Catholic religious orders, which have reinvested members' salaries in the establishment and maintenance of their schools, the cost to Protestants of providing their own secondary schools has been relatively high. The introduction of the concept of a comprehensive school, where capital and current costs would be met fully by the state, presented an opportunity to establish Protestant schools without the burden of heavy costs. Three Protestant comprehensives have been established, two in Dublin and one in Cork, but the intake of pupils in these schools is not exclusively Protestant.

The Department of Education and Science meet both capital and current costs of comprehensive schools in full.

Community schools

Another important finding of the *Investment in Education* report was that there were gaps in the efficiency of the educational system in the use of existing educational resources. In particular, the report referred to duplication of resources and staff in secondary and vocational schools. In a statement to the authorities of secondary and vocational schools in 1966, George Colley, TD, Minister for Education, indicated that the two rigidly separated, post-primary systems could no longer be maintained, although their distinctive character should be retained. He recommended a sharing of accommodation and facilities between schools.[21]

This was taken a stage further when, in 1970, Patrick Faulkner, TD, Minister for Education, announced plans for community schools to be created by agreement rather than legislation. The circular on community schools issued by the Minister indicated that in some areas community schools would result from the amalgamation of existing secondary and vocational schools and in growing suburban areas from the development of a single school rather than the traditional development of separate secondary and vocational schools. The community schools were to be co-educational and non-fee paying with enrolments of 400 up to 1,000.

The community schools concept seemed a logical development that would help to eliminate many of the obvious deficiencies in the educational system. An added attraction was that the capital costs would be covered mainly by the state and, in a period of rising costs, this would be an incentive to religious orders to participate in community schools. Another dimension to the community school concept was the involvement of the community. The community schools were to be focal points in the locality, their facilities being made available outside school hours to the community.

The announcement of plans for community schools gave rise to considerable controversy and opposition was expressed towards the merging of two distinct educational systems. Much of this was undoubtedly influenced by the higher prestige accorded to secondary schools. Not infrequently, parents and religious orders objected to the amalgamation of traditional secondary schools with the vocational system. Controversy also attended the deeds of trust (the legal base for the schools in the absence of legislation) that were to be signed by the main parties.

By 2000 there were 69 community schools (Table 4.2). One of the main factors accounting for the acceptance of the community school concept was the decline in membership of religious orders. As a result it was virtually impossible for them to establish new secondary schools as they had in the past, and increasingly difficult for them to retain a significant presence in the existing secondary schools.

Current expenditure in community schools is borne entirely by the state, as are at least 90 per cent of capital costs, the remainder being met by the religious orders and the VEC.

Management in second-level schools
The local management of second-level schools is far more complex than that at first level where, as noted, boards of management were introduced in 1975. This complexity arises in part from the very different origins, purpose and ethos of the four categories of schools. To add to the confused situation, there are differences even within a category, e.g. between Catholic and Protestant secondary schools.

Section 14 (1) of the Education Act 1998 stipulates that:

It shall be the duty of a patron, for the purposes of ensuring that a recognised school is managed in a spirit of partnership, to appoint

Table 4.2: Number of second-level schools, 1976 and 2000

	1976	*2000*
Secondary	532	419
Vocational	245	247
Comprehensive	15	16
Community	27	69
Total	816	751

Source: Statistical Reports, Department of Education and Science

where practicable a board of management the composition of which is agreed between patrons of schools, national associations of parents, recognised school management organisations, recognised trade unions and staff associations representing teachers and the Minister.

The Act did not seek to impose a uniform model of boards of management on all second-level schools (achieving agreement on that would have been a difficult task). Instead it allows flexibility to suit the needs of particular schools. The following is necessarily a summary of the key management features of each category of school:[22]

- *Secondary schools.* Secondary schools are privately owned, the majority by Catholic religious orders (a minority are owned by Catholic dioceses, Catholic or Protestant lay persons and foundations). The patron/trustees (normally members of the order) hold the property in trust for the order. Since the mid-1980s management boards, consisting of parents, teachers and representatives of religious orders, have been established in some secondary schools. The membership of the board consists of four nominees of the patron/trustees, two elected parents and two elected teachers.
- *Vocational schools.* In addition to representation by local authority elected representatives, the Vocational Education (Amendment) Act, 2001 also provided for representation, as of right, for two parents and two teachers on VECs. It also provided for the appointment by the relevant local authority in consultation with the core membership, of four other members representative of educational, voluntary, VEC staff and commercial interests in the area. Individual vocational schools are under the trusteeship of the local VEC. In May 1974, Richard Burke, TD, Minister for Education, requested all VECs to establish boards of management in each of their schools. By the mid-1990s, boards of management had been established in the majority of vocational schools and they normally consist of six VEC members, two parents and a teacher. These boards are sub-committees of the relevant VEC.
- *Comprehensive schools.* The original instruments and articles of these schools provided for a three-member board of management, i.e. the chief executive of the VEC, a diocesan representative (Catholic or Protestant) and an official from the Department of Education and Science (usually a schools

inspector). There are variations on this model, with some schools having added parents and teachers as non-voting members. This model is under review and is likely to change in order to reflect the partnership concept in other schools.

- *Community schools*. These are normally managed by a board comprising three nominees of religious orders or the diocese, three nominees of the VEC, two elected parents and two elected teachers.

Rationalisation

A number of developments have occurred in the past few decades that have, to some extent, lessened the distinction between the traditional secondary and vocational schools. Thus, the curriculum in these two types of schools is now broadly analogous. Similarly, the establishment of community schools has ensured that a single school now exists in some areas where traditionally secondary and vocational schools would have been established. Nevertheless, it is difficult to justify the present system where there are four different types of schools at second level with different administrative and financial arrangements. Some rationalisation is required.

In 1985, the Department of Education published a Green Paper, *Partners in Education*. It proposed the abolition of the Vocational Education Committees and their replacement by thirteen Local Education Councils (LECs), with a membership representing teachers, parents, school management, youth services, training agencies, trade unions and employers. The LECs would be responsible for co-ordinating all secondary, vocational, comprehensive and community schools in their area, and for the provision, planning and development of second-level education. The areas to be covered by the LECs would embrace a number of counties in some cases.

The Green Paper pointed out that developments in the post-primary education system over the previous two decades had led to the creation of a number of different types of schools, all of which were seeking to provide essentially the same education service to the same public. It commented that:

> In the context of the rationalisation of school facilities in particular this situation has given rise to controversy between school authorities at post primary level, a controversy related to issues of school management rather than to educational considerations.[23]

The Green Paper indicated that the establishment of a regional body would eliminate friction based on the management structure of schools and would provide a better framework for the rationalisation of post-primary facilities and for the delivery of other services.

The reaction to the Green Paper by the various interest groups was not very enthusiastic. Thus, the abolition of the Vocational Education Committees was unacceptable to many members of those committees, especially public elected representatives. Similarly, the reaction of the teachers' unions in second-level schools was muted although the Irish National Teachers' Organisation, representing teachers in primary schools, objected to the plan on the grounds that primary schools were not included in the proposed regionalised structure.

While rationalisation as envisaged by the Green Paper is unlikely to come about in the near future, a certain rationalisation at second level would now appear to be inevitable. This arises mainly from the decline in religious orders and schools under their control. The traditional situation in many towns of a secondary school for girls run by a religious order, a secondary school for boys run by a religious order, and a co-educational vocational educational school is already changing and is likely to change further as the religious orders' involvement in education continues to decline. In 1997 a report by the Conference of Religious of Ireland concluded that within 25 years or less there may not be enough members of religious orders to conduct any school-related function.[24] This in itself will inevitably lead to a rationalisation of the second-level system at local level.

Third-level education

Third-level education in Ireland may be broadly divided into two sectors, i.e. university and non-university.

Non-university sector
The regional Institutes of Technology (formerly the regional technical colleges, the colleges of the Dublin Institute of Technology (DIT), the teacher training colleges and a number of other institutions providing courses in areas such as domestic science, commerce, retail distribution and management studies, provide most further education outside the universities. It is a sector that has grown considerably in the past three decades.

Students in this sector now account for half the total at third level.

The idea of regional technical colleges was first referred to in a policy statement on post-primary education in 1963 by Dr Patrick Hillery, TD, Minister for Education.[25] The intention was to arrange for the provision of a limited number of technological colleges with regional status. The proposal was taken further in 1969 by the report of a steering committee on technical education. The report envisaged the colleges, for the most part, as being second-level institutions but suggested some of them might also provide post-leaving certificate full-time or equivalent part-time courses over one or two years leading to higher technician courses.[26] Both the report of the steering committee and the *Investment in Education* report stressed the need for high level technicians to service a growing industrial sector.

The first regional technical colleges (RTCs) opened in the period 1970–1972. While they were originally intended to reinforce the technical dimension of the second-level system, they quickly found themselves called upon to cater increasingly for third-level demand.

The Regional Technical Colleges Act, 1992 gave greater autonomy to the colleges with their own governing bodies. Hitherto they were effectively sub-committees of their local Vocational Education Committee. During 1997 the status of the RTCs became an issue and each was renamed an Institute of Technology. The courses in these Institutes are now third level and encompass degree, certificate and diploma courses. There are now twelve such Institutes of Technology including the nine established in the 1970s at Athlone, Carlow, Cork, Dundalk, Galway, Letterkenny, Sligo, Tralee, Waterford and newcomers at Limerick (former College of Art, Commerce and Technology), Tallaght and Dún Laoghaire (former College of Art and Design).

Dublin Institute of Technology. The Dublin Institute of Technology (DIT), was established informally in 1978 to bring greater coordination to the work of six third level colleges of the City of Dublin Vocational Education Committee. The six colleges are the Colleges of Technology in Bolton Street and Kevin Street, the Colleges of Catering, of Commerce, of Marketing and Design and of Music. The Dublin Institute of Technology Act, 1992 gave statutory recognition to the development and expanding role of the Institute. From 1998/99 the DIT has degree awarding powers.

Colleges of Education. There are five colleges of education for primary school teachers: St Patrick's, Drumcondra; Church of Ireland College; St Mary's Marino and Froebel College, all in Dublin; and Mary Immaculate College in Limerick (Carysfort Teacher Training College, Dublin, established in 1883, was closed in 1987). There are two colleges for home economics (St Catherine's in Dublin, and St Angela's in Sligo). Thomond College (Limerick) is a specialist college for teachers of physical education and crafts. Both Mary Immaculate College and Thomond College were incorporated into the University of Limerick in 1991. In 1993, St Patrick's College, Drumcondra was included within Dublin City University. Teachers of art are trained in the National College of Art and Design, Dublin. The colleges of education and the two colleges of home economics are associated with the universities for their degree awards.

Two other institutions were part of the non-university sector: the National Institute for Higher Education at Limerick and Dublin. In 1989, however, these became the University of Limerick and Dublin City University, respectively.

Awards in the non-university sector. The National Council for Educational Awards (NCEA) was set up in 1972 on an *ad hoc* basis pending the passing of legislation to establish it on a statutory basis. Following a period of uncertainty concerning its future in the mid-1970s, the NCEA Act was passed in 1978 and came into effect in July 1980. The NCEA was responsible for the co-ordination, development, promotion of technical, industrial, scientific technological and commercial education, and education in art and design outside the universities. It fulfilled this role by the approval of courses and the granting of degrees, diplomas, certificates and other educational awards.

The Higher Education and Training Awards Council (HETAC) was established in June 2001 under the Qualifications (Education and Training) Act, 1999. It is the legal successor to the NCEA. Awards made by the NCEA are deemed to be HETAC awards. Essentially, HETAC is the qualifications awarding body for third-level educational and training institutions outside the university sector.

University sector
There are now seven universities in the Republic:

• University of Dublin with one college, Trinity College (TCD)
• The National University of Ireland (NUI) with four constituent universities at Dublin, Cork, Galway and Maynooth
• Dublin City University
• University of Limerick.

The National University also has five recognised colleges: National College of Art and Design; the Royal College of Surgeons; St Angela's College of Education; Shannon College of Hotel Management and the Institute of Public Administration.

The following is a brief background to the establishment of the older universities:

Trinity College. University of Dublin received its charter from Elizabeth I in 1591. From the beginning it was identified with English rule and the governing class in Ireland. For much of its history, according to F.S.L. Lyons, Trinity was 'intensely conscious of its position as a bastion of the Ascendancy in general and of Anglicanism in particular'.[27] In 1793 Catholics were admitted to degrees in Trinity College and by the mid-nineteenth century they constituted about 10 per cent of the undergraduate body. While the formal name is the University of Dublin, it is more commonly referred to as Trinity or Trinity College (attempts to include other colleges were not successful).

The Queen's Colleges, 1845. In 1845 Sir Robert Peel introduced a Bill providing for the establishment of three 'Queen's Colleges' in Ireland. The colleges were to be established at Belfast, Galway and Cork. There would be no interference with religious convictions, but the establishment, by private endowment, of a theological school within the colleges was permissible. Opposition to the Bill was considerable, particularly from some members of the Irish Catholic hierarchy who feared that lectures in philosophy, history and science were bound to reflect contemporary thought on these subjects. At the Synod of Thurles (1850) the hierarchy condemned the Queen's Colleges and exhorted laymen to avoid them as students or teachers on the grounds that they were dangers to faith and morals. A minority of bishops unsuccessfully appealed against these decisions. Despite ecclesiastical opposition, the three colleges were established.

The Royal University, 1879. The University Education (Ireland) Act, 1879 provided for the formation of a new university (the Royal University) and for the dissolution of the Queen's University. The Royal University was modelled on the University of London, which at the time was purely an examining body. Authority was granted to confer degrees on all students irrespective of where they had studied. The religious difficulty was overcome and Catholics and Protestants presented themselves for examination.

The Catholic University, 1854. At the Synod of Thurles a section of the Catholic hierarchy favoured the establishment of a Catholic university styled on that of Louvain, which had been founded with Papal approval in 1834. Dr John Henry Newman, a distinguished Oxford convert to Catholicism, was invited to become rector of the new university. An application by the hierarchy for a charter for the university was unsuccessful, as was an application for state funds. Newman left Ireland in 1858 and the university declined. In 1890 it was placed in the charge of the Jesuits who administered its affairs until the establishment of the National University in 1908.

The National University of Ireland, 1908. The National University of Ireland was established by the Irish Universities Act, 1908. In the following year the Royal University was formally dissolved. The Act provided for the establishment of two new universities, one in Dublin and one in Belfast. The one in Belfast was to become the Queen's University, replacing the former college of that name. The new National University of Ireland, centred in Dublin, was to take over the Queen's Colleges in Cork and Galway as constituent colleges as well as the new college founded in Dublin to replace the Catholic University. It was further allowed to affiliate 'such institutions as have a standard deemed satisfactory by the University', an arrangement that allowed the subsequent entry of Maynooth. No test whatever of religious belief was to be permitted for any appointment in either of the universities, thus denying the denominational university that the Catholic hierarchy had long demanded.

St Patrick's College, Maynooth. St Patrick's was founded in 1795 as a seminary for the training of the Catholic clergy. It was the only Catholic educational institution to receive state aid at the time. In 1910, under the provisions of the Irish Universities Act, 1908, the College was recognised by the Senate of the National

University as a recognised College of the University in certain faculties. A decision by the hierarchy to admit lay students to courses at Maynooth in 1966/67 led to the wider use of an institution that had hitherto been confined to the training of priests. Since then the number of clerical students has declined while the number of lay students has increased steadily. Under the Universities Act, 1997, St Patrick's College remains but the National University, Maynooth has been made into a separate legal entity.

Trinity College in the twentieth century. The future status of Trinity College became a leading question during the early part of the twentieth century. A Royal Commission of 1907 recommended that Dublin University should be enlarged to include the Queen's Colleges, and that a new college acceptable to the Catholic authorities be founded in Dublin. Opposition to this proposal, however, ensured that Trinity maintained its independence when the National University was established in 1908.

At the National Synod of Maynooth in 1875, the Catholic hierarchy had coupled Trinity College with the Queen's Colleges as places forbidden to Catholic students. Yet for many years the bishops took no active steps towards implementing this decision, apart from periodical instructions to priests to refrain from advising parents to send their children to Trinity College. After 1944, the Archbishop of Dublin began issuing annual condemnations of the attendance of Catholics at Trinity in his lenten pastorals. Such attendance would, he affirmed, be permissible only for 'grave and valid reasons'. The consequence was not only to limit the entry of Catholic students, but that of students from the lower income groups as well. Local authorities proved unwilling to oppose the hierarchy's position by offering scholarships under the 1908 Act to Trinity College, though some were prepared to award them in special circumstances to Protestant candidates alone. The most commonly accepted 'grave and valid reasons' was an inability to take the compulsory matriculation qualification in Irish which was required by the National University. Perhaps the most significant barriers created by the ban were not so much religious as social and it served to isolate Trinity from the life of the vast majority of the Irish people.

One effect of the ban was to lead to an influx of non-Irish undergraduates. In 1965/66, 27 per cent of Trinity's students were from the United Kingdom (excluding Northern Ireland),

and a further 9 per cent were from other countries. In the same year Catholics accounted for 20 per cent of the total number of students. In 1967 the Board of Trinity College decided to limit the entry of non-Irish students, up to a maximum of 10 per cent, to those who had associations with Ireland or those who belonged to educationally developing countries. This measure partly paved the way for the removal of the ban, which occurred in 1970. By 1975/76, only 3 per cent of Trinity's students were from the United Kingdom (excluding Northern Ireland), and a further 6 per cent were from other countries. In the same year Catholics accounted for 65 per cent of students.

Reference has already been made to the former National Institutes for Higher Education at Limerick and Dublin, which were granted university status in 1989. The Higher Education Authority first put forward the idea of an Institute in Limerick in 1969. The Institute began functioning in 1972, offering degrees and diplomas with a strong bias towards technology and European studies. The National Institute for Higher Education in Dublin was established in 1975 and the first students were enrolled in 1980.

Higher Education Authority
The Higher Education Authority was established in 1968 on the recommendation of the Commission of Higher Education but it was not until 1972 that it became a statutory body following the passing of the Higher Education Act, 1971. The Higher Education Authority has two main functions:

- as an advisory body it must monitor, review, advise and play its part generally in furthering the development of higher education and in the coordination of state investment therein
- its central statutory power and function as an executive body is to assess in relation to annual or other periods the financial requirements of the institutions of which it is the funding agency; to recommend for state grants the capital and current amounts so assessed and to allocate to the institutions concerned the state funds provided.

The main source of funding for third-level institutions are state grants which are channelled to them through the Higher Education Authority.

Undergraduate fees were abolished in the two-year period 1995/96 to 1996/97 (see later section on higher education grants). Immediately prior to that they had accounted for about one-third of total income for third level institutions.

Enrolment at third level
The introduction of free post-primary education, the availability of higher education grants, the expansion of the non-university sector, as well as the burgeoning youth population has inevitably meant a substantial increase in the numbers attending third level institutions since the mid-1960s (see Table 4.3). The number of places in private third level colleges that are not state-aided has also grown.

Higher education grants
The report of the Commission on Higher Education contained surveys which indicated that children of manual workers comprised less than one-tenth of university students, farmers' children not more than two-tenths, with the children of non-manual workers accounting for the remainder.[28] Consequently, the Commission recommended a grant scheme which would not only remove financial barriers, but might also help to remove psychological barriers. The Local Authority (Higher Education Grant) Act, 1968 provided for such a scheme, with grants available to students reaching a required standard in the Leaving Certificate examination and whose parents satisfied a means test. The grant, administered by local authorities, operated on a sliding scale related to parental income and number of children in the family. It also distinguished between students living within commuting distances of third-level centres and others.

Another type of funding for higher education is that provided by the European Social Fund (ESF) grants scheme introduced in 1986. This scheme covers one year and two year programmes at National Certificate level in the Institutes of Technology. These ESF grants are not subject to a means test and they cover course fees and a maintenance element related to proximity of the family residence to the third-level college.

By 1992, one-quarter of student new entrants to third-level institutions were in receipt of an ESF grant. In the same year less than half (47.6 per cent) of all new entrants to third-level institutions were not in receipt of any financial aid.[29]

In 1995, Niamh Bhreathnach, Minister for Education, announced the phased abolition of undergraduate fees over the academic years 1995/96 and 1996/97. This was to be financed in part by the phasing out of covenants that provided tax relief to parents who took out such covenants in favour of their children. By 1995 approximately two-thirds of students were not paying fees, with some in receipt of grants and others pursuing courses mainly in Institutes of Technology funded by the ESF grants. The maintenance element of the higher education grants (subject to a means test) has remained an important source for many students following the abolition of third-level fees.

There was no groundswell of opinion in favour of the abolition of third-level fees. If anything the view among education analysts was that it represented a windfall to the middle and higher income groups and would do little to further participation in third level by those from lower income groups.

By the latter part of 2002, the government was having second thoughts about free third-level education. This apparently had as much to do with the need to reduce public expenditure as with a concern that lower socio-economic groups had not reaped the benefit of the abolition of fees by increased participation (see later section on participation at third level). Among the options being actively considered was the introduction of a student loan scheme. Following considerable controversy, the re-introduction of fees was not pursued.

Rationalisation of structures at third level
For over three decades, there has been debate and controversy surrounding the status of different third-level institutions.[30] Between 1967 and 1977 a variety of proposals and counter-proposals were put forward, either by the Minister for Education or others, such as the *Report of the Commission on Higher Education* (1967) and the Higher Education Authority (HEA). Essentially these proposals were concerned with the number of universities and with which colleges should have university status. The classic example of the bewildering changes and proposals were those made by Richard Burke, TD, Minister for Education, 1973–1976. In 1974 he indicated that Trinity College would retain its status as a separate university, University College Dublin would

become an independent university, and the NUI would remain (with constituent colleges in Cork and Galway), i.e. there would be three universities. In July 1976, however, in a complete turnabout in policy, he announced that there were to be five universities (Trinity, UCD, UCC, UCG, and Maynooth).

The results of a national referendum on the seventh amendment to the Constitution held in July 1979 made it possible for the government to introduce legislation providing for the abolition of the NUI and the establishment of independent universities at UCD, UCC and UCG.

As a result of various pieces of legislation, many changes occurred from the late 1980s onwards. These included the establishment of Dublin City University and the University of Limerick (1989), the establishment of the four constituent universities of the NUI (1997), the granting of autonomy to the Dublin Institute of Technology and the Regional Technical Colleges (1992), the redesignation of the Regional Technical Colleges as Institutes of Technology (1998), the abolition of the NCEA and its replacement by HETAC.

Despite these changes, which have brought about a certain amount of rationalisation, debate continues on issues such as autonomy and degree-awarding functions, especially in the non-university sector.

Adult education

With the introduction of important developments in the Irish education system at all levels during the 1960s and early 1970s, it was inevitable that attention would be focused on adult education and, more specifically, on those who, for whatever reason, had terminated their full-time education at an early age.

Formal adult education courses are mainly provided by statutory agencies, notably the VECs. Many other organisations and institutions, both statutory and voluntary, are involved in adult education. These provide a variety of courses from basic literacy to leisure type courses.

A number of policy reports on adult education have been published over the past three decades, the most recent, a White Paper, in 2000.

A report in 1973 estimated that 10 per cent of the adult population participated annually in adult education, indicated that the expenditure on adult education was inadequate to meet even existing needs and recommended separate budgetary provision by the Department of Education. Among its main structural recommendations was the establishment of county education committees.[31]

The *Report of the Commission on Adult Education* was published a decade later in 1984. Its findings indicated that the group which had not participated in any form of education since completing their initial education had within it disproportionately high numbers of older and working class people and rural dwellers, i.e. those who had in general benefited least from initial education compared with their younger, middle class and urban counterparts. The Commission recommended that local adult education boards be established under the VECs with a separate budget to enable priorities to be established on a local basis. It also recommended the establishment of a national education council.[32]

Some progress was made, especially with the appointment of adult education organisers in 1979 under the VECs and the establishment of adult education boards in each VEC area in 1984. However, criticism of lack of investment in the sector continued.

Aontas, the national umbrella organisation representing statutory and voluntary bodies, in a 1989 report stated:

> Adult education in Ireland is underdeveloped ... it is more oriented in range and practice towards the middle classes following hobby and leisure pursuits than a direct means towards improving their life chances. Often those who have most to benefit tend to be excluded.[33]

A Green Paper, published in 1998, was followed by a White Paper in 2000.[34] The White Paper, *Learning for Life*, defined adult education as: 'systematic learning undertaken by adults who return to learning having concluded initial education or training'.

It was critical of the lack of priority given to the sector and the inadequate level of investment by successive governments. Of the 1984 Commission's report it noted that:

> ... it was to have little impact on an education system already straining to cope with a greatly expanded provision for a rapidly increasing youth population and the financial crises of the mid-1980s.[35]

The White Paper proposed the establishment of a statutory agency, the National Adult Learning Council, which would have responsibility for framing and implementing policy and 33 Local Adult Learning Boards. It also proposed increased funding. The White Paper was widely welcomed in adult education circles.

Participation in education

The school-going population has grown considerably since the mid-1960s as a result of the increase in the birth rate up to the early 1980s. This increase in population has been reflected in the growth in numbers of pupils enrolled at first level. However, as the birth rate declined from the early 1980s onwards so also did the numbers attending first level. Consequently, the composition of the school-going population has undergone some change over the past few decades (Table 4.3). In the mid-1960s, first level students accounted for three-quarters of all full-time students; by the late 1990s, however, due to a combination of a decline in the birth rate and increased participation by age, they accounted for under half (48.4 per cent) of the full-time student population. The percentage share at third level has increased from a low base of 3 per cent to 13 per cent over the same period. As a result of recent demographic trends, the overall number of full-time students is set to continue to decline further from the peak year of 1990 when the number reached 1.018 million. Projections indicate reductions in second level to more than counterbalance modest increases in first level and third level.

Table 4.3: Full-time students in education, 1965–1999

	1965		1975		1999	
	No	*%*	*No*	*%*	*No*	*%*
First level	504,900	75.5	550,100	64.4	451,200	48.4
Second level	142,900	21.4	271,000	31.7	358,000	38.5
Third level	20,700	3.1	33,100	3.9	122,400	13.1
Total	668,500		854,200		931,600	

Source: Statistical Reports, Department of Education and Science

While there has been a general increase in the numbers attending second and third level, it is more relevant to examine trends in participation rates. Since the mid-1960s, prior to the introduction of free post-primary education, the participation rates for those aged 15 to 18 years had increased remarkably up to

Table 4.4: Participation in full-time education by age, selected years, 1966–1999

Age	1966	1974	1988	1995	1999
15 years	54.2	77.5	97.1	95.7	96.0
16 years	39.0	60.4	90.3	91.1	91.6
17 years	27.3	43.2	74.2	81.9	80.5
18 years	14.7	22.4	48.3	63.6	63.2
19 years	9.6	12.5	28.5	47.5	47.3

Source: Statistical Reports, Department of Education and Science

the mid-1990s (Table 4.4). Since then the rate of progress has halted and further improvement in participation by age is likely to be more difficult to achieve.

Participation at third level
At third level, serious disparities exist in relation to participation by students from different social classes. One of the first surveys of entrants to third-level education was from the Dublin area in 1978/79. This indicated that about three-quarters of entrants came from the four higher socio-economic groups despite the fact that these groups constituted only one-fifth of the population of Dublin.[36] The study also revealed distinct geographic differences within Dublin, reflecting the socio-economic composition of the population in different areas.

Clancy has carried out a series of four national surveys on participation in third level for the Higher Education Authority at six-year intervals in 1980, 1986, 1992 and 1998. The surveys reveal large disparities by socio-economic group and geographical area in access to higher education (Table 4.5). New entrants to 43 third-level colleges in the Republic were included in the most recent survey in 1998, *College Entry in Focus.*[37]

One of the main findings of the four surveys is that of continuity in the degree to which various groups participate, with some 'over-represented' and others 'under-represented' in terms of their share of the relevant national population. The following are some of the key elements:

- Four groups (farmers, higher professional, lower professional, employers and managers) account for just over half (52.7 per cent) of higher education entrants in 1998 although these

Table 4.5: Participation ratio* by father's socio-economic status of entrants to higher education 1980, 1986, 1992, 1998

Socio-economic group	1980	1986	1992	1998
Farmers	1.48	1.68	1.46	1.63
Other agricultural occupations	0.31	0.47	0.67	0.76
Higher professionals	2.95	2.86	2.36	2.18
Lower professionals	1.65	1.88	1.18	1.05
Employers and managers	2.12	1.80	1.86	1.82
Salaried employees	2.93	2.30	1.33	1.19
Intermediate non-manual workers	1.09	1.10	0.76	0.72
Other non-manual workers	0.45	0.44	0.73	0.69
Skilled manual workers	0.43	0.50	0.77	0.73
Semi-skilled manual workers	0.46	0.42	0.52	0.51
Unskilled manual workers	0.15	0.16	0.34	0.48

* The participation ratio is calculated by relating the number of entrants by socio-economic group to the national population in that group. Where the ratio is 1:0 the socio-economic group is proportionately represented, where it exceeds 1:0 the group is over-represented and where it is less than 1:0 the group is under-represented.

Source: P. Clancy, *College Entry in Focus: A Fourth National Survey of Access to Higher Education* (2001), Table 24, p. 66.

groups constituted one-third (32.2 per cent) of the relevant population.

- Six groups (higher professional, lower professional, employers and managers, salaried employees, farmers and intermediate non-manual) were 'over-represented' in the 1980 survey and, with the exception of the intermediate non-manual group, they remained 'over-represented' in each of the subsequent surveys.
- Excluding the position of the intermediate non-manual group, the 1998 participation of all the 'under-represented' groups is significantly higher than the 1980 rate.
- The two most 'under-represented' groups in 1980 (unskilled manual workers and other agricultural workers) have shown a continuous increase in subsequent surveys.
- While the highest proportionate increase occurred for those lower socio-economic groups that had very low participation in 1980, these same groups still remained a considerable distance behind others in 1998.

The surveys reveal a steady increase in admission rates from 20 per cent in 1980 to 44 per cent in 1998. Much of this is explained by the increased participation at second level, which almost

Table 4.6: Rates of admission to higher education by county of permanent residence, 1980, 1986, 1992, 1998

County		Admission rate		
	1980	1986	1992	1998
Carlow	29	32	39	44
Dublin	17	20	33	38
Kildare	16	24	35	41
Kilkenny	20	27	32	41
Laois	15	23	31	39
Longford	21	30	38	49
Louth	23	25	35	43
Meath	16	25	37	45
Offaly	15	20	32	38
Westmeath	20	31	38	49
Wexford	18	22	34	44
Wicklow	18	23	37	41
Clare	20	30	43	50
Cork	22	28	37	49
Kerry	25	35	43	53
Limerick	20	27	37	50
Tipperary	19	27	36	49
Waterford	23	28	33	41
Galway	28	33	46	57
Leitrim	19	34	42	53
Mayo	23	31	42	56
Roscommon	20	28	41	50
Sligo	25	35	42	56
Cavan	16	24	33	45
Donegal	21	19	27	35
Monaghan	20	24	27	41
Average:	20	25	36	44

Source: P. Clancy, *College Entry in Focus: A Fourth National Survey of Access to Higher Education* (2001), Table 43, p. 111.

inevitably, was bound to be reflected at third level. While all counties shared in this increase, the significant variation by county, first evident in 1980, still held for 1998 (Table 4.6). A regional pattern was evident, with western counties having the highest admission rates and the lowest rates in counties of Ulster and the midland counties of Leinster, including Dublin. It should be noted that students attending third-level institutions in Northern Ireland affect the participation rates, especially in some border counties. When this is taken into account, the rates for

Donegal are increased by 10.5, Monaghan by 8.1 and Louth by 3.2.

Clancy also undertook a separate analysis of admission rates within Dublin as part of the 1992 and 1998 surveys. These revealed large variations by district with a distinct north–south divide. For example, in 1998 five of the postal districts in the south of the city had admission rates in excess of 50 per cent as compared with only one of the districts in the north of the city. Three districts recorded admission rates of less than 10 per cent.

Apart from the essential socio-economic and geographic data highlighted, the surveys contain a range of other informative analysis. For example, there were distinct differences between school type and entrance to third level in 1998, with the transfer rate from leaving certificate students in fee-paying secondary schools the highest (70.6 per cent), followed by non fee-paying secondary schools (59.0 per cent), comprehensive schools (57.0 per cent), community schools (49.5 per cent) and vocational schools (38.0). Furthermore, the 1998 survey was the first to record a female majority (53 per cent) among entrants.

In September 2000 an action group was established by Michael Woods, TD, Minister for Education and Science, to advise on the most appropriate means of increasing third-level participation of students from disadvantaged backgrounds, students with disabilities and mature students. The report of the Action Group, published in July 2001, contained 77 recommendations.[38] Among the recommendations were the following:

- a substantial increases in the rate of maintenance grants to allow more students to qualify (in 2001 approximately 40 per cent of full-time students qualified for maintenance grants)
- by 2006, 1.8 per cent of undergraduates in full-time third-level courses should be students with disabilities
- by 2006, third-level institutions should aim to set aside at least 15 per cent of full-time undergraduate places for mature students (as compared with 5 per cent in 2001).

Concern with access to universities was also reflected in the establishment of a review group by the HEA in 2003. This group will monitor the record of the universities in providing access for all social groups.

It can be argued that the issue of equality of access to all levels of education is not unrelated to public expenditure at different

Table 4.7: Current expenditure on education by level, 1999

	€m	%
First level	1,140.7	34.2
Second level	1,338.4	40.1
Third level	855.2	25.7
Total	3,334.3	100.0

Source: Statistical Report, Department of Education and Science

levels. There is little correlation between the share of current expenditure and the share of students at each level. Thus, third level accounts for 13 per cent of all full-time students but one-quarter of current expenditure (Table 4.7). There are reasons for the unit costs being higher at second level as compared with first level but it is the scale of the difference that has been questioned. The per capita expenditure at first level (i.e. during the years of compulsory schooling) has traditionally been much less than that at second level and significantly less than that at third level. However, the differential has narrowed considerably over the past two decades (Table 4.8). By 2000, expenditure per third-level student was twice that per first-level student as compared with a five-fold differential in 1980.

Not only do those who go on to third level receive the highest subsidies but they are also more likely to be from the higher socio-economic groups and are more likely to obtain more remunerative employment than those who have completed their education at first or second level. In this context increased expenditure and support at first level has been advocated as a means of ensuring greater equality of opportunity in education and mitigating the effects of educational disadvantage.

Table 4.8: Public Expenditure (per capita) on education at first-, second- and third-level education 1980, 1995, 2000

	1980		1995		2000	
	€	Ratio	€	Ratio	€	Ratio
First level	430	1.0	1,640	1.0	2,181	1.0
Second level	826	1.9	2,385	1.5	3,325	1.5
Third level	2,151	5.0	5,050	3.1	4,604	2.1

Source: Proposal for Plan 1984– 1987, National Planning Board (Stationery Office, Dublin, 1984), p. 291; *Statistical Reports,* Department of Education and Science

Educational disadvantage

Tussing argued that reasonable equality of opportunity, insofar as it involves schooling and school expenditure, requires concentration on first level.[39] He maintained that the consequences of inadequate schooling at that level probably cannot be rectified and certainly cannot be rectified at any reasonable cost later on.

Apart from the aim of lowering the general pupil-teacher ratio (reduced from 33:1 in the mid-1960s to 21:0 in the late 1990s) specific measures were introduced from the mid-1980s to lessen the incidence of educational disadvantage. The principal means was through the *Disadvantaged Areas Scheme* whereby certain schools were designated as being disadvantaged. The number of schools designated was added to each year as resources permitted. These schools received higher capitation grants than the ordinary primary schools and there was a concerted effort to reduce the pupil–teacher ratio. By 2002 there were 314 primary schools involved. In 2000 the scheme was replaced by the *Giving Children an Even Break* programme under which the target would be 'individuals at risk' in schools rather than the previous method of designating additional schools. The support provided will be related to the degree of concentration of pupils with educational disadvantage. Schools qualifying are in areas of high unemployment and are generally concentrated in large urban areas.

In addition to the *Giving Children an Even Break* programme, a number of other initiatives have been introduced on a pilot basis. These include:

- The *Home Liaison Scheme*, established in 1990 and extended in 1999 to all designated disadvantaged schools. It involves a preventative strategy that promotes active co-operation between home, school and relevant community agencies in promoting the educational interests of children. By 2001 there were 309 primary schools and 190 second-level schools participating in the scheme.
- *Breaking the Cycle* which commenced in 1996, with the pilot phase ending in 2001. Features of the scheme included a reduction to 15:1 in the pupil teacher ratio in the junior classes in urban areas, and in rural areas the provision of a local co-ordinator to clusters of schools to provide support to pupils at risk of early school leaving. All schools in this scheme, which are

given special financial support packages, are now included in the *Giving Children an Even Break* programme.

In keeping with a growing commitment by government, an Educational Disadvantage Committee was established in 2002 under the Education Act, 1998. The Committee will advise the Minister for Education and Science on policies and strategies to be adopted to identify and correct educational disadvantage. In order to facilitate participation by a wide range of education interests, a larger Educational Disadvantaged Forum was established which would work in close tandem with the Committee and which would primarily provide a means, through public meetings, for all those involved in educational disadvantage to make their views known.

It must be recognised that there are probably limits to which educational policy measures alone can bring about real equality of opportunity. Thus, for example, the provision of additional facilities and supports in schools in disadvantaged areas may not be sufficient in themselves to counteract the influence of other serious social problems in the home environment such as low income, high unemployment and poor housing, which impinge on educational development.

Development of policy

Reference has been made at the beginning of this chapter to the lack of a comprehensive legislative base for the education system. This in itself has, at times, hindered the development of educational policy.

Seán O'Connor, former Secretary of the Department of Education, has pointed out that it is only since the early 1960s that the Minister for Education and the Department of Education began to take a lead role in policy formation. Up to then the Department seemed content to leave the control of the system to the three main interest groups, i.e. the church, teachers' unions and parents. O'Connor indicates that of these groups, the church exerted the most decisive influence, the teachers' union were mainly concerned with working conditions and remuneration, and parents only became involved to protest at inadequate facilities in their local school.[40]

Even when the Department of Education or the Minister assumed a lead role in policy making, difficulties could still arise in obtaining agreement among the various interests. The problems associated with the establishment of management boards in primary schools in the mid-1970s exemplify the difficulties of effecting change by agreement. Similar problems arose in relation to community schools.

Part of the problem was that until the Education Act, 1998 there was an absence of a general legislative framework. The system was therefore open to the criticism that decisions were being made without reference to the Oireachtas. Successive Ministers for Education issued circulars and regulations as administrative measures but these lacked statutory power.

Much of the analysis which influenced developments until recently was contained in reports of independent review bodies, e.g. the *Investment in Education* report, 1965, carried out by the Organisation for Economic Co-operation and Development. Policy documents emanating from the Department of Education itself have been few enough in number until recent years.

The White Paper, *Educational Development* (1980), which had been promised since 1973, had been expected to deal with a range of fundamental issues in the education system. The general reaction to the White Paper, however, was one of disappointment. The following extract from an editorial in the *Irish Press* summarised the popular criticism:

> The White Paper ... is open to serious criticism for what it does not contain. There is no timescale or costing on the proposals and insufficient government commitment to their implementation.[41]

In contrast to the White Paper, the reaction to the *Programme for Action in Education*, 1984–1987, published by the Department of Education following submissions from different interest groups, was more positive. It spelled out a whole series of issues, which the government intended to tackle, and at the same time left scope for further discussion and consultation.

White Paper 1995
The 1990s was a decade in which the education system was subject to a level of scrutiny and debate on a unprecedented scale.[42] It was a decade in which various policy reports were produced and widely discussed, with proposals and counter proposals being made. It was a decade in which all of the interest groups in education were consulted and voiced their views.

In November 1990, Mary O'Rourke, TD, Minister for Education, announced her intention to issue a White Paper to be followed by public discussion and an Education Act. The *Programme for Economic and Social Progress* (1991) reiterated these views but added that a Green Paper, comprehensive in its coverage, would be published in 1991, affording the opportunity to all parties to offer views prior to the publication of a White Paper in 1992 and the introduction of an Education Act.[43]

Following two changes of ministers, leaks of drafts to the media, and the highly unusual step of publishing an introduction to the Green Paper in April to coincide with the Annual Conference of the Teachers' Unions, the Green Paper, *Education for a Changing World*, was finally published in June 1992 by Seamus Brennan, TD, Minister for Education. Apparently, the published version had undergone some changes from the proposals of Mary O'Rourke, TD, former Minister for Education. Among the main proposals were the devolution of power from the Department of Education to school boards which would have to produce a school plan and issue an annual report on its work; the raising of the school leaving age from 15 to 16 years; the establishment of boards of management in all primary and second level schools.

A period of consultation between the various interest groups followed the publication of the Green Paper. The National Education Convention held in Dublin Castle in October 1993 represented a new departure in education. It was the first time that representatives of the Department of Education, the churches, the teachers' unions and parents had come together to tease out issues of common concern. This laid the foundation for the White Paper *Charting our Education Future*, published in 1995.

Among the key proposals were:

- the devolution of powers from the Department of Education to ten regional education boards
- the establishment of a commission to recommend on the rationalisation of the vocational education system
- the underpinning of the rights and responsibilities of school boards of management by legislation
- the extension of the remit of the Higher Education Authority to all publicly funded third-level institutions
- the raising of the school-leaving age from 15 to 16 years.

Reaction to the White Paper was generally positive. Such criticism as there was, related to the failure to provide an indication of the cost of the proposals or how they were to be funded.

A report in 1996 of the Commission on School Accommodation, set up following publication of the White Paper, having examined the vocational education system, recommended a reduction from 38 to 21 in the number of Vocational Education Committees, by the amalgamation of geographic areas.[44] In 1998 the number was reduced to 33 when five of the smaller urban VECs (Bray, Drogheda, Sligo, Tralee, and Wexford) were amalgamated with the relevant county VEC.

Education Act, 1998
An Education Bill to give legislative effect to the main proposals in *Charting our Education Future* was published in January 1997. It proposed the establishment of ten Regional Education Boards, covering geographic areas very similar to the Health Boards. The Bill also proposed to establish school boards of Management on a statutory basis. Opposition to sections of the Bill came mainly from the various Churches who, in an unprecedented move, came together to issue a joint statement. Their main cause of concern was the perceived lessening of the role of the patron in the management of schools. Fianna Fáil and the Progressive Democrats, the opposition parties in the Dáil, also opposed the Bill for a variety of reasons and promised that in government they would abolish the regional education boards if they were established. As events turned out, the Education Bill was not passed before a general election was called in May 1997 and, along with other Bills, consequently lapsed.

Following a change of government in June 1997, a revised Education Bill was published in December 1997. It did not provide for the establishment of regional education boards. The Education Act, 1998 set out the role and responsibilities of the various stakeholders in education such as students, teachers, parents, boards of management. For example, the Act recognises patrons as the owners of schools, recognises the National Parents' Council and recognises that parents, teachers and patrons have a right to be involved in the management of their schools. Throughout the Act there is a strong emphasis on the notion of partnership between all the interests in education.

It could be argued that the Education Act, 1998 did not meet the expectations of fundamental change in the system which the discussion arising from the Green and White Papers had generated. However, the Act '. . . remains the most significant piece of legislation enacted for the educational system, which was put on a statutory basis for the first time'.[45]

Decentralisation

While the establishment of regional education boards was effectively abandoned with the change of government in 1997, the issues that gave rise to the proposal remained. In 2000 a review of the operation of the Department of Education and Science, carried out by Seán Cromien (former secretary-general of the Department of Finance), was highly critical of certain aspects of the Department. The report referred to the Department as 'overwhelmed with detailed day-to-day work which has to be given priority over long-term strategic thinking' and, quoting a member of senior management, where 'the urgent drives out the important'.[46] The Cromien report indicated that the 'problem for the Department has been that it is so centralised that this leads to a degree of dependence by its clients which is quite exceptional,' and that this dependence appears to be encouraged by the Department by its willingness to respond to every claim on its time and attention. The report recommended that specialist bodies be established such as a schools examinations agency, to take the burden off the Department which could then concentrate on policy and strategic planning. It also recommended the establishment of a network of local offices which initially would provide information and integrated services but which ultimately could have a decision-making function. It recognised that this process would take some time. While not going down the road of regionalisation (the issue was not considered as such) the recommendations of the Cromien report represented a strong signal in that direction.

In June 2001, Michael Woods, TD, Minister for Education and Science, announced a number of fundamental reforms that would reduce the detailed workload of the Department and allow it to concentrate on key areas of policy. These included:

- the establishment of a independent examinations agency
- the establishment of a network of regional offices which would be a first point of contact for schools

- education services for children with disabilities to be taken over by a new body, the National Council for Special Education (see section on People with Disabilities, Chapter 6)
- an extension of the remit of the Higher Education Authority to include funding and co-ordination of all publicly-funded third-level colleges (this would include the Institutes of Technology which were funded by the Department).

By 2003, almost 80 years after its establishment, it was clear that fundamental changes in the operation of the Department of Education and Science were about to take place.

Notes

1. There are many excellent works dealing with the development of first-level education and the education system in general. The most comprehensive is J. Coolahan, *Irish Education: History and Structure* (Institute of Public Administration, Dublin, 1981). Other works include: D.H. Akenson, *The Irish Education Experiment* (Routledge and Kegan Paul, London, 1970), which deals with the national system of education in the nineteenth century; N. Atkinson, *Irish Education, a History of Education Institutions* (Hodges Figges, Dublin 1969); P.J. Dowling, *A History of Irish Education* (Mercier Press, Cork), 1971; F.S.L. Lyons, *Ireland Since the Famine* (Fontana, London, 1973) (relevant sections); J. Lee, *The Modernisation of Irish Society, 1848–1919* (Gill and Macmillan), Dublin, 1973, Chapter 1; T.J. McElligot, *Education in Ireland* (Institute of Public Administration, Dublin, 1966).
2. See P.J. Dowling: *The Hedge Schools of Ireland* (Mercier Press, Cork, 1968).
3. See M. Mulryan Moloney, *Nineteenth-Century Education in the Archdocese of Tuam* (Maynooth Studies in Irish Local History, No.36, Irish Acedemic Press, Dublin, 2001).
4. D.H. Akenson, op. cit., Chapter 1.
5. *Report of the Primary Education Review Body* (Stationery Office, Dublin, 1990), p. 93.
6. *Irish Times*, 21 October, 1974.
7. *Report of the Primary Education Review Body*, op. cit., p. 36.
8. *Investment in Education* (Stationery Office, Dublin, 1965), pp. 225–266.
9. NESC Report, No. 19, *Rural Areas; Social Planning Problems* (Stationery Office, Dublin, 1976), pp. 52–53.
10. *Irish Times*, 8 February, 1977.
11. *Rules for National Schools under the Department of Education* (Stationery Office, Dublin, 1965), p. 8.
12. *Programme for Action in Education, 1984–1987* (Stationery Office, Dublin, 1984), p. 16.
13. The block grant is calculated by reference to a complex formula which takes account of the number of day pupils and boarding pupils in Protestant schools.

14. *Investment in Education*, op. cit., p. 150.
15. S. O'Connor, *A Troubled Sky: Reflections on the Irish Educational Scene, 1957–1968* (Educational Research Centre, St Patrick's College, Dublin, 1986), p. 193.
16. J.H. Whyte, *Church and State in Modern Ireland, 1923–1970* (Gill and Macmillan, Dublin, 1971), p. 38.
17. Coolahan, op. cit., p. 103.
18. G. Hussey, *At the Cutting Edge: Cabinet Diaries 1982–1987* (Gill and Macmillan, Dublin, 1990), p. 128.
19. *Investment in Education*, op. cit., pp. 154–168.
20. *Review of National Policies for Education: Ireland* (OECD, Paris, 1969), Appendix iv, p. 122.
21. ibid., p. 129.
22. For further details see Commission on School Accommodation, *Amalgamation of Second-Level Schools*, 2001, pp. 59–64.
23. *Partners in Education* (Stationery Office, Dublin, 1985), p. 10.
24. *Religious Congregations in Irish Education – A Role for the Future?* (Education Commission, Conference of Religious of Ireland, Dublin, 1997), p. 9.
25. *Review of National Policies for Education: Ireland*, op. cit., pp. 124–125.
26. Steering Committee on Technical Education, *Report to the Minister for Education on Regional Technical Colleges* (Stationery Office, Dublin, 1969).
27. Lyons, op. cit., p. 93.
28. *Commission on Higher Education*, 1960–67, Vol. 1, Presentation and Summary of Report (Stationery Office, Dublin, 1967), p. 49.
29. P. Clancy, *Access to College: Patterns of Continuity and Change* (Higher Education Authority, Dublin, 1995), p. 66.
30. For an excellent overview of the various policy issues and developments in the third-level sector see T.White, *Investing in People, Higher Education in Ireland from 1960 to 2000* (Institute of Public Administration, Dublin, 2001).
31. *Adult Education in Ireland* (Stationery Office, 1973).
32. *Lifelong Learning: Report of the Commission on Adult Education* (Stationery Office, Dublin, 1984), p. 9.
33. M. Bassett, B. Brady, T. Fleming, T. Inglis, *For Adults Only: A Case for Adult Education in Ireland* (Aontas, National Association of Adult Education, Dublin, 1989), p. 44.
34. *Green Paper: Adult Education in an Era of Lifelong Learning* (Stationery Office, Dublin, 1998); *Learning for Life, White Paper on Adult Education* (Stationery Office, Dublin, 2000).
35. *Learning for Life*, op. cit., p. 54.
36. P. Clancy and C. Benson, *Higher Education in Dublin: A Study of Some Emerging Needs* (Higher Education Authority, Dublin, 1979), pp. 13–16.
37. P. Clancy, *College Entry in Focus: A Fourth National Survey of Access to Higher Education* (Higher Education Authority, Dublin, 2001).
38. *Report of the Action Group on Access to Third Level Education* (Stationery Office, Dublin, 2001).
39. A.D. Tussing, 'Equity and the Financing of Education' in S. Kennedy (ed.), *One Million Poor?* (Turoe Press, Dublin, 1981), p. 211.
40. S. O'Connor, op. cit., Chapter 1.
41. *Irish Press*, 19 December 1980.

42. For an excellent overview of this period see J.Walshe, *A New Partnership in Education: From Consultation to Legislation in the Nineties* (Institute of Public Administration, Dublin, 1999).

43. *Programme for Economic and Social Progress*, op. cit., pp. 33–34.

44. *Rationalisation of Vocational Education Committees* (Commission on School Accommodation, Report of the Steering Group, 1996).

45. Walshe, op. cit., p. 208.

46. Department of Education and Science, *Review of Department's Operations, Systems and Staffing Needs*, 2000 (Cromien Report).

5

Health Services

Introduction

As in the case of the income maintenance and other social services, the Irish health services evolved over a period of time. The emphasis in this chapter is on recent developments and issues. Consequently, only a summary of the background to the present system is given in this introductory section.

Services in the nineteenth century

It is possible to distinguish between four different elements of health services in the nineteenth century. These were hospital services, mental hospital services, dispensary services and prevention services.[1]

The hospital system had emerged over a period, with some voluntary hospitals established in the eighteenth century. These were established initially by philanthropic individuals and later by religious orders. The hospitals, usually located in the larger urban areas, mostly Dublin, were independent of state control. They provided a service well into the twentieth century and some continue to play a vital role in the national hospital system. They include a number of hospitals in Dublin such as Dr Steevens' Hospital, Mercers Hospital, the Mater Misericordiae Hospital and others in Cork such as the North Infirmary. Many of the smaller voluntary hospitals were closed in the late 1980s (see later section). In addition to the voluntary hospitals, a network of public infirmaries and fever hospitals was developed in the nineteenth century. By the 1830s there were approximately 20 county infirmaries and 70 fever hospitals. A further strand in the hospital system was the workhouse whose medical role gained in importance as the numbers in the workhouses declined towards the latter part of the nineteenth century.

Treatment of mental illness was confined to lunatic asylums. A small number of large asylums was established in the nineteenth century. Among these was the Richmond Institution at Grangegorman in Dublin, established in 1815, and which continued to function well into the twentieth century as St Brendan's Hospital.[2] In addition to these large institutions, district asylums were established in almost all counties.

As already noted in Chapter 2, the central feature of the Poor Law system, established in Ireland in 1838, was the workhouse. However, some other services were developed outside the workhouse and one of the most notable was the dispensary system. Under this system, introduced under the Poor Relief Act, 1851, a network of dispensary districts was established throughout the country. In each of these districts a doctor was employed to provide a free service to the poor of the area. This dispensary system continued up to 1972 and was the forerunner of the present choice-of-doctor scheme for medical cardholders.

For a variety of reasons, the preventive services were limited throughout most of the nineteenth century with the result that outbreaks of infectious diseases wrought havoc. For example, a cholera outbreak in the early 1830s affected large parts of the country, especially Dublin, with devastating consequences – at least 25,000 died in 1832–1833 and there was widespread panic and social disruption.[3] The cause was unknown nor was there any known effective treatment; the link between cholera and polluted water supplies only became established over several decades. By the latter part of the nineteenth century the link between public and personal hygiene and the transmission of disease became firmly established by scientists. This, together with the work of public health reformers, resulted in the Public Health Act, 1878 which introduced measures to ensure proper sanitation, clean water supplies and food hygiene controls in order to prevent the spread of infectious diseases. Subsequent advances were such that by about 1900, 'large scale epidemic disease had become history'.[4]

Services in the twentieth century
Apart from the evolutionary development of the above and allied services to meet changed circumstances and advances in medicine, a number of broad trends was discernible in the health services throughout the twentieth century.

Firstly, there was a gradual shift away from the community, as a focus of health care, to the health needs of the individual. For example, some of the early measures in the nineteenth century were designed not so much to promote health as to prevent community-wide catastrophes resulting from the spread of infectious diseases. Similarly, in mental illness the emphasis was on protecting society rather than rehabilitating the individual.

Secondly, the state became more and more directly involved in the planning and provision of health care. This did not occur without controversy and opposition mainly from the Catholic Church and the medical profession. The classic instance of this was the Mother and Child Scheme that Dr Noel Browne, Minister for Health (1948–1951), proposed to introduce. The Catholic hierarchy opposed the scheme (which would have provided free health services for women before, during and after childbirth and for children up to 16 years), on the grounds that it represented undue state intervention. The medical profession opposed the scheme because it did not want a comprehensive state health service, preferring instead a mix of public and private.[5]

Thirdly, there was a move away from local administration to a more centralised model. The myriad of local administrative units in the nineteenth and early twentieth centuries was gradually rationalised. The number of such units was reduced from 90 in the 1920s to eight following the Health Act, 1970 (see later section). At central level, the Department of Health emerged as a separate government department out of the former Department of Health and Local Government (established in 1924).

Fourthly, the administrative changes at local and regional level reflected a change in funding from local taxation (rates) to central funding. At the beginning of the twentieth century, the health services were largely funded from local taxation, a situation whose shortcomings became increasingly apparent. A gradual shift towards central funding occurred over several decades so that by the late 1970s, local taxation no longer contributed to financing and the services were funded almost entirely through the exchequer from general taxation and a special health levy.

The above trends have been summarised by Barrington:

> In 1900, governmental responsibility for the health of the population was limited to controlling outbreaks of the most serious epidemic diseases and ensuring access by the poor to general practitioner

services and Poor Law infirmaries. By 1970, government had accepted responsibility for providing a high standard of medical care for all sections of the population at no or at a heavily subsidised cost to the recipient.[6]

Health status

While state investment in health services has grown, it is difficult to determine with any precision the extent to which increased public expenditure on health care has led to improved health status in the community. There are, however, some obvious health indicators that have shown dramatic improvement. Thus, for example, life expectancy has increased; infant mortality has been reduced, as has the incidence of infectious diseases, such as tuberculosis. It should be noted, however, that many factors may affect the level of health of the community, e.g. improved living standards in general. It is therefore at least arguable that health standards may well have improved even in the absence of public health programmes.

In recent years there has been an emphasis on the importance of health promotion, i.e. the promotion of positive health rather than the traditional emphasis on curing illness. The Health Education Bureau in a report, *Promoting Health Through Public Policy* (1987), indicated that much of the premature mortality (e.g. due to heart disease and cancer) and illness is associated with lifestyle (e.g. smoking, diet) and the general environment, and is therefore preventable. The Department of Health in its document *Health, The Wider Dimensions* (1986) pointed out that hitherto, the focus of health policy had been too narrow, whereas in fact health is a multi-faceted problem and is linked to a greater or lesser degree to all aspects of life. It therefore recommended a more broadly based approach to health policy.

Two of the key concepts in the Department of Health's strategy document *Shaping a Healthier Future* (1994) are health gain and social gain. The document pointed out that, traditionally, health service objectives have tended to focus on the provision of a level of service rather than on the achievement of a positive outcome. Health gain and social gain are terms used to indicate that patients and clients of health services should receive a clear benefit or outcome from their contact with the system. Health gain is concerned with achieving improvements in health and social gain, thus adding to the quality of life. These concepts were further emphasised in the most recent strategy of the Department of Health and Children, the *Health Strategy: Quality and Fairness, A Health System for You* (2001), which adopted the definition of health used by the World Health Organisation:

> ... a complete state of physical, mental and social well-being and not merely the absence of disease or infirmity.

Health indicators

The 'health' of a population is normally measured by reference to health indicators derived from life expectancy, mortality and morbidity statistics. Only the salient features of the health status of the population are outlined here.[7]

Life expectancy. Life expectancy at birth is one of the most common measures of health status and is used as a basis for international comparisons. Life expectancy has increased substantially since the foundation of the state. By 1995–1997 it stood at 78.6 years for females and 73.0 years for males (as compared with 57.9 for females and 57.4 for males in 1925–1927). This increase may be attributed not only to improvements in health care but also to improvements in housing conditions and general standards of living.

Improvements in life expectancy reflect lower mortality rates in infants and younger children over recent decades. Infant mortality in children under one year of age has fallen from 68 per 1,000 live births in 1947 to 5.8 per 1,000 live births in 2001.

Main causes of mortality. Circulatory disease and cancer account for almost 65 per cent of deaths. As a contribution to overall mortality, cancer has increased over several decades – from 11 per cent in 1950 to 25 per cent in 2001. This trend is projected to continue.

The main causes of premature deaths (deaths under 65 years) in 1999 were cancer or cardiovascular disease (over 60 per cent) and injury/poisoning (16 per cent).

Health inequalities. The *Health Strategy* (2001) indicated:

> Inequalities in health can exist for a variety of reasons, including geographical location, gender, age, ethnicity, hereditary factors and socio-economic status. Poverty, unemployment, education, access to health services and environmental factors including housing and water quality, all play important roles in determining the health of individuals.[8]

There are definite variations by social group in relation to various health status indicators. In general, higher mortality and morbidity are associated with lower socio-economic groups.

Administration

Hensey[9] has already outlined in admirable detail the evolution of the administrative structure for health care in Ireland and, consequently, only the major developments are reviewed here.

State services were first provided in a rudimentary form under the Poor Law (Ireland) Act, 1838. The Poor Law administration provided infirmaries and other forms of medical care in association with the workhouses established in each Poor Law union. Unions were administrative units and the total number covering the present area of the Republic was 126.

In 1872 the Irish Poor Law Commissioners were abolished and replaced by the Irish Local Government Board that assumed control of both Poor Law and health services. Central control became more pronounced following Independence when, in 1924, the Department of Local Government and Public Health was established. In 1947 this Department was effectively divided and three separate departments emerged, i.e. Local Government, Health and Social Welfare.

At local level the administrative structure for health services remained highly complex throughout the nineteenth century and well into the twentieth century. There was a number of agencies with responsibility for various aspects of health care; boards of guardians, for example, which had been established in each Poor Law Union, continued in existence until 1923. By 1940 most health functions at local level had been transferred to county councils and the county manager became responsible for the formulation of local policy on health services. The transfer of responsibility for all health services to local authorities was completed in 1947 when they assumed responsibility in urban areas for preventive health services which up to then had been the domain of urban district councils. In 1947 there were 31 health authorities, corresponding to the same number of county councils and county boroughs. In 1960, however, this number was reduced to 27 when unified health authorities were established within the four counties containing the main cities of Dublin, Cork, Limerick and Waterford; the health functions of Dublin County Council and Dublin County Borough, for example, were amalgamated.

The trend towards a reduction in the number of authorities with responsibility for health services was taken a stage further when the Health Act, 1970 provided for the establishment of eight regional boards.

The reasons for the regionalisation of health functions were outlined in a White Paper in 1966.[10] They were based mainly on the following considerations:

- The state had taken over the major share of the costs of running the services that were increasing substantially every year. It was therefore desirable to have a new administrative framework to combine national and local interests.
- It was becoming more and more obvious that in order to develop the medical service itself, especially in relation to acute hospital care, it would be necessary to have the organisation on an inter-county basis. It was clear that the county as a unit was unsuitable; it was too small an area for the provision of a comprehensive hospital service.
- The removal of health affairs from the general local authority sphere had been foreshadowed as far back as 1947 when the Department of Health was separated from the Department of Local Government and set up as a separate ministry.

Under the provisions of the Health Act, 1970, the administrative structure of the health services was changed as from 1 April 1970. From that date the health services were to be administered by eight health boards, each covering a number of counties as follows:

- Eastern: Dublin, Kildare and Wicklow
- North Eastern: Cavan, Louth, Meath and Monaghan
- South Eastern: Carlow, Kilkenny, Tipperary South, Waterford and Wexford
- Midland: Laois, Longford, Offaly and Westmeath
- Southern: Cork and Kerry
- Mid Western: Limerick, Clare and Tipperary North
- Western: Galway, Mayo and Roscommon
- North Western: Donegal, Leitrim and Sligo

The population of the regions varied with, for example, the Eastern Health Board area having a population approximately six times that of either the Midland or North Western Health Board areas in 1971. The density of population and the location of existing facilities, especially hospitals, however, explain some of these differences.

The membership of each health board represented a combination of three main interests:

- elected representatives drawn from county councils and borough councils; these account for more than half the membership
- professional representatives of the medical, nursing, dental and pharmaceutical interests who are mostly officers of the board
- nominees of the Minister for Health of which there are three on each board.

In the discussions leading to the Health Act, 1970, Erskine Childers, TD, Minister for Health, had bowed to political pressure by conceding just over half the membership of health boards to local elected representatives.[11] In the majority of cases, an elected local representative has been chairperson of each health board (a non-executive position which is filled on an annual basis).

In 2000, the Eastern Regional Health Authority replaced the Eastern Health Board and there was a number of consequential changes to the structures in the eastern region as well as membership of the Authority (see later section).

Each health board has a chief executive officer who is responsible for the day-to-day administration. The chief executive officer has, by statute, personal responsibility for the appointment, supervision and remuneration of staff and for deciding on the entitlement of individuals to health services. In addition, he/she may be delegated authority from the board to perform other functions. Policy decisions on services and expenditure, however, are the responsibility of the board.

Other bodies
As part of the administrative organisation of the health services under the Health Act, 1970, the following bodies were established in addition to the health boards – Comhairle na nOspidéal, three regional hospital boards (based in Dublin, Cork and Galway) and advisory committees.

The functions of Comhairle na nOspidéal include the regulation of the number and type of consultant medical and certain other staff in the hospitals, and advising the Minister for Health on matters relating to the organisation and operation of hospital services.

The regional hospital boards, whose establishment had been recommended in the *Report of the Consultative Council on the General Hospital Services* (1968), were charged with the general organisation and development of hospital services in an efficient manner by the health boards and voluntary organisations. They were not to be concerned with the day-to-day running of the hospitals. The areas covered by these boards were intended to be three regions. However, these boards were never fully activated.

Local advisory committees were established on a county basis and their function was solely advisory. In this way they were intended to represent local interests to the health board. Membership of the committee was made up of local elected representatives, the county manager, members of the medical profession and representatives of voluntary social service organisations. The establishment of these advisory committees can be viewed as a further concession to local elected representatives for the loss of influence in the move from county to regional administration. These committees were abolished in 1988.

Finance

The major source of income for expenditure on health services at present is the exchequer (Table 5.1); up to 1977, however, local taxation was an important and significant source of income.

During the nineteenth century local rates constituted the primary source of income for health services and only towards the end of the century was state aid provided. By 1947, state grants accounted for 16 per cent of the total cost of the services. Post-war developments in the health services necessitated increased state expenditure. Under the Health Services (Financial Provisions) Act, 1947, the state undertook to meet for each health authority the increase in the cost of its services over what that authority had spent in the base year (the financial year ended 31 March 1948), until the cost of the services provided by the authority was being shared equally with the exchequer. The White Paper of 1966 indicated that local rates were not a form of taxation suitable for collecting revenue on the scale required for proposed developments in the health services and recommended instead that the cost of further extensions of the services should not be met by the local rates. By 1970, the exchequer's contribution amounted to 56 per cent of total costs. In 1973 the government decided to remove health charges from local rates over a four-year period and by 1977 the transfer had been completed.

Another source of revenue, the health contribution, was introduced under the Health Contributions Act, 1971 at the request of the Department of Finance which was concerned at the falling contribution from local rates. Up to 1991 the health contribution was based on a percentage of earnings subject to an income limit that was usually adjusted upwards on an annual basis. In 1991, however, the income limit was abolished and the contribution (2.0 per cent) is now levied on total income.

A further source of income since 1973 is derived from receipts under EU regulations. These receipts are mainly in respect of health services provided for people for whom Britain is liable under EU regulations, e.g. recipients of British pensions and dependants of persons employed in Britain.

An important source of revenue for hospitals for several decades was the Hospitals Trust Fund. A number of voluntary hospitals joined forces to run a sweepstake from horse racing in 1930. The venture proved successful and under the Public Hospitals Act, 1933, available surpluses of ensuing sweepstakes were to be payable to the Hospitals Trust Fund, appointed by the Minister for Health and Local Government to administer the funds. The income from the Fund was used mainly for capital expenditure on all hospitals. Up to 1974, voluntary hospitals were financed by capitation grants from the Department of Health and grants from the Hospitals Trust Fund towards revenue deficits. The role of the Hospital Trust Fund in financing hospital development and services had declined considerably in importance when the sweepstake was abolished in the early 1980s. It had, however, made a substantial contribution to the development of hospitals. Barrington has noted:

> The availability of sweepstake money enabled a level of investment in hospitals, which arguably, could not or would not have been provided otherwise.[12]

Almost 90 per cent of funds for health services are derived from the exchequer, with the health contribution and hospital out-patient charges accounting for just over 10 per cent (Table 5.1).

Table 5.1: Sources of finance for statutory non-capital health services, 2001

	€m	%
Exchequer	5,830	86.5
Health contributions and miscellaneous	723	10.7
Receipts under EU regulations	186	2.8
Total	6,739	100.0

Source: Health Statistics, Department of Health and Children

Expenditure by programme

Almost half (47.7 per cent) of current expenditure goes on the general hospital programme while the combined community care sub-programmes account for over one-quarter (28.9 per cent) (Table 5.2). This represents a slight shift in the proportion of resources away from general hospitals in recent years (the hospitals' share in 1993 was 50.8 per cent).

The public cost of health care has been a matter of concern for several decades. For example, in the late 1980s expenditure cutbacks were introduced as part of a general attempt to improve the state of the public finances. As a percentage of GDP, health spending fell from 7.72 per cent in 1980 to 7.04 per cent in 1985 and to 5.72 per cent in 1990. One of the consequences of this was to reduce the number of beds available in acute hospitals. A decade later, however, against a background of economic growth, health expenditure was increased substantially, from €3.4 billion

Table 5.2: Gross* non-capital expenditure on health services, 2002**

Programme	€000	%
Community protection programme	275,355	3.4
Community health service programme	1,331,760	16.7
Community welfare programme	709,845	8.8
Psychiatric programme	570,272	7.1
Programme for the handicapped	969,121	12.1
General hospital programme	3,832,187	47.7
General support programme	339,445	4.2
Total	8,027,985	100.0

* When income from hospital charges and other sources (€293 million) is taken into account the net non-capital expenditure for 2002 is estimated to be €7,734 million.

** Estimated

Source: Health Statistics, Department of Health and Children

in 1997 to €7.7 billion in 2002. By 2002, health expenditure had risen to 7.39 per cent of GDP.

The level of recent increased investment in health has far outstripped that in any other area of social services such as education. Despite this increased investment, most of which went on remuneration for additional and existing staff, the perception, if not the reality, remained that there was only a modest discernible increase in the level of services and that some services were inadequate in many respects. This in turn led to a growing focus on value for money in the health services.

Services

Following their establishment, the work of health boards was divided into three broad programmes, each with a programme manager. The programmes were community care, general hospital and special hospital (the latter to include psychiatric services and services for persons with intellectual and physical/ sensory disabilities). In recent years, however, there has been a move away from this structure to one based on care groups, e.g. acute hospital services, mental health services and services for older people.

The older classification of three broad programmes is still used for analysis of expenditure data by the Department of Health and Children (see Table 5.2). These provide a useful framework for an examination of health services.

It is not possible to cover each of the services for each care group. Instead, some the main features of community care services, acute hospital services and mental health services are considered.

Community Care Programme

The traditional pattern of health services in Ireland placed great emphasis on institutional care. The policy in recent decades, however, has been to emphasise community rather than institutional services. The reasoning behind this was that it was justified on social as well as economic grounds and that an efficient community health and welfare service would reduce the demand for hospital beds.

The community care programme covers a wide range of services and has three sub-programmes, i.e. community protection, community health and community welfare services.

- *Community protection* includes prevention of infectious diseases, child health examinations, health immunisation, health promotion and other preventive services.
- *Community health services* include general practitioner services, refund of drugs scheme, home nursing services, dental, ophthalmic and aural services.
- *Community welfare* includes a range of cash payments (e.g. domiciliary care allowance for children with disabilities), home help services, grants to voluntary welfare organisations, child care services.

The general practitioner service under the community care programme is part of the general medical service (GMS), which accounts for one-third (31.8 per cent) of expenditure on the total community care programme. It is appropriate to consider the nature of this service which is so important to the primary health care needs of almost one-third of the population.

General Medical Service. As already noted, a free general practitioner service for poor persons was provided from 1851 in local dispensary districts. This system continued until the Health Act, 1970 provided for its abolition. The White Paper of 1966 had referred to the advantages of the dispensary system but indicated that the segregation of the population into fee-paying patients (who attended the doctor's surgery) and public patients (who attended the dispensary) outweighed any of its merits.[13] Consequently, the Health Act, 1970 provided for the introduction of a choice-of-doctor scheme under which eligible persons would not be discriminated against in regard to place of treatment. The choice-of-doctor scheme comes under the general medical service (GMS), which also subsumes the service provided by pharmacists to those eligible.

Following negotiations between the Minister for Health and the medical profession, the choice-of-doctor scheme was introduced in 1972. The scheme gave eligible patients, i.e. medical card-holders and their dependants, the choice-of-doctor to the greatest extent practicable and ended the discrimination and stigma attached to the dispensary system. The introduction of the choice-of-doctor scheme has been described, with considerable justification, as 'a major landmark in the history of social development in Ireland'.[14]

In 200[...] were 1,863 doctors and 1,203 pharmacists participating in the scheme. Most of the doctors care for both private and eligible patients, although the ratio between both categories of patients may vary considerably between parts of the country since there is a wide divergence in the distribution of medical cardholders. Up to 1989, participating doctors were paid a fee-per-consultation in accordance with a scale which varied depending on the time at which the service was given and, in the case of domiciliary consultation, on the distance travelled.

Under the dispensary system, most of the doctors supplied drugs, medicines and appliances to eligible patients. Under the GMS, retail pharmaceutical chemists, who have entered into agreement with health boards, are the primary channels of supply of drugs prescribed for eligible persons. Prescriptions are dispensed without charge to the patient and the pharmacist recoups the cost of the drugs and, in addition, is paid a dispensing fee by the health board. In some rural areas where the doctor's practice is located at a considerable distance from the nearest retail pharmacist participating in the scheme, the doctor may dispense the medicines and is paid a dispensing fee for each patient.

Since its inception in 1972, expenditure on the GMS has been a matter of some concern, especially the cost of providing drugs and medicines that have accounted for about two-thirds of the total expenditure on the GMS annually. In 1975 the Minister for Health established a working party to examine prescribing patterns. Their report noted that a number of doctors over-prescribed to a significant extent. This consisted in prescribing too many items, prescribing excessive quantities and constantly prescribing the more expensive drugs without regard to their cost.[15]

A further working party, established by the Minister for Health in 1982, examined methods by which the GMS might be made more cost-effective, with a special emphasis on the way in which doctors were paid.[16] Under a new system of payment introduced in 1989, participating doctors receive a capitation payment in respect of each panel patient, weighted by reference to demographic characteristics (age and sex), and geographic factors (distance of the doctor's principal place of practice from the patient's home). Furthermore, fees are paid for a number of specified procedures. The Irish College of General Practitioners had criticised the fee-per-item system prior to its replacement on the grounds that:

> ... the GP's income depends solely on the number of face-to-face consultations which can be fitted into each day. It medicalises minor illness and induces unhealthy doctor dependence in the patient.[17]

Under the fee-per-item method of payment, there was also an observed relationship between the incidence of consultation and the level of prescribing, i.e. the greater the number of visits to doctors the greater the number of prescriptions. Under the new capitation-based system of payment, the incentive to over-visiting should be removed and it should also reduce prescribing rates by discouraging unnecessary consultation. However, it has been pointed out that:

> Unfortunately, no systematic evaluation is available to indicate whether the contract changes resulted in a reduction in doctors' clinical activity (fewer house calls, less repeat visiting by those with chronic illness, or more referral).[18]

In the area of prescribing, the Department of Health agreed on a drug budgeting scheme for all GMS doctors. Each was given a personal prescribing target and those who reach it are given a 'drug refund' for improving premises, purchasing equipment or pursuing approved professional development.

In 2001 the cost per eligible person was €177 (doctor cost), €371 (pharmacy cost), giving an average total GMS cost of €548 for every person with medical card eligibility (as compared with €443 in 2000). With reference to GMS costs per eligible person, the Deloitte and Touche report on *Audit of the Irish Health Services for Value for Money* (2001) indicated:

> This represents real value for money. If this is seen as a premium paid to GPs to cover their registered population, the cost per person per year is relatively low.[19]

General hospital programme

This programme covers the treatment of patients in medical, surgical and maternity hospitals, including treatment and out-patient consulting clinics associated with these hospitals. These services are provided either directly by health boards in hospitals under their control or by contract with voluntary and private hospitals. There are three categories of hospitals, i.e. public, voluntary public and private.

Public hospitals. These evolved from the infirmaries and the workhouses of the nineteenth-century Poor Law. Following the abolition of the workhouses in the 1920s, a county system of hospitals began to emerge.

Voluntary public hospitals. Some date from the early eighteenth century and some are run by religious orders. They are confined mainly to the larger urban areas, especially Dublin where the greatest demand for services existed and where financial support for their upkeep was also likely to be more readily available. A number of these hospitals were closed in the late 1980s.

Private hospitals. Most of these are run by religious orders and some share the same campus with voluntary public hospitals (e.g. Mater Private Hospital and the Mater Hospital). These private hospitals do not receive direct state subsidies.

Given the manner in which the hospital system evolved over a period of time it is not surprising that rationalisation would have become an issue on several occasions.

The first report of the Hospitals Commission covering the period 1933–1936 recommended against the development of each county hospital but favoured the grouping of hospitals in suitable geographic centres 'irrespective of county boundaries'. It submitted a scheme for the development of 12 main regional centres, county hospitals in areas remote from regional centres and a network of district hospitals in the provincial towns. The Commission was critical of the situation in Dublin where there were too many small hospitals and it recommended the development of two general hospitals in south Dublin and two in north Dublin.[20] These proposals were not pursued, partly because the government had already embarked upon the development of county hospitals.

In 1967, Seán Flanagan, TD, Minister for Health, appointed a consultative council to review the hospital system. The report, published in 1968, is usually referred to as the *Fitzgerald Report* after the chairman of the council, Professor Patrick Fitzgerald.[21] In general, the report indicated that the existing hospital system was defective in staffing, equipment, quality of service and teaching standards. It suggested that the system could only be improved by a radical reorganisation involving, among other things, a considerable reduction in the number of centres providing acute treatment and a planned and co-ordinated hospital organisation embracing both the public and voluntary hospitals. It recommended that the hospital system be reorganised into three regions based on the medical teaching centres in Dublin, Cork and Galway. Each region would have a regional hospital of 600–1,000 beds offering a full range of services supported by a number of general hospitals of about 300 beds throughout the region. General practitioners catering for non-acute cases needing care would staff the existing district hospitals. The existing county hospitals were to be community health centres providing inpatient services as suggested for district hospitals but backed by increased diagnostic facilities and a more comprehensive consultant outpatient organisation.

There was no official commitment to implement the recommendations of the Fitzgerald Report, and in 1973 Brendan Corish, TD, Minister for Health, initiated a process of widespread consultation, involving the medical profession, health boards, and Comhairle na nOspidéal. Guidelines drawn up by Comhairle modified the earlier recommendations of the Fitzgerald Report and proposed, among other things, that the general aim should be to organise acute hospital services with specified minimum staffing so that the population served would be within a radius of 30 miles of the hospital centre. The Minister accepted the Comhairle guidelines as a reasonable basis for improving the hospital service and for decisions on the future system.

Following a process of consultation with all of the interested parties, the General Hospital Development Plan (GHDP) was announced by Brendan Corish, TD, Minister for Health, in 1975. It differed fundamentally from the *Fitzgerald Report* in the number of acute care hospitals to be established. The GHDP envisaged the development of general hospitals in 23 locations (about twice as many as envisaged in the Fitzgerald Report) and speculated on a further number of community hospitals in formats and locations to be decided upon. The plan contained no detail of the future development of hospital services in either Cork or Limerick cities beyond tentative mention of the possibility of a major hospital service in the north-east area of Cork city. In addition, decisions in some other cases were postponed pending further consultation. The major differences between the GHDP and the Fitzgerald Report were distance of population from a general hospital (30 miles versus 60 miles) and, related to that, the number of centres in which general hospitals should be located (23 versus 12).

The GHDP could be viewed as a balance between professional medical opinion and broader political considerations. The *Irish Times* commented:

> Indeed, it is not so much a national plan of any substance as an interim political statement on the state of play at local level.[22]

In its pre-election manifesto of 1977, the Fianna Fáil party included an undertaking 'to preserve the role of the county hospital in providing the necessary level of services for the local community'.[23]

Since the GHDP was not comprehensive and, in the absence of a detailed policy statement from the new government, Comhairle na nOspidéal concluded that the country would in the future be served by a limited number of large specialised hospitals in Dublin, Cork and Galway (at least seven and possibly nine), and by a large number of smaller general hospitals (about 24 or 26). Comhairle indicated that:

> Inherent in such a situation of many small hospitals is the danger that medical deficiencies, spelled out in the Fitzgerald Report and for which that body proposed medical solutions, will continue to exist.[24]

It was largely in the context of cutbacks in public expenditure on the health services that a rationalisation of hospitals occurred in the late 1980s. During this period a number of the public voluntary hospitals and the smaller public district hospitals were closed, often amid considerable controversy. The most notable example was that of Barrington's Hospital in Limerick, a public voluntary hospital that had been established under charter in 1830. The proposal by the Department of Health to close this hospital gave rise to vehement public opposition, with an estimated 20,000 persons attending a demonstration in Limerick city in January 1988 to protest against the closure of the hospital. It also led to the government being defeated on a Private Members' motion in the Dáil in February 1988. The defeat briefly raised the prospect of a general election, but the motion was not binding on the government and the hospital closed in the following month.

The number of acute care hospitals and consequently the number of beds has been reduced, especially since the mid-1980s (Table 5.3). Approximately 4,000 beds were removed from the

Table 5.3: Numbers of acute hospitals beds and average length of stay (ALOS), selected years, 1980–2000

	Beds	ALOS
1980	17,665	9.7
1984	17,633	7.5
1988	13,632	7.0
1991	13,806	6.8
1993	11,809	6.7
2000	11,832	6.6

Source: Acute Hospital Bed Capacity: A National Review (Department of Health and Children, 2002), Table 1.1, p. 18

system between 1984 and 1988 and a further 2,000 were removed between 1991 and 1993. It is highly questionable, however, that all this occurred as a result of any coherent national plan. In practice, the closures of some hospitals were brought about by a combination of the Department of Health reducing budgets to health boards, leaving them no option but to close the smaller hospitals, and simply informing a number of voluntary public hospitals, which it funded directly, that they would have to close.

This absence of national planning led the chief executive of the South Eastern Health Board to comment in 1987 that:

> In the absence of an agreed national plan the effect will be to downgrade all our acute hospitals and instead of a limited number of good hospitals we will have a larger number of poor hospitals.[25]

Rationalisation of hospital services in Dublin along the lines proposed by the GHDP (1975) has been achieved. The Plan allowed for six major general hospitals – the Beaumont, the Mater and the James Connolly Memorial hospitals on the north side and St Vincent's, St James's and Tallaght hospitals on the south side. This rationalisation was a protracted affair that took several years to complete, partly because in some cases it involved the amalgamation of existing hospitals with different traditions and ethos. This was particularly true of Tallaght hospital, opened in 1998 in the south-west suburbs, which is an amalgam of three former city hospitals, the Adelaide, Meath and National Children's hospitals. While this amalgamation is recognised in the formal name, i.e. the Adelaide and Meath Hospital Dublin Incorporating the National Children's Hospital, it is more commonly referred to simply as Tallaght Hospital.

Mental Health Services

For many decades the focus of care in relation to psychiatric illness was the psychiatric hospital. More recently, however, there has been a decline in the number of patients in such hospitals and there is now far greater emphasis on a range of community services. Inpatient treatment is provided in health board psychiatric hospitals, units attached to general hospitals, and a small number of private psychiatric hospitals.

In 1961 a Commission of Inquiry on Mental Illness was appointed to examine and report on the health services available for the mentally ill and to make recommendations on the measures required to improve these services. The Commission's report, published in 1966, indicated that in 1961 there were 7.3 psychiatric beds per 1,000 of the population, which appeared to be the highest in the world.[26] No clear explanation emerged for the exceptional rates of residence in psychiatric hospitals here but the Commission suggested a possible combination of reasons – high rate of emigration, low marriage rates, unemployment, social and geographic isolation in rural areas and unhelpful public attitudes towards mental illness which hinder discharge.

In 1981 the Medico-Social Research Board took a census of patients in psychiatric hospitals. Among the important findings of that census were that approximately one-third were over 65 years of age, a very high proportion (79.5 per cent) were unmarried, and one-fifth were resident in hospitals for 25 years or more.[27]

Another major review of psychiatric services was carried out by a study group between 1981 and 1984. Its report, *The Psychiatric Services: Planning for the Future*, provided a new planning framework for the development of a community-based psychiatric service.[28] The report was widely welcomed. In summary, the report set out guidelines for future development as far as possible in a community setting, with the emphasis on resources being transferred from large psychiatric hospitals to a range of alternative community-based services and to acute general hospitals. Among the key elements in the planning framework were:

- the location of services close to where people work and a strong emphasis on outpatient and day care
- the provision of inpatient treatment in psychiatric units in general hospitals, with the role of the traditional psychiatric

hospitals diminishing as alternative community-based services are developed

- provision of high-support hostels for a small number who will require long-term inpatient care and the provision of appropriate housing in the community
- services to be provided on a sectoral basis for a given population by a multidisciplinary team to be based in each sector.

The report proposed the gradual dismantling of psychiatric institutions and their replacement, as far as possible, by units in general hospitals and the development of community-based services. This approach was in keeping with the general emphasis on community care and the move away from institutional care.

Progress in implementing the recommendations of *Planning for the Future* was slow and the *Green Paper on Mental Health* (1992) noted:

> In most health boards there are some psychiatric services which are comprehensive and community-oriented as defined in *Planning for the Future*, but such services are still not the norm.[29]

The Green Paper also noted that the psychiatric hospital still played a major role in the psychiatric service but that this role was diminishing and changing.

Almost a decade later, the *Health Strategy: Quality and Fairness* (2001) indicated that while considerable progress had been made in many health board areas in implementing the change from institutional to community-based care, as recommended in *Planning for the Future*, few health boards had as yet completed the process.[30]

Implementation of the recommendations in *Planning for the Future* has been monitored in a detailed manner by the Inspector of Mental Hospitals whose annual reports have recorded the progress or lack of it in different parts of the country. In the 2001 report the ongoing replacement of old institutional mental hospitals with acute psychiatric units attached to general hospitals was noted. However, the report also noted that:

> Provision of community-based residential accommodation alternatives to run-down, old-fashioned psychiatric hospital accommodation proceeds somewhat unevenly throughout the country.[31]

Table 5.4: Trends in psychiatric provision, 1984–2000

	Public psychiatric hospitals		Day facilities		Community residences	
	Admissions	Patients	No	Places	No	Places
1984	28,330	11,613	32	800	121	900
2000	21,033	4,139	179	2,349	392	2,934

Source: *Green Paper on Mental Health*, Chapter 2; *Health Statistics* (Department of Health and Children), *Report of the Inspector of Mental Hospitals*

An increasing number of day and community facilities are providing an alternative to long-term care in psychiatric hospitals. This trend is reflected in the continued fall in the number of patients in psychiatric hospitals and the increase in places in day hospitals, day centres and community residences during the 1980s and 1990s (Table 5.4).

By 2002, there were 18 general hospital psychiatric units in operation, with several others at various stages of planning.

The Mental Health Act, 2001 deals mainly with protecting the rights of individuals who may be involuntarily detained in psychiatric hospitals. Under the Act, any person detained involuntarily is entitled to a review after 21 days; a committee of three, including a psychiatrist, a lawyer and one other person will carry out the review. The Mental Health Commission was established in April 2002 under the Mental Health Act, 2001 and its main functions are to ensure that the Act is fully implemented and to establish modern systems of care including quality of services and high standards of clinical practice.

Eligibility for health services

From June 1991, the population has been divided into two categories for eligibility for health services. In Category I, the lowest income group, i.e. medical cardholders and their dependants, accounting for 31 per cent of the population, are entitled to all health services free of charge; the remaining 69 per cent are in Category II and are entitled to a more limited range of services.

The main difference between the two groups is that while the medical card population (Category I) is entitled to a free general practitioner service and hospital service (in public wards of public and voluntary public hospitals), the rest of the population

(Category II) is liable for general practitioner fees but is entitled to a 'free' hospital service (subject to a relatively small maximum annual charge of €400) on the same basis as the medical card population.

It is important to note that there is no statutory basis for determining eligibility based on the two categories above.

Prior to 1991 the system was highly complex, with the population divided into three categories. This situation had evolved over a considerable period of time. From 1851 the low-income group had eligibility for health services under the dispensary system of the Poor Law and in 1953 the middle-income group obtained limited eligibility for services, leaving the higher group without any entitlement. In 1979 further reforms were introduced to simplify the system of eligibility but the three-tiered system remained until 1991.

Medical cards
Persons with full eligibility for health services are defined in the Health Act, 1970 as 'adult persons unable without undue hardship to arrange general practitioner, medical and surgical services for themselves and their dependants and dependants of such persons'. Those with full eligibility receive a General Medical Services card (medical card) that entitles them to free health services. Each health board maintains a register of medical cardholders that is updated regularly. Prior to the establishment of health boards the criteria used in assessing means were not uniform in all administrative areas.

Since 1974, however, the chief executives of health boards have jointly agreed on general guidelines that have been used in determining those categories that have full eligibility. These guidelines have no statutory effect and are issued primarily to inform each health board and the public in general of the broad categories of persons who normally qualify for full eligibility. Entitlement to a medical card is based on assessment of means and community welfare officers of health boards carry out the means test. In practice, means tests are not carried out on recipients of certain social welfare payments who have already been means tested. Each year health boards issue annual income limits for eligibility for medical cards.

Since the improvements in the GMS with the introduction of the choice-of-doctor scheme in 1972, the number of persons with

Table 5.5: Number of persons and percentage of population covered by medical cards, selected years, 1972–2001

	No. of persons	*% of total population*
1972	864,106	29.0
1976	1,193,909	37.0
1980	1,199,599	35.6
1986	1,326,048	37.4
1988	1,324,849	37.4
1990	1,221,284	34.9
1996	1,252,385	34.6
2001	1,199,454	31.2

Source: Annual Reports, The General Medical Service Payments Board

medical card and the total number covered by medical cards, i.e. medical cardholders and their dependants, increased up to the late 1980s (Table 5.5). There are now 1.2 million persons covered by medical cards, representing 31 per cent of the total population.

A number of factors account for the increase throughout the 1970s and early 1980s. Firstly, the take-up of medical cards would have increased as a result of the abolition of the dispensary system to which a certain stigma was attached. Secondly, the introduction of uniform guidelines to determine eligibility for medical cards would also have led to an increase in take-up. Thirdly, during this period there was an increase in the social welfare population, mainly due to the increase in unemployment, and thus, by definition, there was an increase in the lower income group.

There is considerable variation between health boards in relation to the proportion of the population covered by medical cards. These differences broadly reflect income variation within the country. In 2001 the North-Western Health Board area had the highest proportion of population covered by medical cards (46.1 per cent) while the Eastern Health Board area had the lowest (27.6 per cent); of the counties, Donegal had the highest (51.0 per cent) and Dublin the lowest (27.1 per cent).[32]

The *Report of the Commission on Health Funding* (1989) recommended that the criteria for eligibility for medical cards should be uniform throughout the country so that people in similar circumstances would not be treated differently. Eligibility for all services, including discretionary services, should also be the same throughout the country and where charges for such services obtain they should also be uniform.[33] In line with a commitment in the *Programme for Economic and Social Progress* a review of medical card eligibility to ensure uniformity and consistency between all health boards was undertaken.[34] The review, carried out by the health board chief executive officers in 2001, pointed to a number of shortcomings and a lack of consistency in the application of the scheme across health boards. Recommendations of the review include streamlining of applications, improving the standardisation of the medical card applications process to ensure transparency and the provision of information to applicants. The *Health Strategy* (2001) made a commitment to provide a clear statutory framework in relation to eligibility for health and personal social services.[35]

In July 2001 eligibility for medical cards was extended to all persons aged 70 or over irrespective of income. The *Health Strategy* indicated that eligibility would be extended to increase the number of persons on low incomes and to give priority to families with children and particularly children with a disability. A commitment was subsequently made by government to add a further 200,000 persons. This was rescinded in 2002 because of the downturn in the national finances.

Rationalisation

Reference has already been made to the fact that the system of eligibility was highly complex up to June 1991. In fact, an attempt was made in 1974 to rationalise the system into two categories, as was done in 1991. Brendan Corish, TD, Minister for Health, announced that from April 1974 everyone would be entitled to free hospital inpatient and outpatient services. However, the Minister was obliged to defer the introduction of the scheme because of the opposition of hospital consultants. The consultants resisted such change, citing the possible effects on their conditions of employment and on their remuneration in particular.

The *Report of the Commission on Health Funding* argued that people should have available to them a certain level of necessary health services, including primary care, hospital care, long-term care and personal social services. It pointed out, however, that this did not necessarily mean that they should all be publicly funded or delivered by public agencies or provided free of charge. The Commission recommended that the lowest income group (medical cardholders and their dependants) should remain eligible for all necessary health services free of charge. The rest of the population should be eligible for 'core' services. These services would include acute hospital care, long-term care and personal social services; welfare and continuing care services such as those for mothers and children, the elderly, the disabled and the psychiatrically ill (possibly with some charges for these services). The services, to which everyone was already entitled, such as a service for infectious diseases, should remain universally available.

The Commission's recommendations regarding eligibility basically envisaged a two-tier system, i.e. the abolition of Category 3 as then existed. This is similar to what was proposed in the *Programme for Economic and Social Progress*, and which came into effect in June 1991. Unlike 1974, the opposition by hospital consultants to an extension of entitlement to 'free' hospitalisation was more muted on this occasion.

The Commission also recommended that patients would have to opt for either public or private care and should not be allowed to combine them. Those opting for private care should pay the full costs involved.

Health insurance

The Voluntary Health Insurance Board (VHI) was established under the Voluntary Health Insurance Act, 1957 and is charged with providing a health insurance scheme. The VHI is a non-profit-making body and any surplus on its income is devoted to the reduction of insurance premiums or increases in benefits. The VHI was established essentially as a means by which those in the higher income group, who did not have eligibility to health services at the time, would be able to insure themselves against the cost of medical care.

In 1958, one year after its establishment, 57,000 persons were covered by the VHI scheme. The numbers have increased steadily since then so that by 2000 there was a total of 1.488 million subscribers. For some time it was clear that the total membership of the VHI was in excess of the estimated number of people who, strictly speaking, should have taken out insurance to cover themselves against hospital charges. In other words, persons with eligibility for free hospital services had also invested in supplementary cover to enable them to have private or semi-private accommodation and private treatment in hospitals. The rationalisation of the system of eligibility in 1991 did not change this pattern. In fact the numbers in private insurance have continued to grow in line with economic growth and a significant increase in the numbers in employment.

The EU Commission forced competition in private health insurance on a reluctant Department of Health in the early 1990s. In accordance with the Health Insurance Act, 1994, the health insurance market in Ireland was opened up to competition, thus ending the virtual monopoly that the VHI had enjoyed for almost four decades. At the beginning of 1997, BUPA (British Union of Private Assurance) commenced operating in the Irish market and thereby introduced an element of competition into a market hitherto dominated by VHI. Within one year, BUPA had 55,000 subscribers and by 2002 had approximately 300,000 subscribers.

Both the VHI and BUPA operate a community rating system, i.e. all age categories are charged the same premium even though the risk of ill-health obviously varies depending on age.

It is estimated that membership of VHI, BUPA and other smaller health insurance schemes now accounts for approximately 47 per cent of the population.[36] The VHI has by far the largest share of the market.

The White Paper *Private Health Insurance*, published in 1999, set out an ambitious programme for change. This included the transformation of the VHI into a commercial semi-state agency and the retention of a revised system of community-based rating. It also proposed an amendment to the risk equalisation scheme provided for in the Health Insurance Act, 1994, a highly controversial and complex scheme that would prevent insurers targeting mainly young, healthy, and low-risk subscribers. The White Paper acknowledged the 'potential for conflicts of interest to occur' because the Minister for Health and Children is both 'owner' of the VHI and the regulator of the private health insurance market.[37] It therefore proposed the establishment of a Health Insurance Authority to regulate the market. The Health Insurance Authority was established on a statutory basis in 2001.

Access
A feature of the Irish health services has been the public/private mix at primary care and hospital level. While the introduction of the choice-of-doctor scheme in 1972 ended the differences in

access between public and private patients to general practitioners, the same cannot be said for access to inpatient hospital services. The existence of private and public beds, the operation of private health insurance and the work practices of hospital consultants have led to the emergence of a two-tier system. The result has been that those covered by private insurance have had apparent ease in gaining access to hospital care while others have to wait somewhat longer for treatment.

In theory, access to hospital services is available to all especially since 1991 when changes in eligibility categories were introduced. In practice, waiting lists for public patients became the norm throughout the 1990s. At the same time it is established that one of the reasons for the increase in membership of private insurance schemes in the same decade is that private health insurance provides faster access to hospital care and the avoidance of waiting lists.[38]

Because of growing concern with waiting lists, or more particularly, waiting times, for hospital care, a waiting list initiative, backed by additional funding, commenced in 1993. Despite this, the numbers on waiting lists did not decline appreciably throughout the 1990s, with annual average numbers around 30,000. This became an important issue and reinforced a public perception that the system was failing public patients.

Proposals by the Commission on Health Funding envisaged a continued mix of public and private care. The fundamental principle of the majority of the Commission was that it should not be necessary, nor should it be perceived as such, to take out private insurance in order to secure access to treatment. The role of private insurance therefore should be to provide cover for those wishing to avail themselves of private care and to provide cover for costs for which those without medical cards would be liable. The Commission was opposed to public subsidisation of private care when the state is already providing a core service to the entire population. It recommended that payments to the VHI should not qualify for tax relief (the cost of this relief in 1989 was £44m.) and this relief, together with that of certain reimbursed medical expenses, should be phased out.

The Commission on Health Funding also recommended the introduction of a common waiting list for hospitals, arguing that priority of admission should be determined solely by medical need and not by the public or private status of the patient.

Despite increased investment in the health services and the employment of additional staff in the late 1990s, inequalities in access to inpatient hospital services continued and waiting lists remained high. The problem was acknowledged in the White Paper *Private Health Insurance* and was highlighted in a week-long series of articles on the health services in the *Irish Times*.[39] The implications of inequalities in the public/private system for public patients was highlighted in a report by the Society of St Vincent de Paul.[40]

The public/private mix and the public waiting lists were central issues in the *Health Strategy* (2001) (see next section).

Review and policy

As already noted, the health services were subject to extensive review in the 1960s, which led to the landmark Health Act, 1970. Against a background of expenditure restraints and, more recently, of an emphasis on value for money, further reviews and policy formulation have taken place. Two of the more important documents to emerge from this process have been the *Report of the Commission on Health Funding* (1989) and the *Health Strategy: Quality and Fairness, A Health System for You* (2001).

Commission on Health Funding

The Commission on Health Funding was established in June 1987 against a background of public expenditure cutbacks in the health services and growing disquiet among health service unions and the public at large with the consequences of these cutbacks. The establishment of the Commission must also be viewed against a background of reviews in other countries stemming from a concern with the performance of health services and in particular the efficient use of resources.

The Commission's report, published in 1989, examined not only the financing of the health services but also the administration and delivery of services, the quality of services and the mix of public and private health care. The Commission made appropriate recommendations. It stated:

> The kernel of the Commission's conclusions is that the solution to the problem facing the Irish health services does not lie primarily in the system of funding but rather in the way that services are planned, organised and delivered.[41]

The Commission's main recommendations and supporting arguments in relation to financing, administration, eligibility and some other issues are summarised here.

Finance. The Commission concluded that the level of public health funding could not be determined by reference to a fixed proportion of Gross Domestic Product or by reference to international comparison. The level can only be decided in the context of the available resources and the priorities attached by Irish society to different social objectives.

The Commission referred to three main methods of funding health services, i.e. general taxation, social insurance, and private insurance. It pointed out that no country relies exclusively on any of these approaches. The majority of the Commission favoured public funding as the main funding method. It opted for this in preference to private funding on the basis that:

- it would achieve a greater degree of comprehensiveness since the state as central funder is favourably placed to plan and organise the delivery of a unified, integrated service for all categories of patient
- the implementation of policy shifts, such as the transfer of resources from institutional to community care, can be more easily achieved when there is a single major health funder
- equity of contribution towards the cost of services can be achieved by way of progressive taxation or social insurance
- equity of access can be controlled administratively to ensure that necessary services are available to all on the basis of need.

By contrast, the majority felt that a private funding model would not be equitable (there could be discrimination against high-risk groups), comprehensive (arising from problems in enforcing mandatory health insurance) and cost-effective (the international evidence suggests that cost control is not more successful under a private funding model).

Having opted for a public funding model, the choice was then between general taxation and a compulsory health insurance/ earmarked tax system (linking the services provided with their cost). A majority favoured general taxation on the grounds that compulsory health insurance was effectively another tax, offering no real advantages over general taxation. The Commission recommended that the existing health contribution should be abolished. It pointed out that while local taxation was a major source of funding for health services in the past it should not be reintroduced for this purpose since it could hinder national planning of facilities.

Administration. Under the existing structure, the health boards have statutory authority to administer health services in their areas and report to the Department of Health which overviews general policy and funding. This is necessarily a simplified and ideal model. The Commission identified a number of weaknesses in the actual operation of this structure:

- a confusion of political and executive functions
- lack of balance between national and local decision making
- inadequate information and evaluation systems
- inadequate accountability
- insufficient integration of services
- inadequate representation of the consumer viewpoint.

One of the main problems cited by the Commission was that many voluntary agencies providing health services were not funded by health boards and therefore did not report to them: instead they were funded directly by the Department of Health. These included voluntary hospitals (accounting for over half of acute hospital services) and some of the larger voluntary organisations providing services for people with disabilities. The Department of Health and the Minister for Health were consequently involved in the management of services rather than concentrating exclusively on developing and monitoring policy. This is but one instance that has contributed to a situation where communication lines between the Department of Health and health boards are inevitably blurred. The Commission made the general point that accountability in the system as between health boards and the Department lacked clarity. Similarly, the Commission also referred to health boards which by nature of their membership become unnecessarily involved in the management of services.

In order to overcome these weaknesses, the Commission recommended that a new structure be introduced along the following lines:

- The Minister for Health and the Department of Health should formulate health policy and should not be involved in the management of individual services. The range and quality of services and the eligibility for access to them should, as far as possible, be laid down by legislation.

- The management of the health services should be transferred to a new agency, the Health Services Executive Authority, which would be appointed by the Minister. The Authority would be responsible for the management and delivery of health and personal social services in the context of health policies set by the Minister for Health.

- A structure of Area General Managers, responsible to the Authority, should be established covering defined geographical areas in which the manager would be responsible for the delivery of services.

- Existing health boards would be abolished and replaced by health councils composed of elected representatives nominated by local authorities, whose functions would be to represent local interests by influencing policy and by monitoring the quality and adequacy of local services. These councils would have limited powers to delay decisions of the Area General Managers.

It was argued by Joyce and Ham that the weaknesses identified by the Commission could be solved without establishing a Health Services Executive Authority or transforming health boards into health councils. They argued that health management is far more complex than that of other public services, and does not lend itself to a clear split between policy and execution as recommended by the Commission. It requires a political and professional input as is provided by the health board structure. Joyce and Ham recommended:

> ... a strengthening of the Department's policy-making role, a clearer and greater delegation of function from the Department to the health boards, and a change in the statutory responsibility of health boards and the CEOs ... The purpose and mission of the health services must be clearly stated. National policy objectives for health must be developed.[42]

While the NESC supported the general diagnosis of the difficulties within the existing structure, it did not accept that the Commission's proposed structure was entirely consistent with the diagnosis. Thus, for example, it was not clear, according to the NESC, how the danger of local resistance to central policy and competition between regions for resources could be avoided by retaining a political/representation function through health councils. The NESC did not offer a definite view on a particular alternative structure.[43]

Not surprisingly, members of health boards were united in their opposition to the administrative changes proposed by the Commission, arguing that the existing system had worked satisfactorily.[44]

In September 1991, Dr Rory O'Hanlon, TD, Minister for Health, referred to failings in the health service structure as identified by the Commission on Health Funding and the Dublin Hospital Initiative Group, namely the lack of co-ordination between hospital and community-based services, the resultant over-involvement of the Department of Health in day-to-day management issues, and the lost opportunities for achieving efficiencies through greater co-operation between agencies. The Minister indicated that the fragmentation of services and the lack of co-ordination were particularly acute in the Dublin area because of the multiplicity of autonomous agencies involved in the provision of health care. He therefore proposed to establish, through legislation, a single new authority that would be responsible for health and personal social services in the Eastern Health Board area; it would subsume the functions of the health board as well as some of the functions of the Department. The Minister's proposals for the other seven health boards were less clear.[45]

In effect, the Minister accepted the diagnosis of the Commission on Health Funding but the remedy was different to the one prescribed. *Shaping a Healthier Future* (1994) reiterated the policy changes announced by Dr Rory O'Hanlon and promised legislation to establish a new authority in the Eastern region. In November 1996, Michael Noonan, TD, Minister for Health, re-announced the proposals made by his predecessor.

While stopping short of the abolition of health boards and their replacement by a Health Services Executive Authority, deficiencies in the health system as identified by the Commission on Health Funding began to be addressed. The Health (Amendment) (No. 3) Act, 1996 – sometimes referred to as the accountability legislation – had three main objectives:

- to strengthen and improve the arrangements governing financial accountability and expenditure procedures in health boards

- to clarify the respective roles of the members of the health boards and their chief executive officers
- to begin the process of removing the Department of Health from detailed involvement in operational matters.

The process of funding voluntary public hospitals and the main voluntary organisations for people with intellectual disabilities through health boards, rather than directly by the Department of Health, commenced in 1998.

The most significant structural reform of the health services since the Health Act, 1970 occurred with the establishment of the Eastern Regional Health Authority (ERHA) by legislation in 1999. As part of the restructuring, the former Eastern Health Board (covering the counties of Dublin, Kildare and Wicklow) was replaced by three Area Health Boards – the East Coast Area Health Board, the Northern Area Health Board and the South Western Area Health Board. The ERHA, established on 1 March 2000, became responsible for the health and personal social services in the eastern region covering a population of 1.4 million. All of the main voluntary service providers such as hospitals and agencies for the intellectually disabled, most of them previously funded directly by the Department of Health and Children, now came under the aegis of the ERHA. Rather than be involved in the direct provision of services the ERHA was charged with the planning, commissioning, monitoring and evaluation of services provided by the three Area Health Boards and 36 voluntary providers. The direct funding link between the latter and the Department of Health and Children was thus ended, thereby freeing the Department to concentrate on policy and strategic issues.

The Health Strategy 2001
Despite a substantial increase in funding of the health services in the late 1990s there was public disquiet with many aspects, particularly the mix of public and private care in hospitals which gave rise to unacceptable waiting lists for public patients. It was against this background that a national strategy was prepared in consultation with the main providers of services. The process was initiated by Micheál Martin, TD, Minister for Health and Children.

As part of the process, the Department of Health and Children also commissioned a value for money audit from Deloitte and Touche, Management Consultants. The report, *Audit of Value for Money in the Health System*, published in conjunction with the *Health Strategy*, indicated:

> The fundamental problem facing the health services in Ireland and elsewhere is the growth in demand and health care costs. The demand is driven by a range of factors including public expectations, demographics, the availability of new diagnostic and therapeutic approaches to care, and significant technological developments in medicine, including drugs ... The position in Ireland is further exacerbated by a significant level of underfunding of services in the 1980s.[46]

The *Health Strategy: Quality and Fairness, A Health System for You* was launched in November 2001. It represented a comprehensive blueprint for developments for reform of the health services over a ten-year period, setting out core principles, national goals and objectives for implementation through 121 actions. In this it was a far more systematic, comprehensive and goal-orientated strategy than *Shaping a Healthier Future* (1994).

The *Health Strategy* established four guiding principles, i.e. equity, people-centredness, quality and accountability. It dealt with proposed targets, developments and reforms across a range of services.

Inevitably, much of the public focus was on the acute hospital sector where approximately 6,000 beds had been removed due to financial constraints in the late 1980s and early 1990s. The *Health Strategy* promised that an additional 3,000 beds would be provided by 2011 (650 by the end of 2002). All the beds would be designated for public patients. It also proposed the employment of additional hospital consultants.

The *Health Strategy* committed that no adult would have to wait longer than three months for hospital treatment (a commitment to reduce the waiting time to a similar time frame had been made in *Shaping a Healthier Future* in 1994). As one of the means of meeting this target the *Health Strategy* provided for the establishment of a Treatment Purchase Fund to purchase bed capacity from private hospitals in Ireland or abroad. By the end of 2002, a total of 1,920 patients had been treated under the Fund. In summary, the *Health Strategy* proposed that the controversial two-tier system of hospital service, leading to waiting lists for public patients, was to be tackled by a combination of the provision of additional beds, the Treatment Purchase Fund initiative and the appointment of additional consultants rather than the introduction of a common waiting list as recommended by the *Commission on Health Funding*.

There was also a commitment to establish a Hospitals Agency on a statutory basis to prepare a strategic plan for expanding the capacity of acute hospitals and to advise the Minister for Health and Children on issues relating to the organisation and development of all acute hospital services.

Reviewing the structures
As indicated in an earlier section of this chapter, the health board structure evolved from the administrative system of the late nineteenth and early decades of the twentieth centuries. It could be argued that the Health Act, 1970 provided for a logical evolution of an existing system. Since then, however, the necessity of having eight boards (eleven following the establishment of the ERHA in 2000) for a country with a population of less than four million has been raised.

The Department of Health tantalisingly raised this issue in its discussion document *Health, The Wider Dimensions* (1986):

> Given the size of the country and the population, the need for eight separate administrations, each with statutory responsibility for providing the whole range of health and personal social services, has also been questioned.[47]

The Department did not, however, indicate how many health boards there should be nor did it suggest an alternative structure.

The role of health boards was analysed in some depth in the *Report of the Commission on Health Funding* (1989). As noted already, its radical proposals for the replacement of health boards by a Health Services Executive Authority were not accepted. But the issue did not go away.

The Deloitte and Touche report associated with the *Health Strategy* (2001) noted:

> It is difficult to imagine any demand-led service which has grown at the rate of the Irish health service, which is still operating within a structure devised over thirty years ago. The optimum shape of the system including the role and structure of health boards needs to be re-evaluated.[48]

The *Health Strategy* proposed a review of structures that was subsequently undertaken by Prospectus Management Consultants in consultation with the Department of Health and Children. The report, published in 2003, recommended radical changes to existing structures.[49] These recommendations were resonant of those in the Commission on Health Funding but went further.

The main proposals were as follows:

- The abolition of health boards and the establishment of a Health Services Executive to manage the health services as a single national entity
- The establishment of three core areas within the Health Services Executive: a National Hospitals Office, a Primary, Community and Continuing Care Directorate and a National Shared Services Centre
- The establishment of four regional health offices within the Health Services Executive to deliver regional and local services
- The establishment of a Health Information and Quality Authority to promote quality of care throughout the system
- The abolition or merging of a number of other health agencies.

These proposals for reform of health structures were endorsed by government and were regarded as 'essential to the creation of a system that is accountable, effective, efficient and capable of responding to the emerging and ongoing needs of the public'.[50]

Notes

1. This section draws heavily on B. Hensey, *The Health Services of Ireland*, 4th ed. (Institute of Public Administration, Dublin, 1988). Chapter 1.
2. See J. Robins, *Fools and Mad, A History of the Insane in Ireland* (Institute of Public Administration, Dublin, 1986); J. Reynolds, *Grangegorman, Psychiatric Care in Dublin since 1815* (Institute of Public Administration, Dublin, 1992).
3. J. Robins, *The Miasma: Epidemic and Panic in Nineteenth Century Ireland* (Institute of Public Administration, Dublin, 1995) p. 108.
4. Ibid. p. 241.
5. There are various accounts of the controversy surrounding the Mother and Child Scheme. These include relevant sections in R. Barrington, *Health, Medicine and Politics in Ireland, 1900–1970* (Institute of Public Administration, 1987); N. Browne, *Against the Tide* (Gill & Macmillan, Dublin, 1986); G. Deeney, *To Cure and to Care: Memoirs of a Chief Medical Officer* (Glendale Press, Dublin, 1989); J.H. Whyte, *Church and State in Modern Ireland, 1923–1979*, 2nd ed. (Gill & Macmillan, Dublin, 1980), J. Horgan, *Noel Browne, Passionate Outsider* (Gill & Macmillan, Dublin, 2000).
6. Barrington, op. cit., p. 279.

7. The sources for data in this section are *Health Statistics 2002* (Department of Health and Children, Stationery Office, Dublin, 2003) and *Health Strategy: Quality and Fairness, A Health System for You* (Stationery Office, Dublin, 2001).
8. *Health Strategy*, op. cit., p. 31.
9. Hensey, op. cit., Chapters 1–4.
10. *The Health Services and their Further Development* (Stationery Office, Dublin, 1966), pp. 63–64.
11. Barrington, op. cit., p. 274.
12. Ibid., p. 284.
13. *The Health Services and their Further Development*, op. cit., p. 30.
14. *The General Practitioner in Ireland*, Report of the Consultative Council on General Medical Services (Stationery Office, Dublin, 1974), p. 45.
15. *Report of the Working Party on Prescribing and Dispensing in the General Medical Service* (Stationery Office, Dublin, 1974), p. 45.
16. *Report of the Working Party on the General Medical Service* (Stationery Office, Dublin, 1984).
17. *The Future Organisation of General Practice in Ireland: A Discussion Document* (Irish College of General Practitioners, Dublin, 1986), p. 34.
18. M. Boland, 'The Role of General Practice in a Developing Health Service', in J. Robins (ed.), *Reflections on Health: Commemorating Fifty Years of the Department of Health 1947–1997* (Department of Health, 1997), p. 43.
19. Deloitte and Touche, *Value for Money: Audit of the Irish Health System* (Department of Health and Children, 2001) p. 25.
20. Barrington, op. cit., pp. 120–121.
21. *Outline of the Future Hospital System, Report of the Consultative Council on the General Hospital Service* (Stationery Office, Dublin, 1968).
22. *Irish Times*, 21 October, 1975.
23. *Action Plan for National Reconstruction*: Fianna Fáil Manifesto for General Election, 1977, p. 25.
24. Comhairle na nOspidéal, *2nd Report January 1975–December 1978* (Dublin, 1978), p. 24.
25. P. McQuillan, 'What Should We Provide? Service Emphasis to Achieve Objectives'. Paper presented at Conference on Health in the 1990s (Association of Health Boards in Ireland in association with the Institute of Public Administration, 1987), pp. 55–56.
26. *Report of the Commission of Inquiry on Mental Illness* (Stationery Office, Dublin, 1966), p. xv.
27. *The Irish Psychiatric Hospital Census, 1981* (Medico-Social Research Board, Dublin, 1983), pp. 11–12.
28. *The Psychiatric Services: Planning for the Future* (Stationery Office, Dublin, 1984).
29. *Green Paper on Mental Health* (Stationery Office, Dublin, 1992) p. 14.
30. *The Health Strategy: Quality and Fairness* (Stationery Office, Dublin, 2001).
31. *Report of the Inspector of Mental Hospitals 2001* (Stationery Office, Dublin, 2001), p. 4.
32. *Health Statistics 2002*, op. cit., p. 106.
33. *Report of the Commission on Health Funding* (Stationery Office, Dublin, 1989) p. 112.
34. *Programme for Social and Economic Progress* (Stationery Office, Dublin, 1991), p. 28.
35. *Health Strategy*, op. cit., p. 75.

36. Amárach Consulting, *The Private Health Insurance Market in Ireland* (The Health Insurance Authority, 2003) p. 4.
37. White Paper: *Private Health Insurance* (Stationery Office, Dublin, 1999), p. 73.
38. Ibid., p. 8.
39. Maev-Ann Wren, 'An Unhealthy State', *Irish Times*, 2–6 October, 2000.
40. Society of St Vincent de Paul, *Health Inequalities and Poverty*, 2001.
41. *Report of the Commission on Health Funding*, op. cit., p. 15.
42. L. Joyce and C. Ham, 'Enabling Managers to Manage: Health Care Reform in Ireland', *Administration* (Institute of Public Administration, Dublin, Vol. 38, No. 3, 1990), p. 227.
43. NESC Report No. 89, *A Strategy for the Nineties: Economic Stability and Structural Change* (Stationery Office, Dublin, 1990), pp. 285–286.
44. *Health Service News* (Institute of Public Administration, Dublin), Vol. 2, No. 2, May 1990, pp. 4–5.
45. Address by Dr Rory O'Hanlon, TD, Minister for Health, at the launch of the Report of the Dublin Hospital Initiative Group and the announcement of the reorganisation of health services, 18 September 1991.
46. Deloitte and Touche, op. cit., p. 7.
47. *Health: The Wider Dimensions* (Department of Health, 1986), p. 35.
48. Deloitte and Touche, op. cit., p. 8.
49. *Audit of Structures and Functions in the Health System* (Stationery Office, Dublin, 2003).
50. *The Health Service Reform Programme* (Department of Health and Children, 2003), p. 4.

6

Welfare of Certain Groups

Introduction

The basic social services – housing, education, health and income maintenance – cater for needs that are common to all members of society. However, certain groups have special needs, and services over and above the basic ones have evolved to cater for these needs. Such groups include older people, children and persons with disabilities (both intellectual and physical/sensory). While these groups are catered for to some extent by the basic services, special provision is also required. Hence services such as residential care for children or sheltered employment for people with disabilities have been developed.

This chapter examines welfare services for older people, children, people with disabilities, and the Traveller community.

Older people

The term 'older people' is now regarded as acceptable terminology and has replaced terms such as 'elderly' and 'aged'. It is usual to classify those aged 65 or over as older people since this is the generally accepted age of retirement from employment. It is also the age used internationally for comparisons of the proportions of total populations who are older people.

A demographic feature common to most developed nations is the relatively high proportion of people aged 65 and over. This is mainly due to the reduction of mortality rates in infancy and childhood that has led to a considerable increase in life expectancy. The average life expectancy at birth in Ireland during the period 1925–1927 was 57.4 for males and 57.9 for females. By 1995–1997 these had increased to 73.0 and 78.6 respectively. In some European countries the proportionate increase in older people is associated with a declining birth rate and a consequent proportionate decline in the younger age groups. In Ireland, similarly, older people had formed an increasing proportion of the total population up to the 1950s. In 1841, the proportion was approximately 3 per cent, and by 1956 this had increased to 11.2 per cent. While the absolute number of older people has continued to increase, the percentage of such persons in the total population has remained relatively stable in the past few decades. By 1996 it was 11.5 per cent, only marginally higher than 40 years earlier (Table 6.1). This is largely explained by the general population increase over the same period.

Table 6.1: Number of persons aged 65 and over, 1926–1996

Year	Number	% of total population
1926	271,700	9.1
1936	286,684	9.6
1946	314,322	10.6
1956	315,063	11.2
1966	323,007	11.2
1971	329,819	11.1
1981	368,954	10.7
1991	394,830	11.4
1996	413,882	11.5

Source: Census of Population

The percentage of older people varies considerably between urban (defined as towns containing populations of 1,500 or over) and rural areas of the state. In general, western counties have a relatively high proportion of older people compared with other counties. One of the principal reasons for the relatively high proportion of older people in predominantly rural areas has been persistent migration. This migration has been selective in that members of the young adult age group have tended to migrate, leaving behind an unbalanced population structure with disproportionate numbers of older people.

A feature of the population of older people is the increasing proportion living alone. In 1966 there were 35,024 such persons, representing 10.8 per cent of all older people. By 1991 these figures had increased to 96,522 and 24.0 per cent respectively. Those living alone are acknowledged to constitute a vulnerable group with potentially high demands on health and welfare services.

Growing concern over the increasing numbers of older people and the inadequacy of existing services was recognised in 1965 with the appointment of an inter-departmental committee whose function was to examine and report on the general problems of the care of the aged and to make recommendations regarding the improvement and extension of services. The report, *The Care of the Aged*, was published in 1968. The recommendations of the report on improved services were, in the committee's view:

> based on the belief that it is better, and probably much cheaper, to help the aged to live in the community than to provide for them in hospitals or other institutions.[1]

The report reflected the prevailing and increasing emphasis on community as opposed to institutional care.

In 1986, Barry Desmond, TD, the Minister for Health, established a Working Party to review the existing health and welfare services for older people. The Working Party's report, *The Years Ahead: A Policy for the Elderly*, was published in 1988.

Services for older people may be considered under the two broad headings of community and institutional care.

Community services

The *Care of the Aged* report stressed the importance of providing adequate community support services. These would include income maintenance services, housing and general health and welfare services.

Income maintenance. There have been considerable improvements in the income maintenance system for older people over the last few decades. The main state income maintenance schemes are the contributory and non-contributory old age pensions. The former are paid to persons who have been in insurable employment and have made a sufficient number of contributions, while the latter are paid subject to a means test. The retirement pension, introduced in 1970, is also an insurance-based scheme and applies to persons who retire from insurable employment at age 65; at age 66 they can revert to the contributory old age pension. There has been a substantial increase in recipients of these pensions, with numbers reaching over one-quarter of a million in 2001 (Table 6.2). A notable feature of the pension population is the decline in the number of recipients of non-contributory pensions. This is due to the broadening of the social insurance base, and the numbers should decline further as a result of the extension of social insurance to the self-employed in 1988. In the past, this group would have had to resort to the old age non-contributory pension. In the 1970s the qualifying age for the old age pension was reduced from 70 to 66 years and the means test was eased. The effect of these measures led to an increase in the number of recipients.

Table 6.2: Number of recipients of old age and retirement pensions, 1966–2001

Pension	1966	1978	1996	2001
Old age contributory	49,556	61,838	67,988	94,871
Old age non-contributory	112,621	133,669	101,624	89,061
Retirement	-	29,585	69,740	80,326
Total	153,177	225,092	239,352	264,258

Several other improvements in the income maintenance system for older people have been introduced, such as the Living Alone Allowance (1977) and the Age Allowance. The report of the Commission on Social Welfare indicated that payments to older people were the highest of all social welfare groups and that they were closest to the minimally adequate income recommended by the Commision.[2] In a major survey, older people expressed the highest level of satisfaction of any group with their income position.[3] However, *The Years Ahead* pointed out that:

> the general improvement in the income position of the elderly hides wide differences in income among the elderly themselves. The incomes of the elderly span a spectrum from the very wealthy to the very poor.[4]

Housing. Older people have benefited from a general improvement in housing over the past few decades. One of the features of the older people population is that a very high percentage of them own their own dwellings. According to the 1991 census, approximately 80 per cent of older people were owner-occupiers. Since the 1970s, local authorities have allocated 10 per cent of new dwellings to older people and people with disabilities. In some years this figure was exceeded. More recently, the role of providing special housing for older people has been largely taken over by a growing number of voluntary housing associations (see

Chapter 3). These associations have provided housing schemes in urban areas and villages throughout the country.

While there are few older people in the private rented sector, most of those in the former rent-controlled dwellings were older people.[5] Following the abolition of rent control in 1982, their interests, such as security of tenure, have been provided for in legislation. A special rent allowance scheme was introduced to ensure that they would not experience financial hardship because of the abolition of rent control and the subsequent increase in rents (see Chapter 3).

Despite these improvements it is still likely, however, that some of the worst living conditions and lack of household amenities exist in dwellings occupied by older people.

Health and welfare services. A number of developments and improvements have occurred in the health and welfare services since the *Care of the Aged* report was published. These include the introduction of the choice-of-doctor scheme under the General Medical Services. A high proportion (estimated at 70 per cent of older people) have been in receipt of medical cards since the choice of doctor scheme was introduced in 1972. These give an entitlement to all basic health services free of charge. From July 2001 all persons aged 70 and over became entitled to a medical card irrespective of income. Domiciliary services for older people have also improved in recent decades. The Public Health Nursing Service, involving domiciliary visiting, was extended in the 1970s and this has been accompanied by the development of the home help service, meals on wheels and day care services for older people by health boards and voluntary organisations. The main beneficiaries of the home help service are older people living alone. Despite improvements in the community health and welfare services, *The Years Ahead* indicated that less progress had been made in relation to the expansion of dental services, provision of physiotherapy and chiropody, the development of a social work service for older people, and the boarding out of older people. In recommending that the home help service be improved, the report indicated that just over 9,400 of older people were in receipt of this service and that despite its importance in maintaining older people at home in a cost-effective way, the evidence suggested that the service was in fact contracting.

The Years Ahead indicated that the developments that had occurred have resulted in substantial improvements in services for older people that have reinforced their independence and their ability to live at home. It also makes the point that the majority of older people have an adequate income, own their own homes, are active and independent and express considerable satisfaction with their lives. *The Years Ahead* classified the population of older people as follows:

Independent: 78 per cent
Dependent older people at home: 17 per cent
In long-term care: 5 per cent

Institutional services
When the *Care of the Aged* report was published in 1968 a substantial number of older people were in long-term care in county homes, some of which originated as Poor Law workhouses and which catered for all categories of persons with very little assessment of their needs. In effect, they were catch-all institutions catering for a wide variety of older people. The number of patients in these county homes, now referred to as geriatric hospitals, has declined and the accommodation and general standards have been improved. In line with the recommendation in the *Care of the Aged* report, a number of welfare homes were built for older people who did not need full-time care in hospital but who could not live independently on their own at home. *The Years Ahead* indicated that:

> although the county homes have become geriatric hospitals, too much of the atmosphere of the older institution survives in some centres.[6]

Extended care of older people is now provided in a variety of settings – health board geriatric hospitals and homes, district hospitals and welfare homes, voluntary hospitals, and voluntary and private nursing homes. Since the early 1980s there has been a decrease in the number of beds in health board hospitals and homes and a substantial increase in voluntary and private nursing home beds. The growth in nursing homes has been most apparent in the Dublin area where about half of all patients in private nursing homes are concentrated. The majority of the older people in extended care are chronically ill but a significant proportion of them are in care for social reasons.

The Years Ahead recommended that existing geriatric hospitals/ homes, long-stay district hospitals and welfare homes be developed, where appropriate, as community hospitals, i.e. hospitals which would provide a range of services including assessment, rehabilitation, convalescent care, day care, and respite care for relatives. In the larger urban areas, particularly Dublin, the report acknowledged that community hospitals would have to be purpose-built.

The Years Ahead expressed concern about the general level of standards in private and voluntary nursing homes, the relationship between health boards and these homes, and the manner in which they were subvented. Notwithstanding existing legislative safeguards, it recommended that further measures should be adopted such as the introduction of a licensing system and the establishment of an independent inspectorate. The Health (Nursing Homes) Act, 1990 was introduced in response to the needs identified in *The Years Ahead*. The Act provided for the registration and inspection of homes, the introduction of regulations relating to the standards of care and reform of the existing system of subvention to these homes.

Co-ordination
The key to the improved provision of services to older people is co-ordination. In this context *The Years Ahead* recommended the appointment of a district liaison nurse who would co-ordinate services in districts serving up to 30,000 people. It also envisaged the establishment of district teams made up of representatives of the different service providers (e.g. housing, health services). In each health board community care area (made up of several districts) there would be a full-time health official with a qualification as a community physician.

The recommendations of *The Years Ahead* implied the blurring of the traditional distinction between community and institutional services for older people. The model recommended was a continuum of care that is both flexible and responsible and in which residential care complements the supporting care in the community and the family.

The National Council on Ageing and Older People, established by government (as the National Council for the Aged) in 1981, is an advisory body to the Minister for Health on all aspects of ageing and the welfare of older people. It has produced a number of excellent reports on these issues. The Council undertook a review of implementation of recommendations in *The Years Ahead*. The review was highly critical of the lack of progress.[7] It noted that no legislative framework had been established for the development of services, that no agency had taken a lead role in ensuring that recommendations were implemented, that there was considerable regional variation in the implementation status of recommendations and that a new blueprint for the future development policy was required. Ironically, the review pointed out that the only piece of legislation introduced since *The Years Ahead*, i.e. the Health (Nursing Homes) Act, 1990, had led to a growth in institutional rather than community-based care. By contrast the discretionary but essential services such as the home help service lack a legislative base.

The *Health Strategy* (2001) acknowledged that further significant developments were required to meet the demands of the growing population of older people. It indicated that the main gaps in service provision related to:

- community-support services (e.g. paramedic services, community nursing services, health promotion, home help service, day care)
- acute hospitals (e.g. shortages in assessment and rehabilitation beds and day hospital facilities)
- long-stay places (e.g. need for additional community nursing units).[8]

Among the actions outlined in the *Health Strategy* were the provision of additional day centre places, 1,370 additional assessment and rehabilitation beds, 800 additional extended care/community nursing unit places per annum over seven years.

While various projections differ, they all indicate a further increase in the population of older people, with implications for the provision of health and welfare services for this group.

Child care services
This section is concerned with those children who, for whatever reason, are not receiving adequate care and protection at home.

Up to the early 1970s the main statutory means of dealing with these children was to place them in residential care, i.e. in industrial schools or reformatories. Industrial schools dated from 1858 and were designed to cater for young children, while the reformatories, which originated in 1868, were for older delinquent children. These institutions were generally run by religious orders.

In 1970 a report on industrial and reformatory schools (usually referred to as the *Kennedy Report* after the chairman, District Justice Eileen Kennedy) was published. The key recommendation of this report was that:

> The whole aim of the child care system should be geared towards the prevention of family breakdown and the problems consequent on it. The committal or admission of children to residential care should be considered only when there is no satisfactory alternative.[9]

In 1980 the *Report of the Task Force on Child Care Services* was published. This report had its origins in 1974 following a government decision to allocate the main responsibility in relation to child care to the Minister for Health. The Minister established the Task Force to make recommendations on the extension and improvement of services for deprived children and to draw up a Child Care Bill. The Task Force report also emphasised that as far as possible deprived children should be catered for in a family or community setting rather than residential care.

A number of developments have occurred in relation to child care over the past few decades.[10] These are examined under services, administration and legislation.

Services
The philosophy underlined in the Kennedy and Task Force reports has been reflected in policy. The numbers in residential care have fallen and there has been an increased emphasis on family support services. In 1968/69 there were 4,834 children in care. Of these, three-quarters were in residential care and one-quarter in foster care. Within a decade or so these proportions were reversed. In 2000 there were 4,424 children in care. Of these, three-quarters (76.5 per cent) were in foster care, 14.4 per cent were in residential care and the remainder were being provided for by other arrangements. It is interesting to note that the number of children in care has not declined dramatically since the Kennedy report.

With the establishment of health boards, social workers were employed under the Community Care Programme. Their primary focus is child care and child centred family case work with an emphasis on keeping families together in their own homes as far as possible rather than resorting to alternative care. Where this is not possible, the preferred options are adoption or placement with foster parents, with residential care as a last resort.

Many of the industrial and reformatory schools have been closed since the early 1970s, partly in response to the development of community services and in some instances because the religious orders involved decided, sometimes because of their own declining numbers, to opt out of this type of service. The residential centres now are based on group homes rather than the traditional large institutions. The terms 'residential home' and 'special school' have replaced those of industrial and reformatory schools respectively since the early 1970s. The funding of these homes is on a budget basis since 1984 as compared with the capitation system of the past. Furthermore, special courses have been provided for child care workers since the early 1970s. These residential centres are now subject to inspection by the Social Services Inspectorate (see later section).

The Kennedy Report had recommended that the Department of Health (rather than the Department of Education) should be responsible for all residential care facilities. This did not happen until 1982, but the Department of Education has retained responsibility for some special schools.

Administration

The Kennedy Report and the Task Force Report referred to the fact that administrative responsibility for child care services was divided between three government departments – Health, Justice, and Education. Thus, for example, the Department of Health was responsible for personal and social services, while the Department of Justice administered the adoption service and juvenile justice system, and the Department of Education was responsible for the industrial and reformatory schools. Despite the fact that responsibility for developing child care services was assigned to the Department of Health in 1974, administrative responsibility still rests with three departments, though their respective roles have changed somewhat. As already mentioned, for example, the Department of Education and Science now has responsibility for a small number of special schools. The adoption service, formerly under the Department of Justice, was transferred to the Department of Health in 1983.

Both the Kennedy Report and the Task Force Report recommended that the Department of Health should have overall responsibility for all child services and the Task Force Report recommended that a child care authority be established at regional level. Both reports also recommended the establishment of an independent advisory body – the National Children's Council. In order to emphasise its lead role and increased responsibility in relation to child care services, the Department of Health was renamed the Department of Health and Children in 1997. While the child care authorities were not established, a National Children's Office and a National Children's Advisory Council were established in 2001 (see later section).

Legislation

Until recently, the main legislation governing the child care system was the Children Act, 1908. The Kennedy Report had recommended the introduction of a composite children's Act and the terms of reference of the Task Force included the preparation of a new Children's Bill. The Task Force did not prepare this Bill.

Child Care Act, 1991. In 1988 a Child Care Bill was introduced in the Dáil and, following many amendments, was eventually enacted in 1991. The Act has been described as 'a watershed in child care policy in Ireland'.[11] Its purpose was to update the law in relation to the care of children, particularly children who have been assaulted, ill-treated, neglected or sexually abused or who are at risk. Among the main provisions of the Act were the following:

• the placing of a statutory duty on health boards to promote the welfare of children (up to age 18) who are not receiving adequate care and protection
• strengthening the power of health boards to provide child care and family support services
• improved procedures to facilitate immediate intervention where children are in serious danger
• revised provisions for the registration and inspection of residential centres and for the inspection and supervision of pre-school services.

The provisions of the Child Care Act, 1991 were implemented on a phased basis over several years. Incidents of high-profile cases of child abuse (see later section) hastened the implementation:

The Act was not fully implemented until December 1996. The delay was not only due to lack of staff but also had its roots in political inertia. It took three child sexual abuse cases, the 'X' case in 1992, the Kilkenny Incest case in 1993 and the Kelly Fitzgerald case in 1994, to raise public awareness and to finally motivate the government to fully implement the Act.[12]

The Adoption Act, 1988 introduced some limited reforms in that area and the Status of Children Act, 1987 abolished the legal concept of illegitimacy.

The Children Act, 2001. The Children Act, 2001 replaced the Children Act, 1908 and is based on the principle that detention of children should only be used as a last resort. The Act was the result of co-operation between three government departments – Justice, Equality and Law Reform; Health and Children; Education and Science. Implementation of the Act will be overseen by the Department of Health and Children. The Act involves a total overhaul of the juvenile justice system and provides a new legal basis for dealing with children who have behavioural difficulties and children who are offenders. Some of the key sections of the Act are:

- raising the age of criminal responsibility from 7 to 12 years
- the introduction of family conferences to enable children and their families agree on an action plan for the child
- the use of restorative justice where a child offender can face and apologise to a victim
- placing the Garda Diversion Programme on a statutory basis.

Provisions of the Children Act, 2001 will be phased in over a five-year period.

The Special Residential Services Board, provided for in the Act, was established on an administrative basis in April 2000 to co-ordinate special residential services for children on whom detention orders have been imposed or in respect of whom special care orders have been made. These residential services are special schools under the Department of Education and Science and special care units operated by health boards.

The Garda Diversion Programme was initiated in 1963 as the juvenile liaison officer scheme. Its principal aim is to divert young persons from becoming involved in anti-social and/or criminal activity. Under the Programme, if certain criteria are met, a juvenile offender may be cautioned as an alternative to prosecution. In recent years, the age limit for inclusion in the programme was increased from 17 to 18 years. The total number included in the Programme between 1963 and 2001 was 127,853, of which 78 per cent were male.[13] Juvenile offenders admitted to the programme may be cautioned in an informal or formal manner. Where the act committed is of a minor nature, an informal caution is administered by the local Juvenile Liaison Officer, normally at the offender's home. Where the act is more serious, a formal caution is administered by the local District Officer (Superintendent) at a Garda Station in the presence of parents or guardians. Juvenile Liaison Officers take an active interest in youth and other clubs in the community and part of their role is to give talks in schools and other organisations on a range of topics of interest to young people.

There has been considerable improvement in the quality and level of services provided for deprived children since the Kennedy Report. A primary emphasis in child care services since the early 1990s has been on the protection and care of children who are at risk. More recently the focus has shifted to a more preventive approach to child welfare involving support to families and individual children in order to avoid more serious intervention at a later stage. There is now a strong emphasis on preventive measures and early intervention programmes. In this context, a range of services are provided and funded by health boards. These include day nursery provision, neighbourhood youth projects, family support projects and family centres. Furthermore, as already noted in Chapter 4, the Department of Education and Science has targeted children in areas of disadvantage through various programmes.

Child abuse
Since the early 1990s there has been concern about the increased incidence of reported child abuse cases and this has been heightened by a number of high profile cases such as the Kilkenny Incest case (1993). Following this case a number of other instances of sexual or physical abuse of children came to light.

Many of the reported abuses took place in former residential care centres such as industrial schools, while others occurred in ordinary day schools or in the community or home. This led to the drawing-up of guidelines for staff in residential centres and there was a protracted controversy on mandatory reporting of child sex abuse.

Some of the religious orders that had run residential care centres for children issued public apologies. In 1996 the Catholic hierarchy produced a framework for responding to child sexual abuse by priests and religious. In 1997 the Conference of Religious in Ireland established a telephone helpline, Faoiseamh, for those who had been abused in care and in 1998 it received 1,000 calls; by 1999 the number had risen to 5,000.

In 1999, the Department of Health and Children published *Children First: National Guidelines for the Protection and Welfare of Children*. The guidelines were intended to support and guide health professionals, teachers, members of An Garda Síochána and others involved in sporting, cultural, community and voluntary organisations who come in regular contact with children.

The three-part documentary series *States of Fear* on RTÉ in April/May 1999 highlighted the abuse of children in former industrial and reformatory schools.[14] This series generated considerable controversy and public concern and was to have a considerable impact on subsequent policy. The Taoiseach, Bertie Ahern, TD, made a public apology in the Dáil on 11 May 1999, the date of the transmission of the third part of the series, to those who had suffered abuse in institutions:

> On behalf of the state and all its citizens, the government wishes to make a sincere and long overdue apology to the victims of childhood abuse for our collective failure to intervene, to detect their pain, to come to their rescue . . . I want to say to them that they were gravely wronged, and that we must do all we can now to overcome the lasting effects of their ordeal.

A Commission to Inquire into Child Abuse (the Laffoy Commission) was established by legislation in 2000 and held its first public sitting in June 2000. The principal functions of the Commission are to listen to persons who have suffered abuse in childhood in institutions, to conduct an inquiry into abuse of children in institutions and to find out why it occurred and who was responsible. In its interim report of May 2001 the Commission indicated that certain legal issues raised had delayed its work, i.e. a legal expenses scheme and the establishment of a compensation-awarding body. It also indicated that it could not predict how long it would take to afford hearings to all persons who wished to be heard but that it would take longer than the two-year timeframe envisaged by the legislation and that it did not intend to make public any determinations or findings until after the inquiry.[15] By 2003 the Commission's work was continuing.

Arising from the Commission's work and related issues, the government established the Residential Institutions Redress Board under the Residential Institutions Redress Act, 2002 to provide a mechanism for financial compensation for victims of abuse. The work of this Board is separate from that of the Laffoy Commission. As part of an agreement with government, religious orders contributed €128 million (in the form of cash and property) to the compensation fund, with the state having to make up the balance. While the original estimate of total costs arising from claims was €400 million, the final cost may well substantially exceed this.

Against this background, the National Counselling Service was established on a countrywide basis by health boards in 2000 for adults who had experienced childhood abuse. In the first year, almost 2,000 people had sought counselling from this service.[16]

Social Services Inspectorate
In 1999 the Department of Health and Children established the Social Services Inspectorate as an independent body to inspect the social service functions of health boards. In the first phase of its work the Inspectorate is focusing on residential child care provided by health boards. Eventually, its role will encompass a wider range of services, e.g. residential care for older people and people with disabilities.

The Child Care Act, 1991 provides for registration and inspection by health boards of children's residential centres in the voluntary sector and by the Inspectorate in residential centres run by health boards. Since September 2001 all centres are inspected against the National Standards for the Inspection of Children's Residential Centres. Health boards send their inspection reports to the Inspectorate to ensure that equitable standards of inspection are maintained.

By 2001 there were 155 residential centres for children run by statutory agencies or the voluntary sector (as compared with approximately 100 when the Inspectorate was established in 1999). These are community-based children's residential centres, high support and special care units, special arrangements for sibling groups and special arrangements for individual children.

The term 'special arrangement' is provision for a child or children that is neither foster care nor an already established children's residential centre. The Inspectorate has expressed concern at the development of some of these arrangements.[17] The majority of new centres or special arrangements in recent years have been opened by health boards, reflecting the continual withdrawal of religious orders and voluntary committees from the provision of residential child care.[18] A report of each centre inspected is made available on the Inspectorate's website. The overall aim of the Inspectorate is to inspect social services against agreed standards and to support developments that will help these standards to be met.

From inspections carried out up to July 2001, the Inspectorate concluded:

> ... many of the standards for children's residential care are well met and work on improving others is ongoing. However, some standards are still not observed. Furthermore, the standards are applied unevenly across the country.[19]

National Children's Strategy
In November 2000 a National Children's Strategy, *Our Children – Their Lives*, was published. The main components of the strategy are:

- the establishment of an independent statutory body, a National Office for Children, to find solutions for problems, especially where these require the co-operation of several government departments
- an Ombudsman for children who will investigate complaints from the public and will promote good practice in children's services
- a National Children's Advisory Council that will involve children's representatives and representatives of the social partners and researchers.

The National Children's Office was established in 2001. Among its roles, the Office has been assigned lead responsibility for the full implementation of the Children Act, 2001.

The National Children's Advisory Council was established in 2001, with representatives of statutory and voluntary agencies, researchers, parents and children. It has an independent advisory role in relation to the implementation of the National Children's strategy.

The Ombudsman for Children Act, 2002 provided for the establishment of the Office of Ombudsman for Children by April 2004.

By 2003 the emphasis in relation to child welfare was very much on preventive measures and support services for families and children, a very different emphasis from several decades earlier when institutional care was considered the primary response.

People with disabilities

Within the past few decades a number of policy reports have been concerned with persons with disabilitites. These reflect a growing awareness of and concern for the rights of those with disabilities. Increasingly, the thrust of these reports has been on inclusion, i.e. providing the means for persons with disabilities to participate to the greatest extent possible in all aspects of life. This has been accompanied by an increasing emphasis on the rights of such persons and an emphasis on mainstreaming services. The *Health Strategy* (2001) states:

> The principle which underpins policy is to enable each individual with a disability to achieve his or her full potential and maximum independence, including living within the community as independently as possible.[20]

Definition and terminology

The Green Paper *Towards a Full Life* (1984) refers to handicap as:

> A disadvantage for a given individual resulting from an impairment or a disability that limits or prevents fulfillment of a role that is normal (depending on age, sex and social and cultural factors) for that individual.[21]

This definition covers a wide range of physical and intellectual disabilities.

Until the early 1990s the term 'handicap' was used widely to cover both physical and mental disabilities. The *Report of the Review Group, Needs and Abilities* (1990) recommended that the term 'mental handicap' should no longer be used.[22] It suggested 'intellectual disability' as a more appropriate term. Since then the term has gradually acquired acceptance and use. It is worth noting however that by 2003, this change of terminology had not gained general acceptance, even among statutory agencies, and the older terminology was still in use. At the 1998 annual general meeting of the National Association for the Mentally Handicapped of Ireland (NAMHI), an umbrella organisation with over 160 affiliated organisations throughout the country, a motion to alter the name of the organisation was defeated.

Two broad categories of disabilities are now distinguished:

- intellectual disability (formerly mental handicap)
- physical and sensory disability (to cover a wide variety of disabilities such as visual or hearing impairment, physical disabilities arising from congenital causes, accidents, chronic or long-term illness).

While there are issues common to the two categories, each also has particular concerns.

Numbers of persons with disabilities

A *NESC Report* (1980) had stressed the need for a register of people with disabilities as a prerequisite to the planning of services.[23] The Green Paper (1984) indicated that there was no comprehensive source of information on the number of persons with disabilities, and estimated the total number at 150,000.

Intellectual disabilities. The report *Needs and Abilities* (1990) highlighted the need for good quality information. This provided the impetus for the establishment of an intellectual disability database whose relevance and importance was also noted in other policy documents.[24] The national intellectual database was established in 1995. Information from the database gives a better basis for providing services. In 2000 there were 26,760 persons registered on the database.[25]

Physical and sensory disabilities. The need for reliable information on the health service needs of persons with physical and/or sensory disability was also referred to in policy documents.[26] Arising from this a committee was established in 1998 to prepare detailed proposals for the development of a national database. By 2003 work was still in progress on the compilation of the physical and sensory disabilities database.

Services for people with disabilities

A range of services exists for people with disabilities. It is not possible to deal with all of these and only the more salient are examined for each of the two main categories, together with trends in the provision of services and some specific issues such as education, training, income maintenance and legislative safeguards.

The Green Paper (1984) stated:

> There is no disagreement about the philosophy which should underpin the policies and progress for disabled people. The ultimate objective is to equip disabled people to realise their full potential and to participate to the greatest extent possible in the life of the community.[27]

This philosophy has been reiterated in subsequent policy documents.

Despite advances in medical care and community support services, it is recognised that a significant number of persons with disabilities, especially the intellectually disabled, will require long-term care. During the 1970s the main emphasis in the intellectual disability services was on the development of residential facilities. These have been provided largely by voluntary organisations, especially religious orders, and much of the capital for this development came from the Department of Health and health boards.[28] From the 1980s, however, the emphasis was on providing a comprehensive network of services with a continuum of care. This would include sheltered housing, hostel accommodation, short-term residential care and a range of community support services.

Services for the physical and sensory disabled

The health boards are responsible for a range of services for people with physical and sensory disabilities, e.g. residential care and rehabilitative training. The boards either provide these directly or arrange for them to be provided by voluntary and private organisations.

The main thrust of the report of the review group, *Towards an Independent Future* (1996), was the development of services to enable people with a physical or sensory disability to live as independently as possible in the community. It recommended that priority be given to the provision of more day care, respite care, nursing and therapy services, personal assistants and residential accommodation to achieve this goal.[29]

While the state's involvement in the provision of services is considerable and has been growing in recent decades, voluntary organisations have made, and continue to make, substantial contributions in this area. There are several separate organisations specifically concerned with different types of disabilities, e.g. cerebral palsy, spina bifida, multiple sclerosis. Over 200 of these organisations are affiliated to the Disability Federation of Ireland (formerly the Union of Voluntary Organisations for the Handicapped), an umbrella body which acts as an advocate for the voluntary disability sector.

Services for the intellectually disabled
The main initiative for the provision of services for the intellectually disabled has come from voluntary organisations including religious orders, and parents and friends associations. These organisations provide a range of services, e.g. residential care, training and day care centres, and specialist services. Approximately 160 organisations are affiliated to the National Association for the Mentally Handicapped of Ireland (NAMHI), which promotes development of services based on individual need in the least restrictive environment. It also provides information and advice.

The current emphasis in policy on intellectual disability is the development of community-based alternatives to institutional care. At present persons with intellectual disability are catered for in different settings, i.e. psychiatric hospitals, special residential centres, hostels and supervised lodgings, and there is an increasing emphasis on day care provision. *Needs and Abilities* (1990) estimated that there were over 11,000 persons in residential, day care and training centres and that, at the minimum, a further 600 residential and 1,000 day places were required to cater for accumulated and emerging needs, transfer from inappropriate settings (such as psychiatric hospitals) and further support services. It recommended that these additional places be provided over four years commencing in 1990.[30] These targets were achieved by 1992.

While the number of places in residential care and day centres has grown considerably over the past decade or so, the demand for such places continues. This is due to a number of factors such as improved medical technology and treatment and longer life expectancy of those with intellectual disability. It is an area of special concern for ageing parents.

Statistics from the *Annual Report of the National Intellectual Disability Database* for 2000 indicated that of a total of 26,760 persons registered, 89.8 per cent (23,769 persons) were in receipt of services, 1.8 per cent (475 persons) were not receiving a service and 8.4 per cent (2,250 persons) did not have current service requirements.[31] The report also provided a needs assessment for the period 2001–2005 dealing with three categories, i.e. unmet need, service change and the needs of those resident in psychiatric hospitals (806 in 2000) who require to be transferred out of the psychiatric services to more appropriate settings.

Education. The NESC Report (1980) recommended that as far as possible children with disabilities should be educated with other children.[32] There are special classes attached to ordinary schools and a number of special schools especially for children with intellectual disability. The official policy of the Department of Education and Science is now one of integration of children with disabilities, where this is possible, while retaining the option of segregation where necessary. The report of the *Primary Education Review Body* (1990) commented that there were limits to the degree of integration possible and that, in many instances, partial integration may be the only feasible option.[33]

Section 9 of the Education Act, 1998 provides that recognised schools shall provide education to students which is appropriate to their abilities and needs and they should use available resources to ensure that the educational needs of all students, including those with a disability or other special educational needs, are identified and provided for.

In 2002 an Education for Persons with Disabilities Bill was published. Its provisions are designed to ensure that, to the greatest extent practicable, people with disabilities shall have the same right to avail of, and benefit from, appropriate education, as do their peers who do not have disabilities. The Bill also provides for the establishment of an independent National Council for Special Education that would assume responsibility for special education in place of the Department of Education and Science. This Bill had arisen out of controversy surrounding a landmark legal case in 2000 in which the rights of a young adult, Jamie Sinnott (then aged 23), to an education had been upheld by the

High Court. The government appealed the decision in 2001 to the Supreme Court which ruled that the state was only obliged to provide education up to age 18.

Training and employment. Since the mid-1970s there has been increased emphasis on the training and employment of disabled persons. The Report on *Training and Employing the Handicapped* (1975) stated:

> A great many handicapped persons are willing and able to work. Some require special training, others need special conditions of employment. The important thing is that no one should be denied the opportunity to work even if it requires a special effort by society to enable them to do so.[34]

The report recommended the establishment of community workshops with the dual function of training and sheltered employment. These workshops were developed by the Rehab Group (established in 1949 as an independent voluntary body with training facilities in centres throughout the country), health boards and other voluntary organisations. They were intended to prepare persons with various disabilities for open employment while at the same time providing long-term sheltered employment for those who could achieve a reasonable level of production. The availability of finance from the European Social Fund has been an added stimulus to the provision of training for persons with disabilities. Funding from this source was phased out in the late 1990s and ceased in 2000.

In 1977 the government introduced a quota scheme for the public service with a target of 3 per cent of jobs for disabled persons by the end of 1982. Two decades later this target had been reached in the civil service but not in the broader public service.[35] *The Report of the Commission on the Status of People with Disabilities* recommended that the 3 per cent quota be fully attained within three years (i.e. by 1999). The lack of commitment and progress in this area is exemplified by the fact that there is no annual publication of compliance with the quota.[36]

In line with a recommendation in the *Report of the Commission on the Status of People with Disabilities* on mainstreaming services, the Department of Enterprise, Trade and Employment was assigned overall responsibility for vocational training and employment needs of people with disabilities in 2000. This is carried out by FÁS, the Training and Employment Authority, which is under the aegis of that department. FÁS has taken over some of the functions of the former National Rehabilitation Board. Responsibility for foundation training such as life skills programmes and sheltered occupational services for persons in the health services' day care programmes continues to belong to the Department of Health and Children. This rehabilitative training is carried out in a variety of settings by health boards and voluntary organisations throughout the country.

Income maintenance

At present the Department of Social and Family Affairs and the Department of Health and Children administer income maintenance payments for persons with disabilities. Thus, the Department of Social and Family Affairs administers the blind pension, and health boards a blind welfare allowance. A NESC Report (1980) argued that only one agency should administer payments.[37] The Green Paper was also critical of the lack of uniformity in the existing payments system and, in recommending that the disabled person's maintenance allowance (DPMA) be transferred to the Department of Social and Family Affairs, argued that the centralisation of administration would lead to a more consistent approach.[38] The *Report of the Commission on Social Welfare* also commented on the duplication of functions between the two government departments and recommended that, in general, income maintenance payments should be the responsibility of the Department of Social and Family Affairs.[39] The *Report of the Commission on the Status of People with Disabilities* (1996) recommended that a unified scheme, a non-means tested disability pension, be introduced to replace the three main existing payments (invalidity pension, blind pension and DPMA), to provide support for people with disabilities who are incapable of work in the long term due to disability.[40] However, it is most unlikely that a non-means tested disability pension will be introduced.[41]

Prior to 1996, health boards administered the disabled person's maintenance allowance (DPMA), in effect a long-term sickness scheme, while the Department of Social Welfare (as it then was) administered the insurance-based disability benefit and invalidity pension. Since 1996 the Department has assumed responsibility for the DPMA, which has been renamed disability allowance.

Access and mobility

The Green Paper (1984) pointed out that, with few exceptions, the physical surroundings have been designed for the active and healthy, with little regard for the special needs of persons with disabilities, older people, expectant mothers and others whose mobility is impaired or underdeveloped. It suggested that these problems arose more from insufficient understanding and awareness than from deliberate policy. There is now a greater awareness of the need to provide a barrier-free environment. From the early 1980s the Office of Public Works has been directed to ensure that all new buildings are fully accessible to people with disabilities and to arrange modification and adaptation of existing buildings where possible. The Green Paper acknowledged that making the public transport system accessible was beset with difficulties, both practical and financial.

Commission on the Status of People with Disabilities

In 1993 a Commission on the Status of People with Disabilities was established and its main term of reference was:

> To advise the government on practical measures to ensure that people with a disability can exercise their rights to participate, to the fullest extent of their potential, in economic, social and cultural life.

The report of the Commission, *A Strategy for Equality*, was published in 1996. Throughout the report there is a strong emphasis on the rights of people with disabilities and it noted that:

> People with disabilities are the neglected citizens of Ireland. On the eve of the twenty-first century, many of them suffer intolerable conditions because of outdated social and economic policies and unthinking public attitudes ... Public attitudes towards disability are still based on charity rather than on rights, and the odds are stacked against people with disabilities at every turn. Whether their status is looked at in terms of economics, information, education, mobility, or housing they are seen to be treated as second-class citizens.[42]

The Commission estimated that there were 360,000 people with a disability and argued that the problems encountered by them did not centre on physical pain or discomfort. Instead, frustration arose from the sense that people with disabilities were being put in a position of having to deal with a myriad of social barriers in addition to their disabling conditions. The Commission proposed a range of legislative and other changes to improve and promote the rights of people with disabilities. In particular it recommended an amendment to the Constitution to guarantee the right of equality and prohibit discrimination. The Commission, while acknowledging that the report was ambitious, made over 400 recommendations which, when implemented, 'should change the world for many people with disabilities, including their families and carers'. The Commission also recommended the introduction of a Disability Act. The *Irish Times* in commenting on the report stated:

> In a society shot through with barriers to disabled people made up more often of apathy, insolence and ignorance than of hostility – a constitutional amendment would provide the disability movement with a powerful weapon with which to attack those barriers. Even in the absence of a constitutional amendment, a Disabilities Act, as recommended by the commission, could do much to tackle the pervasive discrimination which is the lot of those with disabilities.[43]

The government's commitment to implementing the recommendations of the report was reflected in the establishment of an inter-departmental task force and a monitoring body.

In January 1997, a permanent Council for the Status of People with Disabilities was established. Renamed People with Disabilities in Ireland in 2000, it is a representative structure through which people with disabilities can influence the decision-making process on matters of concern to them.

There is also the Forum of People with Disabilities, a rights-based organisation that works to promote the choices, rights and identity of people with disabilities.

Legislative safeguards

The Green Paper (1984) noted that while other countries had legislation to safeguard the rights of disabled persons, it would need to be demonstrated clearly here that such measures would contribute in a practical way to an improvement in their conditions. It further stated:

> The most important thing which any disadvantaged minority needs is goodwill and understanding. The government are convinced that the promotion of the rights of disabled people can be best achieved by general agreement rather than by measures of compulsion.[44]

This conclusion was rejected by some organisations. For example, the Union of Voluntary Organisations for the Handicapped (later renamed Disability Federation of Ireland), in its response to the Green paper, argued that a basic framework of rights should be set out in a Rights of Persons with Disabilities Act.[45] Subsequently, the case for legislation gathered momentum. As already noted, the *Report of the Commission on the Status of People with Disabilities* recommended the introduction of a Disability Act which would set out the rights of people with disabilities together with a means of redress for those whose rights are denied.

In February 2002 a Disabilities Bill designed to provide a framework for the assessment of need and provision of services for people with disabilities was withdrawn by government in the face of mounting criticism from voluntary organisations and opposition political parties. Various provisions of the Bill had been critcised. For example, it envisaged a time scale ranging from 5 to 13 years in seeking to make transport, buildings and services accessible. Above all, the proposed legislation did not guarantee rights and also prohibited persons with disabilities from taking civil actions against the state. Even the statutory National Disability Authority (see next section) had called for changes to the Bill. Of the Bill the *Irish Times* commented:

> . . . it has been withdrawn as a result of intense political and public pressure. Criticisms of the Bill centred on the long delays before many of its provisions would take effect; the fact that the rights of the disabled would not be legally enforceable and a lack of clarity about what would be required of service providers . . . this Bill is effectively dead.[46]

Subsequent to the withdrawal of the Bill a consultative process was initiated in order to arrive at a consensus on the provisions of legislation.

Disability is one of the nine grounds under which discrimination is prohibited under the Employment Equality Act, 1998 and the Equal Status Act, 2000 (see Chapter 9).

National Disability Authority
The *Report of the Commission on the Status of People with Disabilities* recommended the establishment of a National Disability Authority to 'monitor the impact of public policy and services on people with a disability'. The National Disability Authority was established in 2000 as a statutory body by the National Disability Authority Act, 1999. It has subsumed some of the functions of the former National Rehabilitation Board and comes under the aegis

of the Department of Justice, Equality and Law Reform. Its aim is to ensure that the rights and entitlements of people with disabilities are protected.

Within its broad remit, the Authority will act as a central national body to assist in the co-ordination and development of disability policy; it will undertake research and develop statistical information for the planning, delivery and monitoring of disability programmes and services.

The Traveller community

A report on travelling people by the Economic and Social Research Institute in1986 commented:

> The central conclusion of this study is an inescapable one: the circumstances of the Irish travelling people are intolerable. No humane and decent society, once made aware of such circumstances, could permit them to persist.[47]

This minority group is frequently the subject of popular criticism, prejudice and discrimination. Over the past few decades the number of travelling families has risen considerably and their general lifestyle has undergone considerable change. Up to the 1950s travellers were essentially rural-based but since then there has been a gradual shift to urban areas as the basis of their activities in rural areas was undermined.

There have been three major official reports on travellers – *Report of the Commission on Itinerancy* (1963), *Report of the Travelling People Review Body* (1983) and *Report of the Task Force on the Travelling Community* (1995). Some of the issues highlighted in these reports and subsequent developments are examined here.

Commission on Itinerancy and Review Body
Definition. The Commission on Itinerancy defined an itinerant as:

> A person who had no fixed place of abode and habitually wandered from place to place but excluding travelling show people and travelling entertainers.[48]

The Review Body pointed out that such a definition was inadequate because so many travellers had a permanent place to live. It used the term 'traveller' to designate membership of an identifiable group, pointing out that abandonment of the nomadic way of life does not automatically entail the renunciation of the traveller ethic or integration with the settled community.[49] The term 'traveller' is the accepted one among travellers themselves.

Origins. The Commission stated that the existence of travellers in Ireland is ascribed to many causes, e.g. dispossession in various plantations, descendants of journeying craftsmen, eviction, and famine. Some may be descendants of early poets and bards and craftsmen such as smiths and tanners. Others are likely to have originated in the period from the sixteenth to the nineteenth century when large numbers of peasants were either unable to meet their own subsistence needs or to pay the large rents demanded by landlords and were forced from the land. In addition, there may be other reasons why people adopted a nomadic lifestyle, e.g. as a result of personal social deviancy, such as alcoholism.[50]

Numbers. Censuses of travellers have been undertaken in various years, not always coinciding with the general census of population. More recently, as part of the accommodation programme, annual counts have taken place. Between 1960 and 2001 the number of traveller families has more than trebled, from 1,198 to 5,150 (see Table 6.3). One-quarter of traveller families now live in Dublin.

Health status. Both the Commission and the Review Body indicated that travellers have a much lower life expectancy than the population in general and that the ratio of infant and child deaths to all traveller deaths is very high. Some of this is accounted for by the type of accommodation used by travellers and the health hazards associated with living on the roadside.

In 1987 the Health Research Board carried out a study of the health status of travellers. Among the findings were the following:

- Only 2 per cent of travellers were aged 65 or over as compared with 10.7 per cent of the total population.
- Life expectancy for male and female travellers is 62 years and 65 years, compared with 72 and 77 years for males and females generally.
- Travellers have a two-and-a-half times greater chance of dying in a given year than settled people.
- The birth rate among travellers is over double the national rate, i.e. 34.9 per thousand as compared with 16.6.

The study concluded:

The picture which emerges of the travelling people in 1987 from this report is of a group who marry at a very young age and have many children. From before birth to old age they have high mortality rates, particularly from accidents, metabolic and congenital problems, but also from the other major causes of death. Female travellers have especially high mortality compared to settled women. Those members of the travelling community who do not live in houses, approximately 50 per cent, have even higher mortality ratios than housed travellers, especially females and particularly from accidents.[51]

The Review Body recommended that health boards should provide special care and advice for travellers in relation to the care of mothers and children, availability of immunisation services, the treatment of handicapping conditions in children, family planning, and should educate them as to the health hazards of caravans as permanent accommodation for a large family.

Education. The Commission on Itinerancy stated simply that almost all travellers were completely illiterate.[52] In 1960 only 160 children out of a total of 1,640 between the ages of 6 and 14 years were attending school. The Commission indicated that illiteracy accentuated the travellers' isolation from the settled population and in itself made all the more difficult any attempt to change over to the settled way of life. By 1980 much progress had been made, with about 3,500 children attending school (about half the total) in special classes or special schools that had been established. The Review Body noted, however, that progress to second-level education was very rare and that there was little improvement in the educational standards of adults, of whom about 90 per cent were illiterate.[53]

The Fifth Report of the Committee to Monitor the Implementation of Government Policy on Travelling People (1990) noted that there were four special primary schools and 143 special classes for travellers operating in primary schools throughout the country. The Committee commented that new measures were required to improve the participation levels of travellers' children at post-primary level. By 1989 there were 27 special training centres throughout the country for young travellers. These centres, funded by FÁS and the Department of Education (through Vocational Education Committees), were established and operated with the involvement of the National Association of Training Centres for Travelling People.

Employment. While there are some self-employed travellers, the majority are in receipt of unemployment assistance payments and there are relatively few in formal employment. This is due to a number of factors, e.g. illiteracy, lack of skills, and prejudice among employers. Many travellers are involved in scrap collection, which the Review Body considered a valuable service to the community. It recommended that facilities be provided for this purpose near their housing, or in special centres for heavy scrap.[54]

Settlement and accommodation. The Commission on Itinerancy recommended that: 'The immediate objective should be to provide dwellings as soon as possible for all families who desire to settle'.[55]

The Commission also noted that an overwhelming majority was in favour of settling. The Review Body noted that nothing that had happened since 1963 had lessened the correctness of the Commission's assessment. The Review Body also noted that while progress had been made there also had been failures and 'the greatest failure has resulted from the relative inaction of some local authorities who are slow in implementing government policy'.[56] By 2001 there were almost as many families on the roadside as forty years earlier (Table 6.3). However, this is against a background of a substantial increase in the number of traveller families over this period.

The Review Body also noted that the majority wished to live in houses (either alongside the settled community or in group housing), a minority in caravans on authorised sites with sanitary

Table 6.3: Number of traveller families by type of accommodation 1960–2001*

Families	1960	1980	2001
Local authority housing*	56	1,210	2,941
Permanent halting sites	-	131	1,192
On the roadside	1,142**	1,149	1,017
Total	1,198	2,490	5,150

*   Includes families in local authority standard housing, local authority group housing, private houses assisted by the local authorities and housing provided by voluntary bodies assisted by local authorities.
**   Includes 60 families in motor trailers, 738 families in horsedrawn caravans and 335 families in tents.
Sources: Commission on Itinerancy (1963); Report of the Travelling People Review Body (1983); Reports of the National Traveller Accommodation Consultative Committee.

and other facilities, and a small number wanted to continue travelling but to have available authorised sites on which they could remain for as long as they wished. The settlement of travellers requires the commitment of local authority members and officials. Where they are favourable to the provision of housing or authorised sites they may come under intense pressure not only from the public (mostly residents) but also from industrial and commercial interests. This has frequently resulted in plans being modified or abandoned.

Relationships with settled community
Relationships between travellers and the settled population have been characterised by prejudice and discrimination on the one hand, and isolation on the other. The Review Body noted that:

> The general population of the country has very little detailed knowledge of travellers and the problems they face … fear of travellers is in large measure groundless, where there is irrefutable evidence that those who settle in houses usually create no special problems.[57]

The Review Body even considered the possibility of having special legislation enacted to outlaw discrimination against travellers but concluded, for various reasons, that this was not feasible.[58] What was not considered feasible in the early 1980s, however, was considered necessary over a decade later. Discrimination against members of the Traveller community is prohibited under the Employment Equality Act, 1998 and the Equal Status Act, 2000 (see Chapter 9).

Traveller representation
In the 1960s a number of voluntary organisations, usually settlement committees, were established. In 1969 the first Council of Itinerant Settlement was set up and in 1973 this became the National Council for Travelling People. Some of the organisations also began to focus on educational projects. There has been a significant change in recent years in that travellers have begun to organise themselves, become politically active and lobby for their rights.[59] They have also been represented on various groups, such as the National Council for Travelling People, the Review Body, the Monitoring Committee and, more recently, the Task Force on the Travelling Community. In 1990 the National Council for Travelling People voted to disband themselves. Arising from this

the Irish Travellers' Movement was subsequently established as a national network of organisations and individuals working with the traveller community. Pavee Point is a resource centre which aims to improve the quality of life and living circumstances of travellers. Representation by travellers on a variety of committees is now an established principle.

Task Force Report

In 1993 the government disbanded the Monitoring Committee and replaced it by a Task Force on the Travelling Community whose membership included traveller representatives. The *Task Force* published an interim report in January 1994 and its final report was published in June 1995. Unlike previous reports, that of the *Task Force* took the view that travellers were a group with a distinct culture and identity. The report identified policy strategies that reflected this.

On the issue of accommodation the report emphasised the need for transient sites and the importance of focusing on the way travellers use their living space. The report identified the need for a significant increase in accommodation and recommended the provision of 3,100 units to include 1,000 bays on transient sites, 1,200 bays on permanent sites and 900 houses in group housing schemes or standard housing estates. On education, the report focused on the need for an inter-cultural, anti-racist curriculum and, except in special circumstances, was strongly in favour of integration. On the traveller economy, the report also referred to the theme of culture and emphasised the distinctive contribution of traveller activities in recycling (especially scrap metal), trading and horse dealing.

In an addendum to the Task Force report a number of non-traveller members stated:

> Part of the conflict is also due to the failure of travellers and traveller organisations to recognise that today's society finds it difficult to accept a lower standard of conduct from a section of the community who consciously pursue a way of life which sets its members apart from ordinary citizens, appear to expect that their way of life takes precedence over that of settled persons, and which carries no responsibility towards the area in which they happen to reside.[60]

The *Task Force* report recommended traveller participation in the new structures necessary to implement its recommendations:

- a traveller accommodation agency
- a traveller education service
- a traveller health advisory committee.

The main purpose of the Housing (Traveller Accommodation) Act, 1998 was to provide a legislative framework within which the accommodation needs of travellers would be met in a reasonable period of time. The Act also provided for the establishment of The National Traveller Accommodation Consultative Committee on a statutory basis to advise the Minister for the Environment and Local Government on general matters concerning the accommodation for travellers and to oversee the implementation of traveller accommodation programmes. Under the Act a five-year programme of traveller accommodation was adopted in 2000 for implementation by local authorities. The Annual Report of the Committee for 2001 indicated that the number of traveller families living on the roadside had decreased for the second year in succession, from 1,207 in 1999 to 1,093 in 2000 and to 1,017 in 2001. It also indicated that the numbers would decrease considerably further as the local authorities progressed the implementation of their accommodation programmes.

A Traveller Health Advisory Committee was established in 1998 and was instrumental in the preparation of *Traveller Health: A National Strategy 2002–2005*, published in 2002. The strategy listed 122 actions to be taken to improve the health status of travellers and is to be reviewed annually by the Department of Health and Children in association with the Traveller Health Advisory Committee and health boards. The strategy acknowledged that: 'For a variety of reasons, the traveller population has experienced a level of health which falls short of that enjoyed by the general population'.[61]

The strategy also acknowledged that in the past, the health services have responded in a fragmented and often inappropriate manner to the special needs of travellers and that discrimination, on an individual and institutional level, is also a factor in the lack of an effective response to traveller health needs. It refers to one of the key targets set in the National Anti-Poverty Strategy (see Chapter 8) to reduce the gap in life expectancy between the traveller community and the general population by at least 10 per cent by 2007. It recognises that implementation of the strategy will be crucial in meeting this target.

While structures were established in relation to accommodation and health, no similar structure was established in education. The Department of Education and Science decided not to establish a traveller education service because it considered that services for travellers were already being delivered in an integrated manner by sections within the Department.[62]

The First Progress Report on the Task Force contained an indictment of the lack of improvement:

> About one-quarter of all traveller families continue to live their day-to-day lives in very poor conditions. Five years after the publication of the Task Force Report, there is a lack of real improvement on the ground. This and the daily reality of discrimination makes it very difficult for a large section of the traveller community to have faith in the promises contained within the recommendations of the Task Force Report ... It raises very serious questions both at home and abroad of our society and why we have been unable to make significant improvements in the quality of life for the traveller community.[63]

Notably, the progress report also stated that the views expressed in the quotation from the ESRI report at the beginning of this section were still relevant in 2000.

Notes
1. *Care of the Aged* (Stationery Office, Dublin, 1968) p. 13.
2. *Report of the Commission on Social Welfare* (Stationery Office, Dublin 1986), p. 191.
3. N. Fogarty, L. Ryan, J. Lee, *Irish Values and Attitudes* (Dominican Press, Dublin, 1984), p. 25.
4. *The Years Ahead: Policy for the Elderly* (Stationery Office, Dublin, 1988), p. 19.
5. See, for example, *Rent Tribunal, Annual Report and Accounts, 1985* (Stationery Office, Dublin, 1985), p. 8.
6. *The Years Ahead*, op. cit., p. 24.
7. *The Years Ahead Report: A Review of the Implementation of its Recommendations* (National Council on Ageing and Older People,1997), pp. 3–32.
8. *Quality and Fairness, A Health Strategy for You* (Stationery Office, Dublin, 2001) p. 149.
9. *Report on the Industrial and Reformatory Schools System* (Stationery Office, Dublin, 1970), p. 6.
10. See R. Gilligan, *Irish Child Care Services: Policy, Practice and Provision* (Institute of Public Administration, Dublin, 1991).
11. V. Richardson, 'Children and Social Policy' in S. Quin et al., *Contemporary Irish Social Policy* (University College Dublin Press, 1999), Chapter 8, p. 182.
12. Ibid. p. 183.
13. *Annual Report of An Garda Síochána 2001* (Stationery Office, Dublin, 2002) p. 105.

14. See also M. Raftery and E. O'Sullivan, *Suffer Little Children, The Inside Story of Ireland's Industrial Schools* (New Island Books, Dublin, 1999). This book expands on many areas dealt with by the *States of Fear* series.

15. Commission to Inquire into Child Abuse, *Interim Report, May 2001*, pp. 2, 24.

16. *First Report: The National Counselling Service for Adults who have experienced childhood abuse* (The Health Boards Executive, 2002), p. 32.

17. *Annual Report 2001, Social Services Inspectorate*, pp. 13–14.

18. Ibid. pp. 12,16.

19. Ibid. p. 44.

20. *Health Strategy*, op. cit., p. 141.

21. *Towards a Full Life: Green Paper on Services for Disabled People* (Stationery Office, Dublin, 1984), p. 18.

22. *Needs and Abilities, A Policy for the Intellectually Disabled: Report of the Review Group on Mental Handicap Services* (Stationery Office, Dublin, 1990) pp. 13–14.

23. NESC Report No. 50, *Major Issues in Planning Services for Mentally and Physically Handicapped Persons* (Stationery Office, Dublin, 1980), p. 12.

24. See *Shaping a Healthier Future* (Stationery Office, Dublin, 1994), pp. 70–71; *Enhancing the Partnership: Report of the Working Group on the Implementation of the Health Strategy in Relation to Persons with a Mental Handicap* (Department of Health, 1996), p. 5.

25. *Annual Report, National Intellectual Database 2000* (The Health Research Board, Dublin, 2001), p. 4.

26. *Shaping a Healthier Future*, op. cit., p. 72; *Towards an Independent Future, Report of the Review Group on Health and Personal Social Services for People with Physical and Sensory Disabilities* (Stationery Office, Dublin,1996), p. 33.

27. *Towards a Full Life*, op. cit., p. 21.

28. For an account of the evolution of and issues concerned with statutory and voluntary residential services for persons with mental illness and intellectual disability see A. Ryan, *Walls of Silence* (Red Lion Press, Kilkenny, 1999).

29. *Towards an Independent Future*, op. cit., pp. 6–13.

30. *Needs and Abilities*, op. cit., p. 58.

31. *Annual Report, National Intellectual Database 2000*, op. cit., p. 12.

32. *NESC Report*, No. 50, op. cit., p. 12.

33. *Report of the Primary Education Review Body* (Stationery Office, Dublin 1990), p. 60.

34. *Training and Employing the Handicapped*: Report of a Working Party established by the Minister for Health (Stationery Office, Dublin, 1975), preface.

35. *Partnership 2000 for Inclusion, Employment and Competitiveness* (Stationery Office, Dublin, 1996), p. 32.

36. *Towards Equal Citizenship, Progress Report on the Implementation of the Recommendations of the Commission on the Status of People with Disabilities* (Stationery Office, Dublin, 1999) pp. 81–82.

37. *NESC Report*, No. 50, op. cit., p. 15.

38. *Towards a Full Life*, op. cit., pp. 72–73.

39. *Report of the Commission on Social Welfare*, op. cit., Chapter 19.

40. *A Strategy for Equality: Report of the Commission on the Status of People with Disabilities* (Stationery Office, Dublin, 1996), p. 127.

41. *Towards Equal Citizenship*, op. cit., pp. 56–58.

42. *A Strategy for Equality*, op. cit., p. 5.

43. *Irish Times*, November 19, 1996.

44. *Towards a Full Life*, op. cit., p. 112.
45. *Response to the Green Paper on Services for Disabled People* (Union of Voluntary Organisations for the Handicapped, Dublin, 1985), pp. 31–32.
46. *Irish Times*, February 20, 2002.
47. D.B. Rottman, A.D. Tussing, and M.M. Wiley, *The Population Structure and Living Circumstances of Irish Travellers: Results from the 1981 Census of Traveller Families* (Economic and Social Research Institute, Dublin, 1986), p. 73.
48. *Report of the Commission on Itinerancy* (Stationery Office, Dublin, 1963), pp. 12–13.
49. *Report of the Travelling People Review Body* (Stationery Office, Dublin, 1983), pp. 5–6.
50. *Report of the Commission on Itinerancy*, op. cit., pp. 34–35.
51. *The Travellers' Health Status Study: Vital Statistics of Travelling People*, 1987 (The Health Research Board, Dublin, 1989), p. 24.
52. *Report of the Commission on Itinerancy*, op. cit., p. 64.
53. *Report of the Travelling People Review Body*, op. cit., pp. 59–60
54. *Report of the Travelling People Review Body*, op. cit., pp. 81–82.
55. *Report of the Commission on Itinerancy*, op. cit., p. 61.
56. *Report of the Travelling People Review Body*, op. cit., p. 38.
57. *Report of the Travelling People Review Body*, op. cit., p. 35.
58. Under the Prohibition of Incitement to Racial, Religious or National Hatred Act, 1989, the travelling people are cited as a group about whom offensive material cannot be published.
59. S.B. Gmelch, 'From Poverty Sub-culture to Political Lobby: the Traveller Rights Movement in Ireland', in C. Curtin and T.M. Wilson, *Ireland from Below: Social Change and Rural Communities* (Galway University Press, 1990).
60. Report of the Task Force on the Travelling Community (Stationery Office, Dublin, 1995) p. 289.
61. *Traveller Health: A National Strategy 2002–2005* (Department of Health and Children, 2002) p. 2.
62. *First Progress Report of the Committee to Monitor and Co-ordinate the Implementation of the Recommendations of the Task Force on the Travelling Community* (Stationery Office, Dublin, 2000) p. 53.
63. Ibid. p. 8.

7

The Role of Voluntary Social Service Organisations

Introduction

Voluntary organisations continue to play a lead role in the provision of social services. That role is considered in this chapter.

There is a strong tradition of voluntary activity in Ireland. While this activity is widespread, its precise extent is not known. For example, there is no formal system of registration for charitable organisations, although charitable status is granted to organisations by the Revenue Commissioners for tax purposes solely. The role of voluntary social service organisations is considerable in Ireland, especially if it includes that of religious orders, whose influence on the development of the education and health services has been significant.

In most cases, voluntary organisations complement the work of statutory agencies. Despite the growth in statutory services over several decades the voluntary sector still flourishes and many new organisations have been established within the past few decades.

There is, of course, great diversity within the voluntary sector in relation to the aims, resources, scope of activity and type of personnel. Some employ full-time paid staff, others rely on unpaid volunteers and some have a combination of full-time staff and volunteers. Some rely solely on voluntary contributions from the public but the majority receive some statutory grants. Some focus on particular client groups such as older people, while others cater for a variety of groups. Some are national organisations with branches throughout the country, while others have a narrower geographic base.

Categories of voluntary organisations

Faughnan has produced a classification framework for voluntary organisations which reflects diversity in relation to dominant functions.[1] Her classification is as follows:

Mutual support and self-help organisations. These are based on a common interest or need. An example is GROW, the community health movement, which has a network of groups that meet on a regular basis.

Local development associations. These associations operate within a particular geographic locality and are concerned with promoting the development of that area by collective action.

Resource and service-providing organisations. According to Faughnan, these organisations represent the largest category of voluntary activity in Ireland judged by most criteria, e.g. the largest arena for volunteer involvement. It is also a category with the greatest diversity. These organisations operate either at a local or national level. The largest organisation of this kind is the Society of St Vincent de Paul, with approximately 1,100 conferences (branches) throughout the country and 10,000 members. While the main focus of the Society is on support for low-income families, it provides a wide range of services, e.g. sheltered housing for older people and holiday homes for children.

Representative and co-ordinating organisations. These organisations act in some cases as co-ordinating bodies or, more commonly, as resource agents for affiliated members of a particular category of voluntary activity and as a focal point for liaising with government or government agencies in order to bring about policy changes. Even here there is also diversity in relation to the functions and mode of operation between these representative organisations. The Disability Federation of Ireland (already referred to in the section on people with disabilities) has over 200 organisations affiliated to it and its general objectives are to promote the welfare of persons with disabilities.

Campaigning bodies. Many of the representatives of service organisations are also involved in campaigning for improvement in services. In practice there are few organisations whose sole function is to lobby for change. The National Campaign for the Homeless, representing a variety of voluntary organisations, was established to influence and monitor policy in relation to homelessness in the 1980s.

Funding organisations. Within the past decade or so a number of funds or trusts have been established to support the activities and projects of voluntary organisations. These include the Ireland Funds, the Irish Youth Foundation, and the People in Need Trust. In many instances, the grants (frequently of a once-off nature) given by these organisations supplement the financial assistance provided by statutory bodies.

Evolution of voluntary activity

Faughnan has identified three main strands that influenced the development of the voluntary sector in Ireland.

Firstly, as already noted, the contribution of religious orders, commencing in the nineteenth century following Catholic emancipation, has been significant – especially in the health services and education. In addition, philanthropic individuals were responsible for the establishment of voluntary hospitals in the nineteenth century. Apart from establishing voluntary hospitals, religious orders were pre-eminent in the field of residential care for the mentally handicapped and deprived children. Secondly, a strong community self-help tradition with a base in rural Ireland emerged in the twentieth century. A notable example of this was Muintir na Tíre, a community-based movement established in the 1930s which sought improvement in all aspects of community life. Thirdly, the development of statutory services, especially those of health boards in the 1970s, provided a focal point for voluntary activity. The establishment of community care programmes under health boards provided the impetus to a greater focus for voluntary organisations operating in the general welfare area, e.g. organisations providing services for older people and deprived children.

In 1971, Erskine Childers, TD, Minister for Health, established the National Social Service Council with a broad remit as the focal point for voluntary social services. The NSSC helped to promote the establishment of social service councils (local co-ordinating bodies) throughout the country. Having been restructured in 1981 as the National Social Service Board and given a statutory basis in 1984, the Board's functions were limited to the development of information services in 1988, following an abortive attempt by the government to disband it.

Continued relevance of voluntary organisations

Paradoxically, as the role of state services has increased, that of the voluntary sector has not diminished; it has in fact also increased. Among the reasons for that are the following:

- The general pattern has been that voluntary organisations have pioneered the provision of services, with the state becoming involved in a supportive role at a later stage. The pioneering role remains relevant as new social problems emerge and as others are redefined.
- Even if it were desirable, it is highly unlikely that the state could afford to completely replace the work of voluntary organisations. In many instances voluntary organisations supplement the basic services provided by the state.
- Voluntary activity provides an outlet for the altruism of many people.
- It is generally recognised that voluntary organisations can respond to social need in a more flexible manner than statutory agencies.

While the voluntary sector has obvious strengths, one of the inherent weaknesses of the system is that there may be an uneven geographic spread of organisations. While some areas may be relatively well served by voluntary groups, others may be less so. This applies in particular to services for persons with disabilities where the voluntary sector has played a pre-eminent role. A further weakness is the lack of accountability – financial or general – in many cases.

Funding of voluntary organisations

Depending on the type of activity engaged in, there are different sources of funding for voluntary organisations. These include the European Social Fund and Lottery funding. The main sources of recurrent funds for the majority of voluntary organisations providing welfare services, however, are health boards. Section 65 of the Health Act, 1953 provides that health authorities may support organisations providing services 'similar or ancillary' to those of the health authority. These Section 65 grants are in effect discretionary and there are no established criteria or guidelines for them. In practice, therefore, considerable variation may exist in relation to the level of funding provided. The balance of funding required by voluntary organisations is raised in a variety of ways from the public.

Statutory/voluntary relationships

Despite its significant, if unquantifiable role, in the provision of services it is surprising that there is no clear policy framework in which the voluntary sector can develop. There is a need for a broad plan that spells out the role of voluntary services in the total provision of welfare services.

In 1976 Brendan Corish, TD, Minister for Health, indicated that a policy document on the scope and structure of welfare services and the respective roles and relationships of the statutory and voluntary organisations in the planning and provision of these services would be prepared.[2] No such document emerged.

The short-lived Fine Gael/Labour Coalition government of June 1981 to March 1982 had in its programme a commitment to introduce a charter for voluntary services which would provide a framework for the relationship between the statutory and voluntary agencies.[3] This charter was not pursued following the change of government in March 1982 or the return of the Fine Gael/Labour government in December 1982.

It was against this background that the National Social Service Board produced a discussion document on voluntary social services in Ireland.[4] This called for an integrated approach to the development of welfare services, with statutory and voluntary bodies working together. It referred to the need for greater consultation and planning between both types of agencies at local level, community care area and health board area. It suggested, for example, that the director of community care should meet with representatives of voluntary bodies in the area at least annually. At these meetings information could be exchanged on needs and services and some indication of the level of funding available could also be discussed. The document referred to the unsatisfactory nature of funding under Section 65 grants and recommended that guidelines be established as to what type of activity would be funded, for how long and subject to what conditions.

The *Programme for Economic and Social Progress* (1991) stated that, having regard to the contribution that voluntary organisations make in the delivery of services and combating poverty, the government would draw up a charter for voluntary social services which would set out a clear framework for partnership between the state and voluntary activity and develop a cohesive strategy for supporting voluntary activity. It also indicated that a White Paper outlining the government's proposals in this area would be prepared.[5] In May 1991, Michael Woods, TD, Minister for Social Welfare, initiated a process of consultation with voluntary organisations in relation to the proposed charter.

Because of the changing context, the government subsequently decided that it would be more appropriate to publish a Green Paper rather than a White Paper. *Supporting Voluntary Activity* was published in May 1997.[6] The Green Paper outlined the diversity of the community and voluntary sector, the range of state funding and support available to the sector. It suggested two sets of guidelines that are of relevance to the relationship between the statutory sector and the voluntary/community sector. The first set dealt with guidelines to inform statutory agencies in their relationship with the voluntary/community sector. For example, each government Department and agency should identify and outline its role in relation to the voluntary and community sector and its future plans. The second set concerned guidelines to inform the voluntary and community sector. For example, there should be openness, accountability and transparency in the work of the various organisations.

The Green Paper also outlined suggested principles to apply to the funding of the voluntary and community sector. For example, all grants by statutory agencies should be advertised and eligibility criteria should be published.

When the Green Paper was launched in 1997 the intention was to have a year-long consultation process leading to a White Paper. In the event, the White Paper was not published until 2000.[7] Some of the main features of the White Paper were as follows:

- Formal recognition of the role of the community and voluntary sector in contributing to the creation of a vibrant, participative democracy and civil society
- Introduction of mechanisms in all relevant public service areas for consultation with the community and voluntary sector groups and allow the communities they represent to have an input to policy-making
- Multi-annual funding to become the norm for agreed priority services and community development activities. This would

mean a major move away from the existing unsatisfactory and *ad hoc* funding schemes experienced by many voluntary groups
• Designation of voluntary activity units in relevant government Departments to support the relationship with the community and voluntary sector.

An Implementation and Advisory Group, drawn from relevant government departments, statutory agencies and the community and voluntary sector was established to oversee the implementation of the White Paper decisions and to pursue other issues that arise.

Up to 2002, responsibility for grants (other than Section 65 grants) to many voluntary organisations rested with the Department of Social, Community and Family Affairs. In that year, in the context of departmental reorganisations following the general election, the 'community' function, including responsibility for implementation of the White Paper proposals, was transferred to the Department of Community, Rural and Gaeltacht Affairs.

Notes

1. P. Faughnan, *Partners in Progress: Voluntary Organisations in the Social Service Field* (Social Science Research Centre, University College Dublin, 1990), Section 1.
2. *Dáil Debates*, 29 April, 1976.
3. *Fine Gael–Labour, Programme for Government, 1981–86*.
4. *The Development of Voluntary Social Services in Ireland: A Discussion Document* (National Social Service Board, Dublin, 1982).
5. *Programme for Economic and Social Progress* (Stationery Office, Dublin, 1991), p. 24.
6. *Green Paper: Supporting Voluntary Activity* (Stationery Office, Dublin, 1997).
7. *White Paper, A Framework for Supporting Voluntary Activity and for Delivering the Relationship between the State and the Community and Voluntary Sector* (Stationery Office, Dublin, 2000).

8

Poverty and Exclusion

Income poverty

While there is no universally accepted definition of poverty, it is most popularly regarded as lack of sufficient income. But what might be regarded as poverty in developed countries could be quite different to that in, for example, an under-developed Third World country.

It is now accepted in various research reports that poverty is viewed as exclusion, through lack of resources, from the generally approved standards and styles of living in society as a whole. This approach is based on the fact that perceptions of acceptable and minimum standards change over time and between countries with various levels of per capita incomes. Townsend, one of the foremost writers on the subject, has defined poverty in relative terms, the poor being:

> Individuals and families whose resources, over time, fall seriously short of the resources commanded by the average individual or family in the community in which they live.[1]

The official definition adopted in Ireland is as follows:

> People are living in poverty if their income and resources (material, cultural and social) are so inadequate as to preclude them from having a standard of living which is regarded as acceptable by Irish society generally. As a result of inadequate income and resources, people may be excluded from participating in activities which are considered the norm for other people in society.[2]

Measurement of poverty

If poverty is defined in relative terms it follows that the measurement of the extent of poverty is usually formulated in relation to average incomes in society. Thus, for example, some countries estimate the extent of poverty as the proportion of households/families whose income falls below half of mean income in the population in general. Use of half-average income, however, is no more than convention – it has no analytical basis. Furthermore, the use of a poverty threshold (such as 50 per cent or 60 per cent of mean income) does not give an authoritative 'poverty line', i.e. a line below which people are poor. In practice, the term 'poverty line' is used popularly but has no official or precise meaning.

Various studies have been carried out in Ireland since the early 1970s to estimate the proportion of the population living in poverty. In more recent years, however, a combination of income poverty lines and basic deprivation indicators, developed by the Economic and Social Research Institute, has been used. These indicators include a lack of at least one of a number of items, e.g. lack of adequate heating, lack of a warm overcoat.

A study in 1994 indicated that by using relative income poverty lines, between 21 per cent and 34 per cent of the population were living on incomes below the 50 per cent to 60 per cent of average disposable income (£64 to £77 per week respectively for a single adult in 1994). For the same year, however, by using a combination of income poverty lines and basic deprivation indicators, 9 per cent to 15 per cent of the population could be said to be living in poverty. This section 'can be identified as consistently poor, whose income is low and whose ability to draw on accumulated resources is extremely limited.'[3] These were used as benchmark statistics in the *National Anti-Poverty Strategy* of 1997.

Poverty as an issue
In the 1950s and 1960s several studies in the USA indicated that, despite increasing affluence following World War II, poverty and inequalities persisted. This 'rediscovery', as Sinfield[4] described it, led to poverty becoming a socially accepted subject for debate and research, to the establishment of pressure groups and eventually to attempts by governments to find a solution to the problem. In Ireland, poverty may be said to have been 'rediscovered' at a conference on poverty organised by the Council for Social Welfare and held in Kilkenny in 1971.

The conference sparked off what was to be a growing national debate on how the plight of the poor in society could be resolved.

Perhaps the most important paper read at the conference was *The Extent of Poverty in Ireland* by Ó Cinnéide, in which the author estimated that at least one-quarter of the population was living below the poverty line, based on income maintenance rates of payment in Ireland (the Republic and Northern Ireland in 1971).[5] The social, cultural and educational deprivation associated with poverty was described in other conference papers.[6] It was felt that the causes and effects of poverty in Ireland were not clearly understood and that there was need for further research.

Thereafter the issue became politicised and was taken up, especially by the Labour Party, which, with Fine Gael, formed the Coalition Government of 1973/77.[7] One of the fourteen points in the pre-election joint policy statement of the two parties referred to the elimination of poverty and the ending of social injustice as major priorities. At that government's instigation, the Social Action Programme of the EC was expanded to include pilot anti-poverty schemes. In 1974, Frank Cluskey, TD, Parliamentary Secretary to the Minister for Social Welfare, and a member of the Labour Party, established an advisory committee, the National Committee on Pilot Schemes to Combat Poverty (NCPSCP) to initiate and co-ordinate pilot schemes to combat poverty. The Committee became known popularly as Combat Poverty and within a short time became, in effect, an executive body that planned and administered projects and employed the necessary staff. The objectives of Combat Poverty were:

- to bring about practical intervention in areas of deprivation or among groups in need
- to increase public awareness of the problems of poverty
- to contribute to the evolution of effective, long-term policies against poverty.

Of the various projects initiated by Combat Poverty, Ó Cinnéide concluded:

> One is left with an impression of real but unspecifiable gains for a few.[8]

He also pointed out that the greatest failure of Combat Poverty was that it did not increase public awareness of poverty.

At the end of 1980 the work of Combat Poverty was terminated, partly, because EC funds for further projects were no longer available. The Committee's final report called for the establishment of a national agency to further develop and expand the work of the pilot schemes.

In 1986 the Combat Poverty Agency was established on a statutory basis reporting to the Minister for Social Welfare. Under the Act, the Agency has four general functions:

- advice and recommendations to the Minister (for Social Welfare) on all aspects of economic and social planning in relation to poverty
- initiation and evaluation of measures aimed at overcoming poverty
- promotion, commission and interpretation of research into poverty
- promotion of greater public understanding of poverty.

The Agency recognised that, because of limited resources available, it could not be a major funding source for measures designed to tackle the problem of poverty. Instead it viewed its role as clarifying the causes and effects of poverty and pointing towards solutions.[9] Since its establishment, the Agency has commissioned various studies on aspects of poverty and has been to the forefront in highlighting poverty issues.

National Anti-Poverty Strategy

Poverty as an issue assumed greater significance with the publication of *Sharing in Progress: National Anti-Poverty Strategy* by the government in April 1997. This followed from Ireland's participation in the United Nations World Summit meeting in Copenhagen in 1995 at which the government agreed to implement a national anti-poverty strategy. The National Anti-Poverty Strategy (NAPS) was signed by the three leaders of the coalition parties in government (John Bruton, Dick Spring and Proinsias de Rossa). The strategy was based on research, mostly commissioned by the Combat Poverty Agency, and widespread consultation with all interest groups. It was the first comprehensive document by government on the issue of poverty.

The strategy set a global target over the period 1997–2007 to considerably reduce the numbers of those who are 'consistently poor', from 9 to 15 per cent to less than 5 to 10 per cent, as measured by the Economic and Social Research Institute (ESRI).[10] The measurement of poverty adopted by the ESRI was to take 50 per cent and 60 per cent of disposable income, together with one of nine indicators such as lack of a warm overcoat or lack of a good meal in the day.

NAPS also identified five key areas, in each of which an overall goal, targets and policy actions were outlined. The areas were:

- Educational disadvantage
- Unemployment, particularly long-term unemployment
- Income adequacy
- Disadvantaged urban areas
- Rural poverty.

An overall goal in education, for example, was to eliminate early school leaving so that 90 per cent of children would complete the senior cycle by the year 2000, rising to 98 per cent by 2007. A further objective was that within a period of five years, no student would have serious literacy and numeracy problems.

The strategy is underpinned by a Cabinet Sub-Committee, chaired by the Taoiseach, an inter-departmental policy committee comprised of senior officers and a NAPS unit in the Department of Social and Family Affairs. Progress on implementation is to be monitored by the National Economic and Social Forum.

Reviews on the progress of NAPS have been ongoing. The report of the inter-departmental policy committee for 1999/2000 indicated that by then some targets had been easily met, especially those related to unemployment. Other targets proved more difficult to meet. For example, in education, there had been little progress in meeting the target for senior cycle completion and, ironically, one of the reasons for this was the 'pull factor' of abundant employment arising from the growth in employment opportunities. As part of the review, further targets were set and new areas were brought under NAPS. These included housing and homelessness, child poverty, women living in poverty, older people, poverty and ill-health.

In 2002 a revised National Anti-Poverty Strategy was published. It indicated that over the period 1994–2000, the proportion of the population in consistent poverty fell from 15.1 per cent to 6.2 per cent.[11] It set new targets to reduce, and if possible to eliminate, consistent poverty.

One of the key commitments of the revised NAPS was to achieve a rate of €150 per week in 2002 terms for the lowest rates of social welfare to be met by 2007.

The following are examples of some of the targets set for different sectors and groups:

- *Unemployment*. To eliminate long-term unemployment (unemployment for a period of one year or more) as soon as circumstances permit but not later than 2007
- *Housing*. To deliver 41,500 local authority housing units starts (including acquisitions) between 2000 and 2006
- *Education*. To reduce the number of young people who leave the school system early, so that the percentage of those who complete upper second level or equivalent will reach 85 per cent by 2003 and 90 per cent by 2006
- *Travellers*. To reduce the difference in life expectancy between travellers and the whole population by at least 10 per cent by 2007. In effect this means an increase of about one year in the life expectancy of travellers. Another target was that the transfer rate of travellers to post-primary schools would be increased to 95 per cent by 2004
- *Older people*. To make available, by end of 2007, adequate heating systems in all local authority rented dwellings provided for older people.

The National Anti-Poverty Strategy is arguably the most significant social policy document ever published by government. It has given the issue of poverty and exclusion a far greater prominence than heretofore. Its significance lies in the fact that targets have been established in relation to a number of areas, that there is a commitment to implementation and that a framework has been established to ensure that it remains high up on the national agenda. The achievement of the targets in the National Anti-Poverty Strategy would go a long way towards the reduction of inequalities in Irish society.

Notes

1. P. Townsend, 'Poverty as Relative Deprivation: Resources and Style of Living' in D. Wedderburn (ed.), *Poverty, Inequality and Class Structure* (Cambridge University Press, 1974), p. 15; see also P. Townsend, *Poverty in the United Kingdom: A Survey of Household Resources and Standards of Living* (Penguin Books, 1979), p. 31.
2. *Sharing in Progress: National Anti-Poverty Strategy* (Stationery Office, Dublin 1997), p. 3.
3. Ibid., Appendix 2, p. 33.

4. A. Sinfield, 'We the People and They the Poor, Comparative View of Poverty Research: The Extent of Poverty in Ireland', *Social Studies*, Vol. 4, No. 1 (1975), pp. 3–9.

5. S. Ó Cinnéide, 'The Extent of Poverty in Ireland', *Social Studies*, Vol. 1, No. 4 (1972), pp. 281–400.

6. All the conference papers were published in *Social Studies*, Vol. 1, No. 4 (1972). A second conference on poverty was held in Kilkenny in 1974 and the papers are published in *Social Studies*, Vol. 4, No. 1 (1975). A third conference was also organised by the Council for Social Welfare, held in Kilkenny in 1981 and the papers were published in *Conference on Poverty, 1981* (Council for Social Welfare, Dublin, 1982).

7. See S. Ó Cinnéide, 'Poverty and Policy: North and South', *Administration*, Vol. 33, No. 3 (Institute of Public Administration, Dublin, 1985), pp. 378–412.

8. Ibid, p. 393.

9. *Strategic Plan* (Combat Poverty Agency, Dublin, 1987), p. 2.

10. Sharing in Progress, op. cit., p. 9.

11. *Building an Inclusive Society: Review of the National Anti-Poverty Strategy under the Programme for Prosperity and Fairness* (Department of Social, Community and Family Affairs, 2002), p. 8.

9

Equality Issues

Introduction

Over the past few decades attention has been focused on equality issues. Initially the focus was on equality of opportunity for women and the ending of all forms of discrimination. In Ireland, the first public acknowledgement that a problem existed was the setting up of the Commission on the Status of Women in 1970. The terms of reference were:

> To examine and report on the status of women in Irish society, to make recommendations on the steps necessary to ensure the participation of women on equal terms and conditions with men in the political, social, cultural and economic life of the country.

The Commission was established against a background of growing awareness of areas of discrimination against women as highlighted by the burgeoning Irish Women's Liberation Movement, founded in 1970.[1] The Commission's report was published in 1972.

In 1983, a Working Party was established to 'review the existing situation in relation to measures affecting women's affairs and family law reform, identifying areas requiring action'. The Working Party was chaired by Nuala Fennell, TD, Minister of State for Women's Affairs and Family Law Reform, and the report, entitled *Irish Women: Agenda for Practical Action*, was published in 1985.

In 1990, a second Commission on the Status of Women was established. Its terms of reference were similar to those of the first Commission, the implementation of whose recommendations it was expected to review. It was also charged with paying special attention to the needs of women in the home. The second Commission's Report was published in 1993.

The focus in this chapter will be on some of the main areas in which women were discriminated against, the progress made in these areas and the more recent measures to ensure equality in other areas.

Report of the Commission on the Status of Women

The Report of the Commission on the Status of Women contained 49 recommendations and 17 suggestions designed to eliminate all forms of discrimination against women in such areas as employment, social welfare, education and the taxation codes. By comparison with other Commission reports, it can be said that the Commission on the Status of Women achieved considerable success in terms of recommendations implemented. This could be due to a number of factors, e.g. the influence of the Women's Movement at the time, the political will to implement the recommendations, and the fact that many of the recommendations did not so much involve additional expenditure as changes in practices. Another reason for the success lies in the fact that the Minister for Labour was given overall responsibility for co-ordinating the follow-up action on the report. The Minister, Michael O'Leary, TD, in turn established the Women's Representative Committee to monitor progress on the implementation of the recommendations. The committee published two progress reports and its existence was undoubtedly influential in ensuring progress.

Employment

A number of the recommendations in the first Commission's Report dealt with the question of employment.

One of the most significant developments here was the introduction of equal pay under the Anti-Discrimination (Pay) Act, 1974.

Another development was the Employment Equality Act, 1977, which made it unlawful to discriminate on grounds of sex or marriage in recruitment for employment, conditions of employment, training or work experience or in promotion or the classification of jobs.

The Employment Equality Act also provided for the setting up of an Employment Equality Agency (EEA). The functions of the EEA which came into operation in October 1977 were to work towards the elimination of discrimination in employment, to promote equality of opportunity in employment between men and women, and to keep under review the working of the Anti-Discrimination (Pay) Act and the Employment Equality Act.

The annual reports of the EEA contain interesting information on equality of opportunity (or lack of it) in employment. In the first few reports the EEA referred to the large number of discriminatory advertisements by employers. The EEA had to carry out formal investigations in certain cases, e.g. in CIÉ, which eventually led to the employment of women as bus conductors.[2]

In general, despite the developments that have occurred, women tend to be concentrated in a narrow range of occupational activities, e.g. a high proportion of women in the industrial sector are employed in the textile, clothing and food-processing industries. These are areas where pay is traditionally low, job mobility and promotion almost non-existent, and training opportunities limited.

Social welfare
The first Commission's Report contained 16 recommendations relating to social welfare entitlements and payments. The majority of these have been implemented. Thus, for example, schemes of social assistance for wives of prisoners and unmarried mothers were introduced. The remaining forms of discrimination were largely removed with the implementation of the EC (EU) Directive on equal treatment of men and women in relation to matters of social security in 1986. Up to then married women received less employment benefit and for a shorter period than men did.

In general, the recommendations made were implemented fairly quickly, but one of the most obvious forms of discrimination had to await an EC (EU) Directive. Ironically, member states of the EC were given six years to implement this, i.e. by the end of 1984, but Ireland did not begin to comply until 1986.

Women and the law
A number of recommendations were made to safeguard the rights of women in relation to family and property. Thus, for example, the Family Law (Maintenance of Spouses and Children) Act, 1976 placed a joint obligation on both spouses to support the family. The Family Home Protection Act, 1976 prevented the sale of the

family home by one spouse without the consent of the other spouse.

The Commission, in its report, recommended that women should be qualified and liable for jury service on the same terms as men. It also endorsed the recommendation of the Committee on Court Practice and Procedure that the property qualification for jurors should be abolished and that inclusion in the electoral register should be the only qualification test for jury service.

Under the Juries Act, 1975, which came into operation in 1976, all citizens, with a few special exceptions, are now eligible for jury service without discrimination based on sex or property qualifications.

The taxation code

Up to 1980, married couples, when both were working, were effectively discriminated against as compared with two single persons, under the income taxation code. In practice they paid more tax because the woman's earnings were lumped together with her husband's, treated as one income and thereby liable to the highest rate of tax.

As a result of the Supreme Court judgment in the Murphy case of 1979, sections of the Income Tax Act dealing with the taxation of married couples were deemed to be unconstitutional. From the tax year 1980/81, married couples were treated on the same basis as two single persons.

This was one area where discrimination was only grudgingly removed, mainly because of the cost implications to the Exchequer.

Health

There were few recommendations on health services made by the Commission. One of them, relating to family planning, was subsequently to arouse considerable controversy, though this was not due solely to the Commission's recommendation. It merely reflected a growing demand for the legalising of the sale of contraceptives. The Commission recommended that:

> information and expert advice on family planning should be available through medical and other appropriate channels to families throughout the country. Such advice should respect the moral and personal attitudes of each married couple, and medical requirements (contraceptives), arising out of the married couple's decision on family

planning, should be available under control and through channels to be determined by the Department of Health.

Following considerable controversy, the Health (Family Planning) Act, 1979 came into effect the following year. This Act was restrictive in relation to the channels through which contraceptives were made available, e.g. all contraceptive devices could only be made available on a doctor's prescription. The Act was amended, against much opposition, in 1985, to make contraceptives more freely available. It was also amended in 1992, without any opposition, to liberalise the law even further.

Education
As in health, there were few recommendations made by the Commission in relation to education. It had recommended that co-education should be introduced wherever possible at primary level. It also recommended that the joint training of male and female teachers should be introduced where possible. Subsequently, the teacher training colleges, hitherto confined to single sexes, became co-educational. Ironically, the vast majority of entrants to teacher training colleges in subsequent years were female.

Implementation
In general, considerable progress was made within a decade in implementing recommendations made in the Report of the Commission on the Status of Women. Overt forms of discrimination were largely eliminated. Progress on implementation was due to a number of factors. These included:

- the role of the Council for the Status of Women, established in 1973, to campaign for implementation of the recommendations. The Council was later renamed the National Women's Council of Ireland. It is the representative body for over 150 women's organisations and its principal function is to promote equality for women
- the role of the reports issued by the Women's Representative Committee, established by the Minister for Labour in 1974 to monitor progress towards implementation of the recommendations. The reports, recounting progress or lack of it on each recommendation together with commentary, by various gov-

ernment departments, proved a vital impetus to publicly tracking implementation. Its final report was published in 1977.

The Working Party Report of 1985 was more concerned with the creation of positive opportunities for women. In that sense, it differed in many respects from the Commission's Report of 1972. Many of the recommendations in the Working Party Report were either very detailed or were of an exhortatory nature, e.g. the IDA should give special attention to the needs of women for industrial jobs, and retailers should give consideration to the needs of women with prams and children.

Second Commission's Report

The *Second Report of the Commission on the Status of Women*, published in 1993, contained 210 recommendations. The following were five of the key recommendations:

- Article 41.2.2 of the Constitution (stipulating that the state should ensure that mothers are not obliged through economic necessity to work outside the home to the neglect of their duties in the home) should be deleted from the Constitution
- An Equal Status Act should be introduced
- A second referendum on divorce should be held
- A comprehensive child care service, without which there can be no equality of opportunity in the workplace, should be set up
- Quota systems and reserved seats should be introduced by the political parties to secure a minimum 40 per cent representation of any one sex.

In a reservation to the Report, three of the 19 members of the Commission believed the Report was unbalanced in favour of helping and validating the woman who is in the paid workforce.

Progress in relation to the five key recommendations has been somewhat mixed.

In relation to Article 41.2.2 of the Constitution, the All-Party Oireachtas Committee on the Constitution recommened that this Article and its sub-sections be recast to include various elements reflecting current thinking and practice in relation to the family. It recommended that Article 41.2 be revised in gender-neutral form which might provide that:

The state recognises that home and family life give society a support without which the common good cannot be achieved. The state shall endeavour to support persons caring for others within the home.[3]

In 1986 a referendum was carried out to amend the Constitution in order to provide for divorce in certain circumstances. The measure was defeated, 63.5 per cent to 36.5 per cent. Almost ten years later a further referendum was held in 1995. On this occasion the measure was passed narrowly by the electorate, with 50.28 per cent for and 49.72 per cent against. The ensuing legislation, the Family Law (Divorce) Act, 1996, provided for divorce where a couple had effectively been separated for five years or more. On the eve of the passing of this legislation the *Irish Times* commented:

> The Dáil moved a step closer to the creation of a pluralist, tolerant and caring society yesterday when it approved the final stages of the Family Law (Divorce) Bill, 1996. After 16 years of political agitation by pro-divorce groups, a succession of court actions and two ill-natured referendums spread over 9 years, one of the most divisive social issues was quietly and firmly determined.[4]

The increase in participation by women in the work force, stimulated by growth in the economy in the late 1990s, led to a demand for affordable child care for working parents. The *Report of the Partnership 2000 Expert Working Group on Child Care*, published in 1999, recommended tax allowances for parents and tax breaks for employers. However, the government in 1999 and 2000 sought instead to increase the supply of child care places. This mainly took the form of capital grants for the provision of places. Some groups continued to press for direct financial support to families to enable them meet the costs of child care. This was acceded to in a limited way by substantial increases in the monthly child benefit in 2001 and 2002, a proposal which the Expert Working Group had ruled out on grounds of cost!

The recommendation to introduce a gender quota system has not meet with any success. At a conference to mark International Women's Day in 2002 it was evident that proposals for mandatory gender quotas by the National Women's Council of Ireland commanded support only among the smaller political parties.[5]

Revised equality legislation

While the focus in the 1970s and 1980s was on forms of discrimination related to gender and marital status, the demand for measures to deal with discrimination in other areas increased during the 1990s.

Following considerable debate two important pieces of legislation were introduced which not only replaced existing legislation but also broadened the focus of discrimination. These were the Employment Equality Act, 1998 and the Equal Status Act, 2000.

An Employment Equality Bill was published in 1996 but, prior to being passed into law, was referred by the President, Mary Robinson, to the Supreme Court in April 1997 to decide whether the Bill or any of its provisions were repugnant to the Constitution. A number of sections in the Bill had given rise to concerns, especially a section that would allow schools to appoint only teachers who conformed to the religious ethos of the school. In the event the Supreme Court ruled that sections of the Bill were repugnant to the Constitution. Interestingly, the principal section which concerned the Supreme Court was that relating to the employment of persons with disabilities rather than, as widely expected, the section dealing with the employment of teachers; the Court ruled that the employment of a person with a disability could impose an unreasonable cost burden on an employer.[5] A revised Employment Equality Bill was passed in 1998.

The Employment Equality Act, 1998 effectively repealed and replaced the Anti-Discrimination (Pay) Act, 1974 and the Employment Equality Act, 1977.

The Employment Equality Act outlaws direct and indirect discrimination at work and in employment conditions on nine distinct grounds, i.e.

- gender
- marital status
- family status
- age
- disability
- race
- sexual orientation
- religious belief
- membership of the traveller community.

The Act provides for a number of exceptions to the principle of equal treatment. For example, an employer is not prevented from discriminating on age or disability grounds where there is clear actuarial and other evidence of significantly increased costs for the employer. Similarly, there is an exemption for religious, educational and medical institutions run by religious bodies where the discrimination is essential for the maintenance of the religious ethos of the institution.

The Equal Status Bill, 1997 was also held to be unconstitutional for broadly similar reasons as the Employment Equality Bill. A revised Equal Status Bill was passed in 2000. The Equal Status Act, 2000 deals with discrimination in areas other than employment and covers advertising, collective agreements, the provision of goods and services, education, property and other opportunities to which the public have access. Discrimination is also outlawed on nine distinct grounds, i.e. gender, marital status, family status, age, disability, race, sexual orientation, religious belief and membership of the traveller community.

Discrimination in both the Employment Equality Act and the Equal Status Act is defined as the treatment of one person in a less favourable way than another person is, has been or would be treated on any of the nine grounds.

The legislation also prohibits sexual harassment and/or harassment.

Equality Authority

The Equality Authority (which subsumes the work of the former Employment Equality Agency) was established in October 2000 and works with employers, employees, trade unions, service providers and others to develop equality policies and best practice. It also provides advice, assistance and legal representation to those who may have a grievance under the legislation.

The Office of the Director of Equality Investigations was established as an independent statutory office under the Employment Equality Act, 1998. It offers an accessible and impartial forum to remedy unlawful discrimination. The Office investigates or mediates on complaints arising under equality legislation (including the Equal Status Act).

The first annual report of the Equality Authority (covering the period mid-October to end-December 2000) indicated that 202 cases were brought under the Employment Equality Act and that the largest group (59.4 per cent) was on grounds of gender. The report also indicated that 14 cases were initiated under the Equal

Status Act; six of these were on the grounds of membership of the traveller community and related to access to licensed premises (pubs), shops and housing.

The second annual report of the Equality Authority for 2001 recorded an increase in new cases, 300 under the Employment Equality Act and 661 under the Equal Status Act, with the largest groups concerning gender (34.6 per cent) and traveller community (72.5 per cent) respectively. The report noted that in relation to cases under the Equal Status Act,

> The overwhelming volume of cases arising was unexpected and unprecedented particularly in the area of refusal of service by publicans to members of the traveller community.[6]

The third annual report of the Equality Authority indicated that discrimination in employment on the grounds of gender remained the largest single category of the 489 cases of complaint. This accounted for over one-quarter (28.2 per cent) of cases, followed by discrimination on race grounds (24.4 per cent), and discrimination on disability grounds (20.6 per cent). A total of 795 cases was taken under the Equal Status Act and the majority (413) related to licensed premises with about three-quarters of the complainants being members of the traveller community.[7]

As part of its function of bringing about positive change by eliminating discrimination, the Authority published an equality strategy for older people in 2002. It noted that the work of the Authority had '... highlighted a widespread ageism in Irish society in particular experienced by older people. Strong negative stereotypes of older people persist'.[8]

Equality issues have broadened considerably from the narrow focus on gender and employment of the early 1970s.

One of the factors that gave added impetus to the broadening of the equality agenda during the 1990s was the changing nature of the Irish population which began to reflect far greater diversity than ever before. Irish society began to change from a relatively homogeneous culture to a multi-racial and multi-cultural society. With significant improvement in the economy from the mid-1990s onwards, labour shortages emerged which necessitated the active recruitment of non-nationals. In addition, the number of applications from asylum seekers/refugees increased dramatically throughout the 1990s, from 39 in 1992 to a peak of 10,938 in 2000 (the number in 2001 was 10,325).[9] While all applications for refugee status were not granted, the number was nonetheless sufficient to make an impact not only in Dublin but also in various parts of the country. These factors gave rise to a more culturally diverse population. Different cultural norms and traditions have had to be accommodated.

Apart from the legislation to underpin equality there was also a perceptible change in terminology and labelling to reflect a more inclusive, less stigmatising society. Examples include 'intellectual disability' (rather than 'mental handicap') and 'older persons' (rather than 'the aged' or 'the elderly').

As if to emphasise the evolving nature of the equality agenda, a report of the National Economic and Social Forum in 2002 recommended that the existing nine grounds on which discrimination is outlawed should be extended to cover socio-economic status, trade union membership, criminal conviction and political opinion.[10]

Notes

1. For background see *Irishwomen Into Focus*, Office of the Minister of State for Women's Affairs, Department of the Taoiseach, 1987, pp. 4–13.
2. The All-Party Committee on the Constitution, *The Constitution Review Group: Recommendations/Conclusions*, 1996, pp. 74–75.
3. *Irish Times*, September 26, 1996.
4. *Irish Times*, March 9, 2002.
5. *Irish Law Times*, Vol. 15, No. 6, June 1997.
6. The Equality Authority, *Annual Report 2001*, p. 40.
7. The Equality Authority, *Annual Report 2002*, pp. 18–21.
8. The Equality Authority, *Implementing Equality for Older People*, 2002, p. i.
9. Office of the Refugee Applications Commissioner, *Annual Report 2001*, p. 8.
10. National Economic and Social Forum, *A Strategic Policy Framework for Equality Issues*, Report No. 23, 2002.

Bibliography

General

Bourke, H., The People Under the Poor Law in 19th Century Ireland (The Women's Education Bureau, 1987).

Coughlan, A., *Aims of Social Policy*, Tuairim Pamphlet, 1966.

Fahey, T. and J. Fitzgerald, *Social Welfare Implications of Demographic Trends* (Combat Poverty Agency, Dublin, 1997).

Kaim-Caudle, P., *Social Policy in the Irish Republic* (Routledge & Kegan Paul, London 1967).

Kearney, C.P., *Selectivity Issues in Irish Social Services* (Family Study Centre, University College Dublin, 1991).

Kennedy, F., *Public Social Expenditure in Ireland* (Economic and Social Research Institute, Dublin, 1975).

Kennedy, F., *Cottage to Creche, Family Change in Ireland* (Institute of Public Administration, Dublin, 2001).

Kiely, G., A. O'Donnell, P. Kennedy and S. Quin, *Irish Social Policy in Context* (University College Dublin Press, 1999).

NESC Report No.8, *An Approach to Social Policy* (Stationery Office, Dublin, 1976).

NESC Report No.61, Irish Social Policies: Priorities for Future Development (Stationery Office, Dublin, 1981).

Quin. S., P. Kennedy, A. O'Donnell and G. Kiely, *Contemporary Irish Social Policy* (University College Dublin Press, 1999).

Reynolds, B. and S. Healy, *Social Policy in Ireland: Principles, Practices and Problems* (Conference of Religious in Ireland, 1998).

Sustaining Progress, Social Partnership Agreement 2003–2005 (Stationery Office, Dublin, 2003).

White, J.H., *Church and State in Modern Ireland* (Gill & Macmillan, Dublin, 1971).

Income maintenance

Annual Reports, Social Welfare Appeals Office.

Callan, T., B. Nolan *et al. Poverty, Income and Welfare in Ireland* (Economic and Social Research Institute, Dublin, 1989).

Callan, T., B. Nolan and C.T. Whelan, *A Review of the Commission on Social Welfare's Minimum Adequate Income* (Economic and Social Research Institute, Dublin, 1996).

Farrelly, D., *Social Insurance and Assistance in Ireland* (Institute of Public Administration, Dublin, 1964).

Green Paper, *Basic Income* (Stationery Office, Dublin, 2002).

Ó Cinnéide, S., *A Law for the Poor* (Institute of Public Administration, Dublin, 1970).

Report of the Commission on Social Welfare (Stationery Office, Dublin, 1986).

Report of the Review Group on the Treatment of Households in the Social Welfare Code (Stationery Office, Dublin, 1991).

Reynolds, B. and S.J. Healy (eds), *Poverty and Family Income Policy* (Conference of Major Religious Superiors, 1988).

Report of the Expert Working Group on the Integration of the Tax and Social Welfare Systems (Stationery Office, Dublin, 1996).

Statistical Information on Social Welfare Services (Stationery Office, Dublin).

Housing

Annual Housing Statistics Bulletin (Department of the Environment and Local Government).

A Plan for Social Housing (Department of the Environment, 1991).

Baker, T.J. and L.M. O'Brien, *The Irish Housing System: A Critical Overview* (Economic and Social Research Institute, Dublin, 1979).

Blackwell, J. (ed.), *Towards an Efficient and Equitable Housing Policy* (Institute of Public Administration, Dublin, 1989).

Fahey, T., 'Social Housing in Ireland: The Need for an Expanded Role?' in *Irish Banking Review*, Autumn, 1999.

Fahey, T., 'Housing and Local Government' in Daly, M. (ed.), *County and Town, One Hundred Years of Local Government in Ireland* (Institute of Public Administration, Dublin, 2001).

Homelessness, An Integrated Strategy (Department of the Environment and Local Government, Dublin, 2000).

Homeless Preventative Strategy: A strategy to prevent homelessness among: Patients leaving hospital and mental health care, Adult prisoners and young offenders leaving custody, Young people leaving care (Stationery Office, Dublin, 2002).

NESC Report No. 23, *Report on Housing Subsidies* (Stationery Office, Dublin, 1977).

NESC Report No. 87, *A Review of Housing Policy* (Stationery Office, Dublin, 1989).

NESF Report No. 18, *Social and Affordable Housing and Accommodation: Building the Future* (Stationery Office, Dublin, 2000).

O'Brien, N. and B. Dillon, *Private Rented: The Forgotten Sector* (Threshold, Dublin, 1982).

Report of the Commission on the Private Rented Residential Sector (Stationery Office, Dublin, 2000).

Shaping the Future: An Action Plan on Homelessness in Dublin 2001–2003 (Homeless Agency, 2001).

Social Housing – The Way Ahead (Department of the Environment, 1995).

Blackwell, J. and S. Kennedy (eds), *Focus on Homelessness* (Columba Press, Dublin, 1988).

Education

Bassett, M., B. Brady, T. Fleming, and T. Englis, *For Adults Only: A Case for Adult Education in Ireland* (Aontas, National Association of Adult Education, Dublin, 1989).

Coolahan, J., *Irish Education: History and Structure* (Institute of Public Administration, Dublin, 1981).

Clancy, P., *College Entry in Focus: A Fourth National Survey of Access to Higher Education* (Higher Education Authority, Dublin, 2001).

Commission on Higher Education 1960–67 (Stationery Office, Dublin, 1967).

Investment in Education (Stationery Office, Dublin, 1965).

Lifelong Learning: Report of the Commission on Adult Education (Stationery Office, Dublin, 1984).

Learning for Life, White Paper on Adult Education (Stationery Office, Dublin, 2000).

Mulcahy, D. and D. O'Sullivan (eds), *Irish Educational Policy: Process and Substance* (Institute of Public Administration, Dublin, 1977).

O'Connor, S., *A Troubled Sky: Reflections on the Irish Educational Scene, 1957–1968* (Education Research Centre, St. Patrick's College, Dublin, 1986).

Green Paper, Partners in Education (Stationery Office, Dublin, 1985).

Report on the National Education Convention (Stationery Office, Dublin, 1994).

Programme for Action in Education 1984–1987 (Stationery Office, Dublin, 1984).

Report of the Primary Education Review Body (Stationery Office, Dublin, 1981).

Report of the Action Group on Access to Third Level Education (Stationery Office, Dublin, 2001).

Tussing, A.D., *Irish Educational Expenditure: Past, Present and Future* (Economic and Social Research Institute, Dublin, 1978).

White Paper: Education for a Changing World (Stationery Office, Dublin, 1995).

Walshe, J., *A New Partnership in Education, From Consultation to Legislation in the Nineties* (Institute of Public Administration, Dublin, 1999).

White, T., *Investing in People, Higher Education in Ireland from 1960 to 2000* (Institute of Public Administration, Dublin, 2001).

Health services

Audit of Structures and Functions in the Health System (Stationery Office, Dublin, 2003).

Barrington, R., *Health, Medicine and Politics in Ireland 1900–1970* (Institute of Public Administration, Dublin, 1987).

Community Care Services: an Overview (Stationery Office, Dublin, 1987).

Green Paper on Mental Health (Stationery Office, Dublin, 1992).

The Health Service Reform Programme (Department of Health and Children, 2003).

Health, the Wider Dimensions (Department of Health, 1986).

Hensey, B., *The Health Services of Ireland* (Institute of Public Administration, Dublin, 1988).

Outline of the Future Hospitals System – Report of the Consultative Council on the General Hospital Service (Stationery Office, Dublin, 1968).

Report of the Working Party on the General Medical Service (Stationery Office, Dublin, 1984).

Robins, J. (ed.), *Reflections on Health; Commemorating Fifty Years of the Department of Health 1947–1997* (Department of Health, 1997).

Report of the Commission on Health Funding (Stationery Office, Dublin, 1989).

Shaping a Healthier Future (Department of Health, 1994).

The Health Services and their Further Development (Stationery Office, Dublin, 1966).

The Psychiatric Service: Planning for the Future (Stationery Office, Dublin, 1984).

Wren, M., *Unhealthy State. Anatomy of a Sick Society* (New Island Books, Dublin, 2003).

Welfare of certain groups

Annual Reports, National Traveller Accommodation Consultative Committee.

A Strategy for Equality: Report of the Commission on the Status of People with Disabilities (Stationery Office, Dublin, 1996).

Care of the Aged (Stationery Office, Dublin, 1968).

First Progress Report of the Committee to Monitor and Co-ordinate the Implementation of the Recommendations of the Task Force on the Travelling Community (Stationery Office, Dublin, 2000).

Gilligan, R., *Irish Child Care Services: Policy, Practice and Provision* (Institute of Public Administration, Dublin, 1991).

Needs and Abilities, A Policy for the Intellectually Disabled: Report of the Review Group on Mental Handicap Services (Stationery Office, Dublin, 1990).

NESC Report No. 50, *Major Issues of Planning Service for Mentally and Physically Handicapped Persons* (Stationery Office, Dublin, 1980).

Raftery, M. and E. O'Sullivan, *Suffer the Little Children: The Inside Story of Ireland's Industrial Schools* (New Island Books, Dublin, 1999).

Report of the Committee to Monitor the Implementation of Government Policy on Travelling People.

Report of the Commission on Itinerancy (Stationery Office, Dublin, 1963).

Report of the Industrial and Reformatory School System (Stationery Office, Dublin, 1970).

Report of the Travelling People Review Body (Stationery Office, Dublin, 1983).

Report of the Task Force on the Travelling Community (Stationery office, Dublin, 1995).

Rottman, D.B., A.D. Tussing and M.M. Wiley, *The Population Structure and Living Circumstances of Irish Travellers: Results from the 1981 Census of Traveller Families* (Economic and Social Research Institute, Dublin, 1986).

The Years Ahead: Policy for the Elderly (Stationery Office, Dublin, 1988).

The Years Ahead Report: A Review of the Implementation of its Recommendations (National Council on Ageing and Older People, 1997).

Towards a Full Life: Green Paper on Services for Disabled People (Stationery Office, Dublin, 1984).

Towards an Independent Future: Report of the Review Group on Health and Personal Social Services for People with Physical and Sensory Disability (Stationery Office, Dublin, 1996).

Towards equal Citizenship: Progess Report on the Implementation of the Recommendations of the Commission on the Status of People with Disabilities (Stationery Office, Dublin, 1999).

Training and Employing the Handicapped: Report of a Working Party established by the Minister for Health (Stationery Office, Dublin, 1975).

Traveller Health: A National Strategy 2002–2005 (Department of Health and Children, 2002).

Voluntary organisations

Faughnan, P., *Partners in Progress: Voluntary Organisations in the Social Service Field* (Social Science Research Centre, University College Dublin, 1990).

Supporting Voluntary Activity: A White Paper on a Framework for Supporting Voluntary Activity and for Developing the Relationship between the State and the Community and Voluntary Sector (Stationery Office, Dublin, 2000).

Voluntary Social Service in Ireland: A Discussion Document (National Social Service Board, Dublin, 1982).

Poverty and exclusion

Building an Inclusive Society: Review of the National Anti-Poverty Strategy under the Programme for Prosperity and Fairness (Stationery Office, Dublin, 2002).

Ó Cinnéide, S., 'Poverty and Policy North and South', *Administration*, Vol. 33, No. 3 (Institute of Public Administration, Dublin, 1985).

Sharing in Progress: National Anti-Poverty Strategy (Stationery Office, Dublin, 1997).

Equality issues

Annual Reports, Equality Authority.

NESF Report No. 23, *A Strategic Framework for Equality Issues*, 2002.

Index